MANGA
FOR SUCCESS

BUSINESS PROBLEM-SOLVING AND STRATEGY

AUTHOR
TAKAYUKI KITO
KEISUKE YAMABE

ARTWORK BY
ENMO TAKENAWA

WILEY

For general information on our other products and services or for technical support, please contact our Customer Care Department within the United States at (800) 762-2974, outside the United States at (317) 572-3993 or fax (317) 572-4002.

Wiley also publishes its books in a variety of electronic formats. Some content that appears in print may not be available in electronic formats. For more information about Wiley products, visit our web site at www.wiley.com.

Library of Congress Cataloging-in-Publication Data is Available:
ISBN 9781394176168 (Paperback)
ISBN 9781394176175 (ePub)
ISBN 9781394176182 (ePDF)

Cover Design: JMA Management Center Inc.
Cover Images: JMA Management Center Inc.
© ShEd Artworks/Shutterstock

SKY10042727_030923

CONTENTS

...I CAN'T.

I CAN'T JUST ABANDON EVERYONE WHEN MAT-SUI-YA IS IN TROUBLE!

STEP 1 Analyze the Situation

STORY 2 Knowing Your Enemy Is Knowing Yourself – 50

A BUSINESS STRATEGY THAT CANNOT BE EXECUTED IS NOTHING BUT A PIE IN THE SKY.

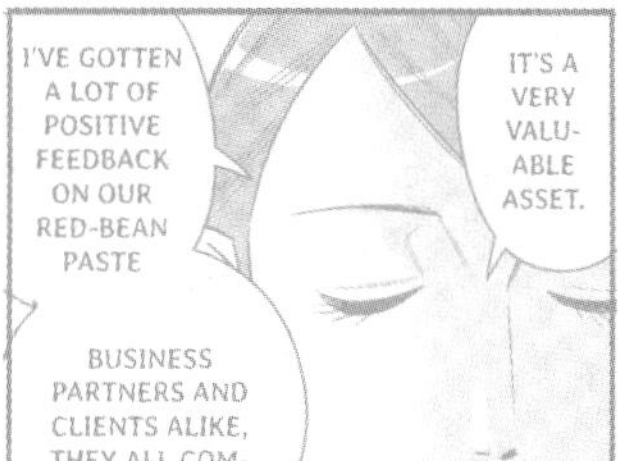
I'VE GOTTEN A LOT OF POSITIVE FEEDBACK ON OUR RED-BEAN PASTE
IT'S A VERY VALU-ABLE ASSET.
BUSINESS PARTNERS AND CLIENTS ALIKE, THEY ALL COM-PLIMENT ANN.

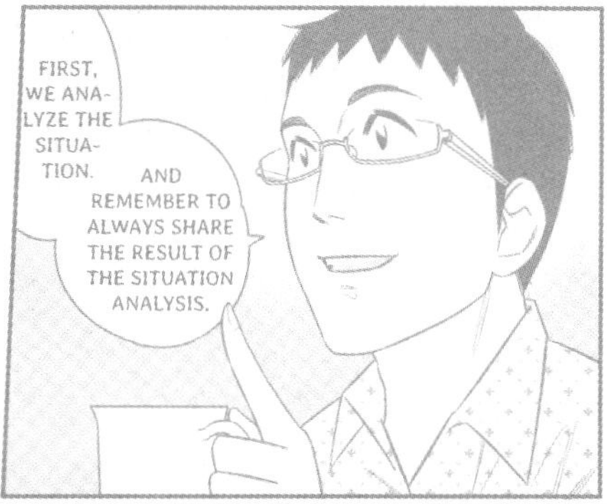
FIRST, WE ANA-LYZE THE SITUA-TION.
AND REMEMBER TO ALWAYS SHARE THE RESULT OF THE SITUATION ANALYSIS.

STEP 2 — Forming Strategic Options

STORY 3 How to Save a Company in Trouble? · 118

THAT'S EASY FOR YOU TO SAY... YOU JUST GIVE OUT ORDERS.

WE ARE THE ONES WHO COME FACE-TO-FACE WITH THE CLIENTS. IT'S NOT ALWAYS ABOUT RATIONALITY.

...I WILL HAVE A WORD WITH THE CEO MYSELF REGARDING THIS.

STEP 3 Review and Select Options

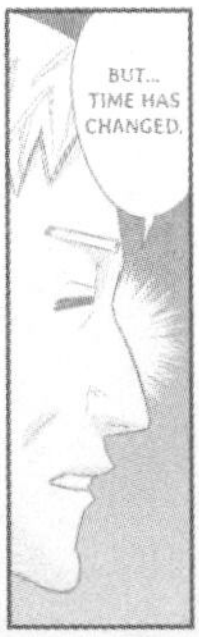

BUT... TIME HAS CHANGED.

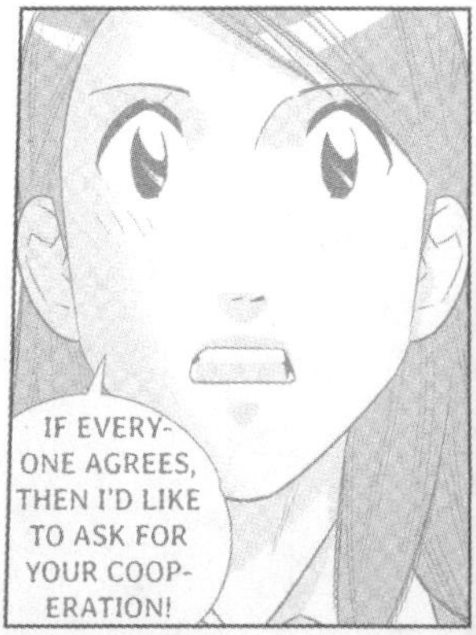

IF EVERY-ONE AGREES, THEN I'D LIKE TO ASK FOR YOUR COOP-ERATION!

STEP 4 How to Translate Options into Plans and Actions

WE ARE ON THE HOMESTRETCH NOW.

LET'S COME UP WITH SPECIFIC EXECUTIONS AND ACTIONS BASED ON THESE PRINCIPLES.

IN REGARDS TO THE FUTURE LOAN, INAHO BANK IS DEMANDING YOU RESIGN FROM YOUR POSITION.

Preface

What would you do if you were assigned to come up with a business strategy out of the blue? Maybe some of you readers are already racking your brains day and night trying to come up with one.

What is a business strategy, and how do you make an effective one? Regardless of your background, if you have picked up this book, you are probably facing such tasks and challenges.

A business strategy is important as it can greatly influence a company's future. However, it is very difficult to truly understand its core elements and apply them to think up a strategy that has a competitive edge. It's only natural to get baffled by how complex it is. There is no such thing as a single correct answer, and no deus ex machina that can solve all your problems.

For 15 years, we have been assisting various companies as professional business consultants. Even for those of us who specialize in this field and constantly think of our clients' business strategies, we keep getting stumped and hit numerous walls. Creating a business strategy and executing it to achieve the desired result is certainly not an easy task.

There are many books and articles out there on business strategies providing beneficial hints and suggestions. However, as consultants who have helped many companies with their strategies, we know that being able to deal flexibly with situations on the front line is not an easy feat.

This book is about offering tips on creating a business strategy that is applicable on the front line. If you are looking for brand-new concepts, frilly terms, or groundbreaking ideas, then we believe this book is not for you. However, if you are a business operator or a team manager, or you are involved in business planning and development and need to come up with a good applicable business strategy, you will find this book very useful. Even if you're not directly involved in strategy building, this book will help you gain a better understanding of how a company executes their strategy and how it might influence your everyday tasks.

Additionally, this book might also provide some insights for those interested in business consulting, as it is a culmination of our on-site experiences and what we have learned from day-to-day operations as business consultants. By reading this book, you will learn the point of view of a business consultant and gain a better understanding of how to support your clients in building business strategies.

The ultimate goal for this book is to provide our readers with tools to create a business strategy that can be executed and yield the desired result. We have written the tips and tricks of the trade as plainly and straightforwardly as possible. Of course, it is not an easy task. Building a business strategy is a complicated task that requires more than just reading a book. However, it is exactly because of that, we decided that we wanted this book to be more practical so that it can help readers in creating a realistically applicable business strategy.

As we mentioned before, there are a lot of books on business strategy out there. We simply feel that most of them do not offer anything that is directly applicable. With that in mind, we have written a book that can offer you practical ideas applicable on the front line right away. Regardless of whether you decide that this book meets its goal or not, we hope to be able to contribute even just a little bit to the development of your business.

Roland Berger LLC
Partner Takayuki Kito
Partner Keisuke Yamabe

PROLOGUE

What Is a Business Strategy?

STORY 1 **Help Me, Senpai!**

A BUSINESS STRATEGY THAT CANNOT BE EXECUTED IS NOTHING BUT A PIE IN THE SKY.

...I CAN'T.

I CAN'T JUST ABANDON EVERYONE WHEN MATSUI-YA IS IN TROUBLE!

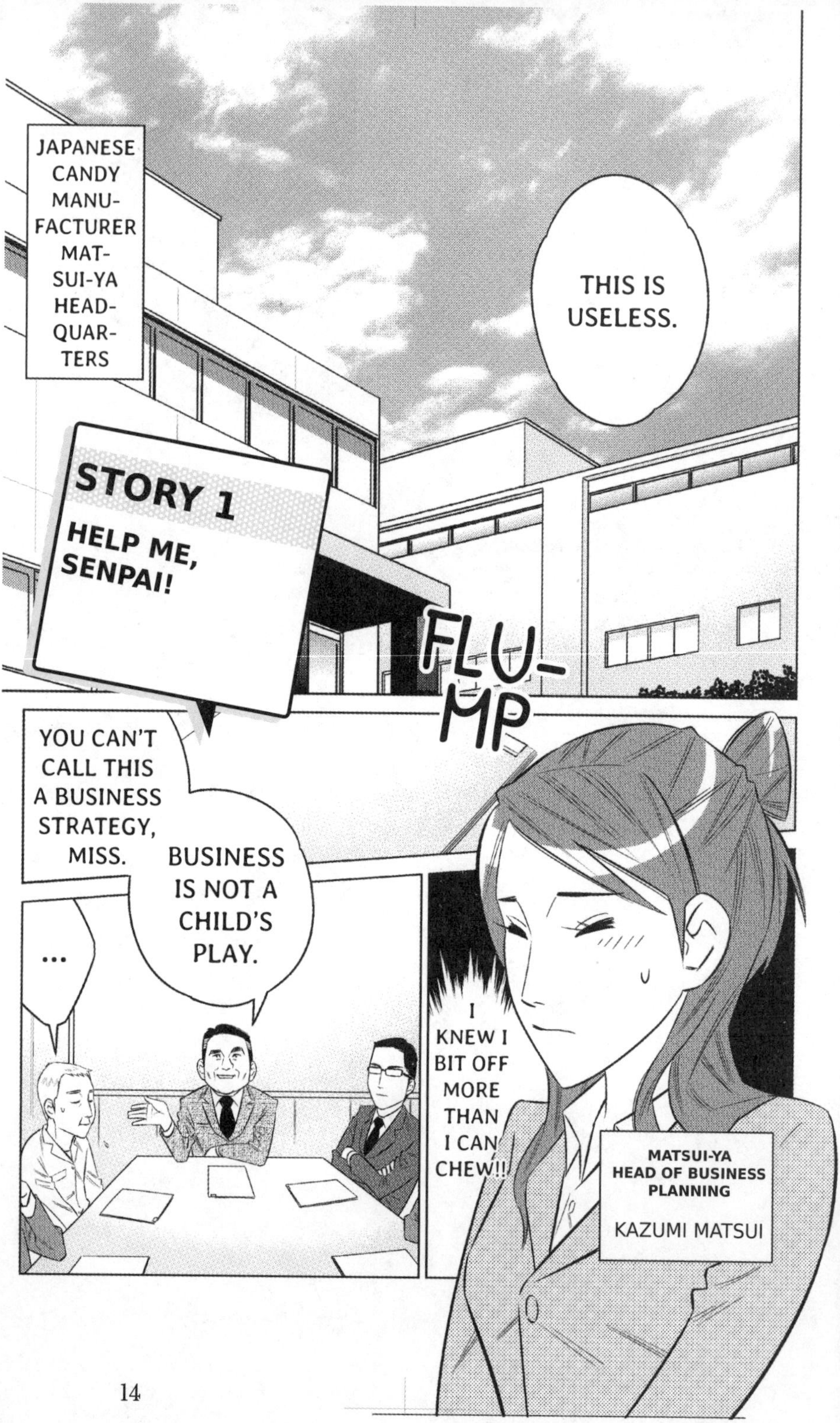
JAPANESE CANDY MANU-FACTURER MAT-SUI-YA HEAD-QUAR-TERS
THIS IS USELESS.
STORY 1
HELP ME, SENPAI!
FLU-MP
YOU CAN'T CALL THIS A BUSINESS STRATEGY, MISS.
BUSINESS IS NOT A CHILD'S PLAY.
...
I KNEW I BIT OFF MORE THAN I CAN CHEW!!
MATSUI-YA HEAD OF BUSINESS PLANNING
KAZUMI MATSUI

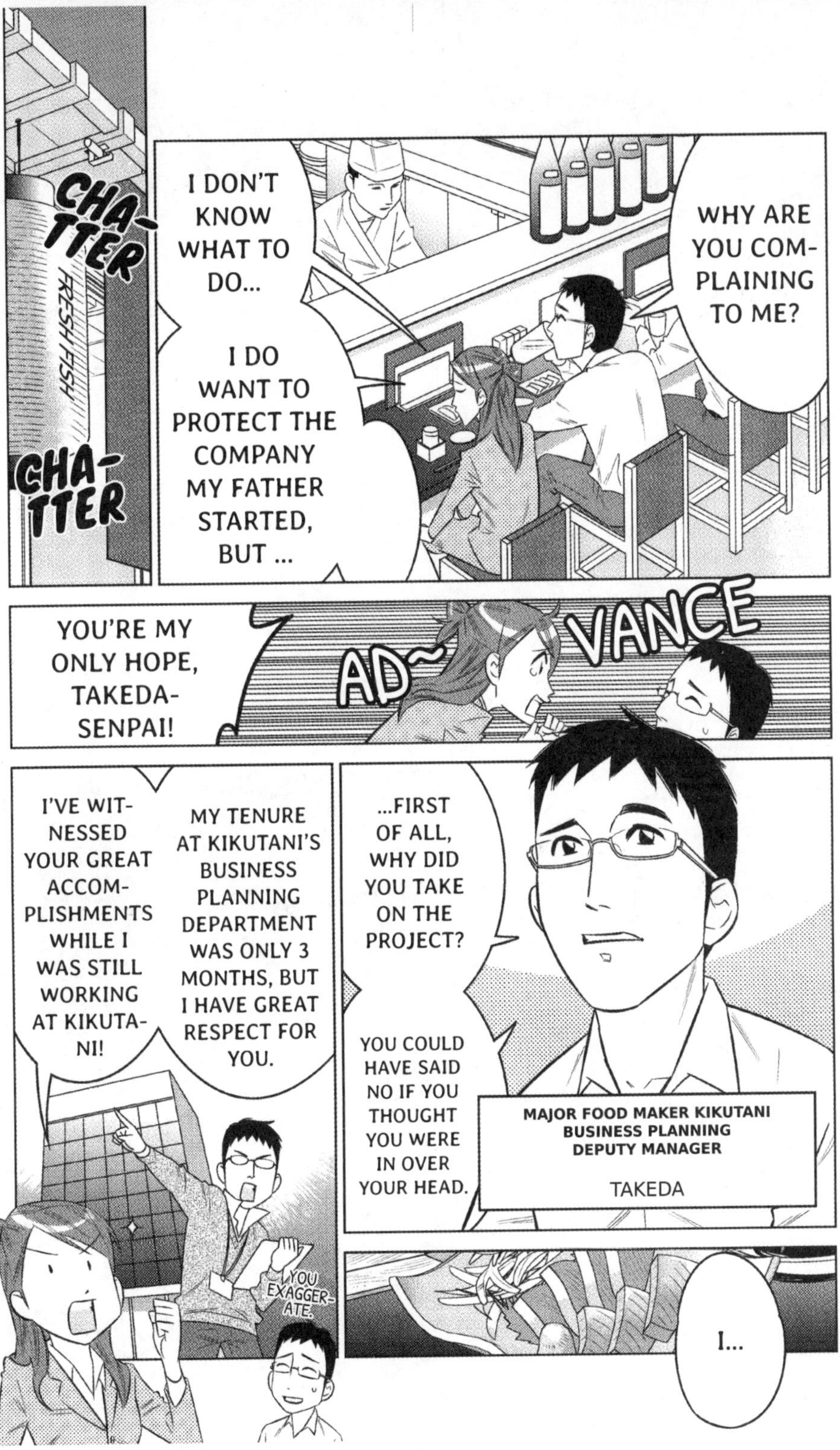
CHA-TTER
FRESH FISH
CHA-TTER
I DON'T KNOW WHAT TO DO...
I DO WANT TO PROTECT THE COMPANY MY FATHER STARTED, BUT ...
WHY ARE YOU COMPLAINING TO ME?
YOU'RE MY ONLY HOPE, TAKEDA-SENPAI!
AD~VANCE
I'VE WITNESSED YOUR GREAT ACCOMPLISHMENTS WHILE I WAS STILL WORKING AT KIKUTANI!
MY TENURE AT KIKUTANI'S BUSINESS PLANNING DEPARTMENT WAS ONLY 3 MONTHS, BUT I HAVE GREAT RESPECT FOR YOU.
YOU EXAGGERATE.
...FIRST OF ALL, WHY DID YOU TAKE ON THE PROJECT?
YOU COULD HAVE SAID NO IF YOU THOUGHT YOU WERE IN OVER YOUR HEAD.
MAJOR FOOD MAKER KIKUTANI BUSINESS PLANNING DEPUTY MANAGER
TAKEDA
I...

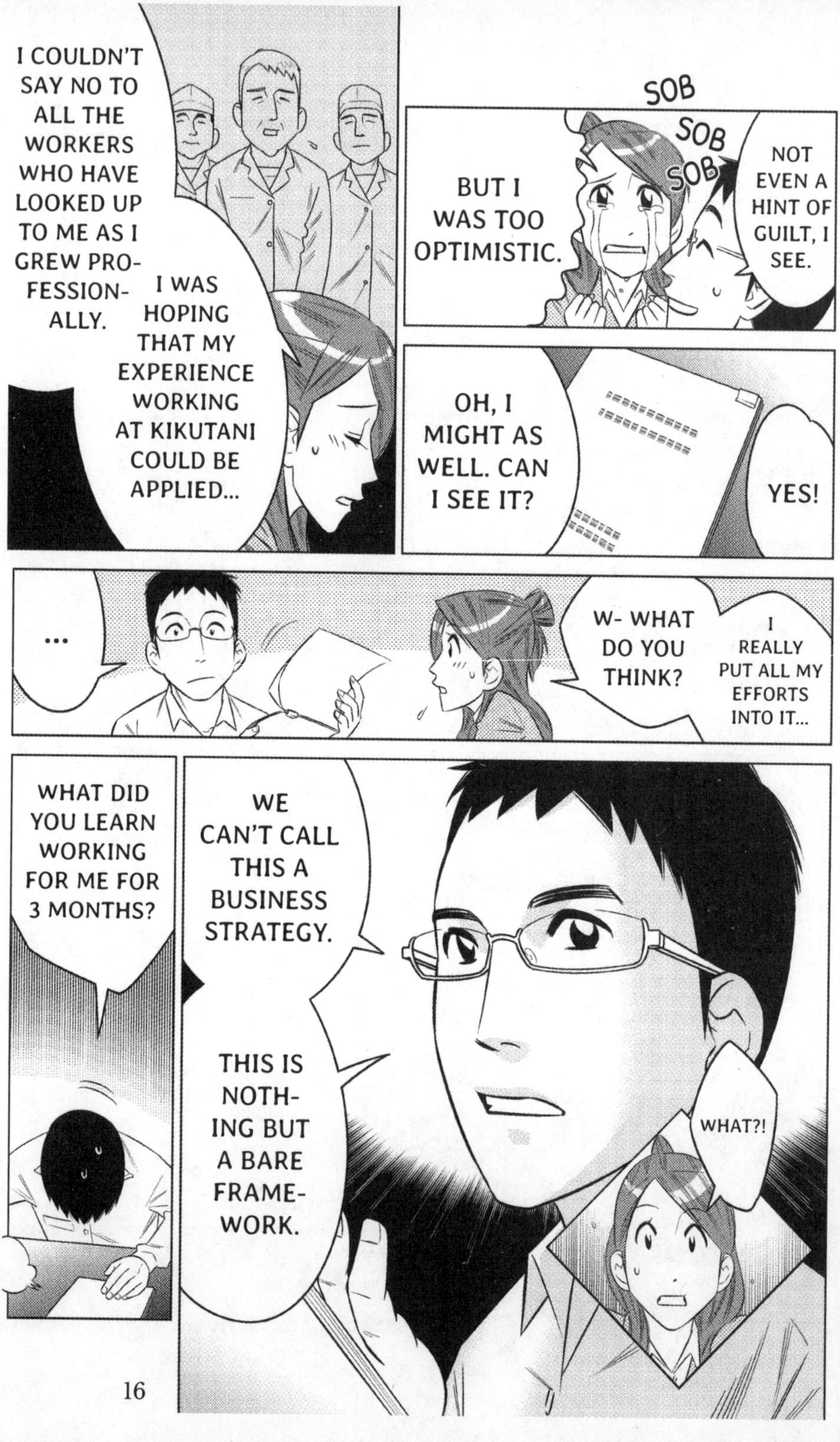
I COULDN'T SAY NO TO ALL THE WORKERS WHO HAVE LOOKED UP TO ME AS I GREW PRO-FESSION-ALLY.
I WAS HOPING THAT MY EXPERIENCE WORKING AT KIKUTANI COULD BE APPLIED...
BUT I WAS TOO OPTIMISTIC.
SOB SOB SOB
NOT EVEN A HINT OF GUILT, I SEE.
OH, I MIGHT AS WELL. CAN I SEE IT?
YES!
...
W- WHAT DO YOU THINK?
I REALLY PUT ALL MY EFFORTS INTO IT...
WHAT DID YOU LEARN WORKING FOR ME FOR 3 MONTHS?
WE CAN'T CALL THIS A BUSINESS STRATEGY.
THIS IS NOTH-ING BUT A BARE FRAME-WORK.
WHAT?!

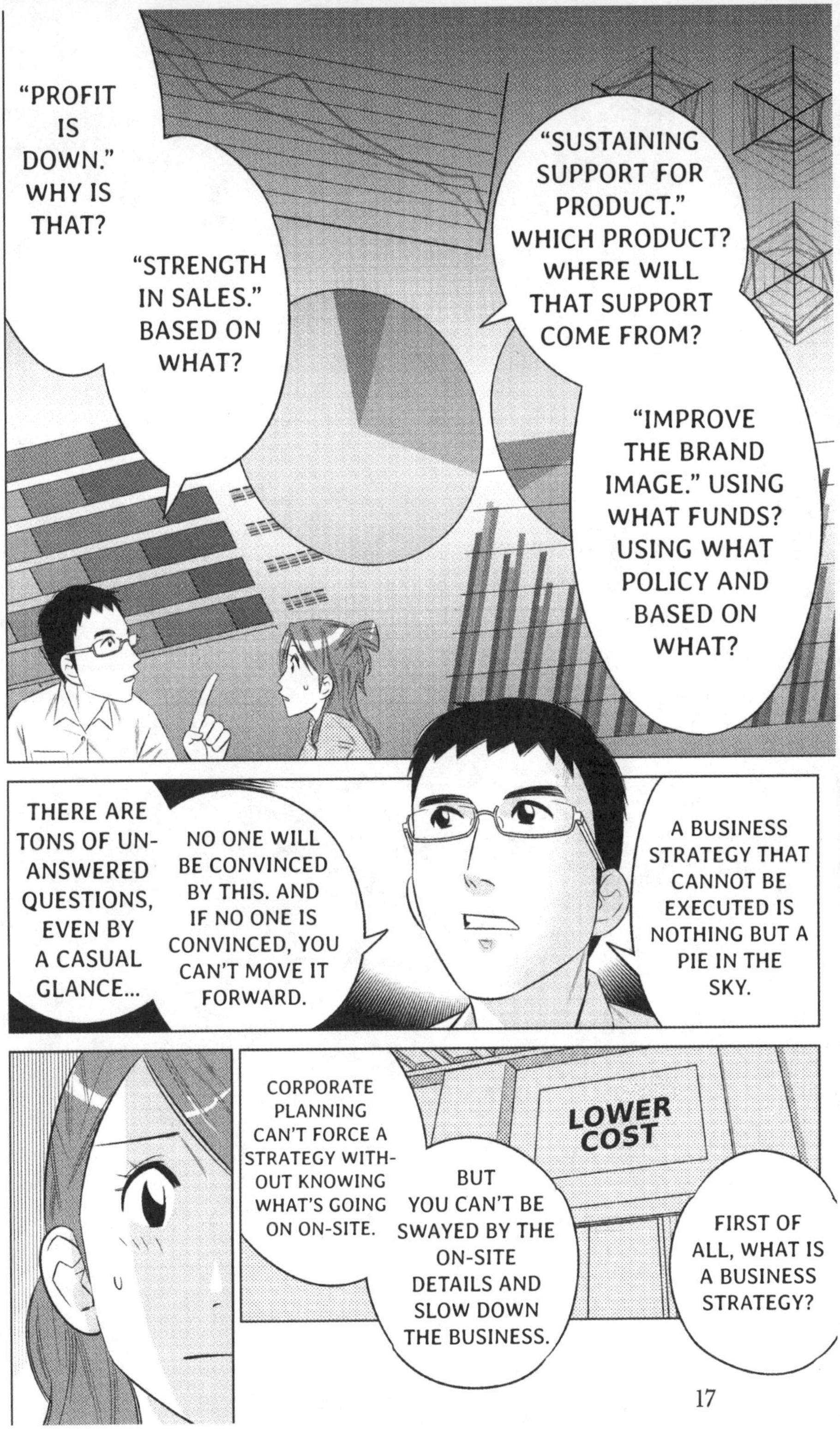
"PROFIT IS DOWN." WHY IS THAT?
"STRENGTH IN SALES." BASED ON WHAT?
"SUSTAINING SUPPORT FOR PRODUCT." WHICH PRODUCT? WHERE WILL THAT SUPPORT COME FROM?
"IMPROVE THE BRAND IMAGE." USING WHAT FUNDS? USING WHAT POLICY AND BASED ON WHAT?
THERE ARE TONS OF UN-ANSWERED QUESTIONS, EVEN BY A CASUAL GLANCE...
NO ONE WILL BE CONVINCED BY THIS. AND IF NO ONE IS CONVINCED, YOU CAN'T MOVE IT FORWARD.
A BUSINESS STRATEGY THAT CANNOT BE EXECUTED IS NOTHING BUT A PIE IN THE SKY.
CORPORATE PLANNING CAN'T FORCE A STRATEGY WITH-OUT KNOWING WHAT'S GOING ON ON-SITE.
LOWER COST
BUT YOU CAN'T BE SWAYED BY THE ON-SITE DETAILS AND SLOW DOWN THE BUSINESS.
FIRST OF ALL, WHAT IS A BUSINESS STRATEGY?

A BUSINESS STRATEGY IS A BLUEPRINT AND A SCENARIO FOR STRENGTHENING AND SUSTAINING THE COMPANY'S PRIORITIES.

YOU HAVE TO PRESENT A STRATEGY PROPOSAL THAT EVERYONE FROM THE TOP DOWN CAN AGREE ON BY INCLUDING REALISTIC EXECUTION PLANS...

ONLY THEN YOU CAN CALL IT A "BUSINESS STRATEGY."

IT'S ALSO A FRAMEWORK FOR THE ALLOCATION OF THE LIMITED RESOURCES.

AFTER ALL, YOU CAN'T PUT EVERYTHING IN MOTION ALL AT ONCE.

YOU HAVE TO MAKE A CLEAR DISTINCTION OF WHAT'S IMPORTANT AND WHAT'S NOT.

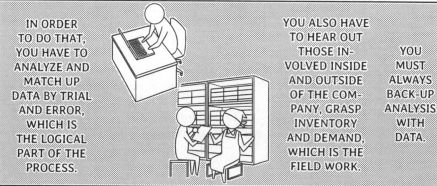

IN ORDER TO DO THAT, YOU HAVE TO ANALYZE AND MATCH UP DATA BY TRIAL AND ERROR, WHICH IS THE LOGICAL PART OF THE PROCESS.

YOU ALSO HAVE TO HEAR OUT THOSE INVOLVED INSIDE AND OUTSIDE OF THE COMPANY, GRASP INVENTORY AND DEMAND, WHICH IS THE FIELD WORK.

YOU MUST ALWAYS BACK-UP ANALYSIS WITH DATA.

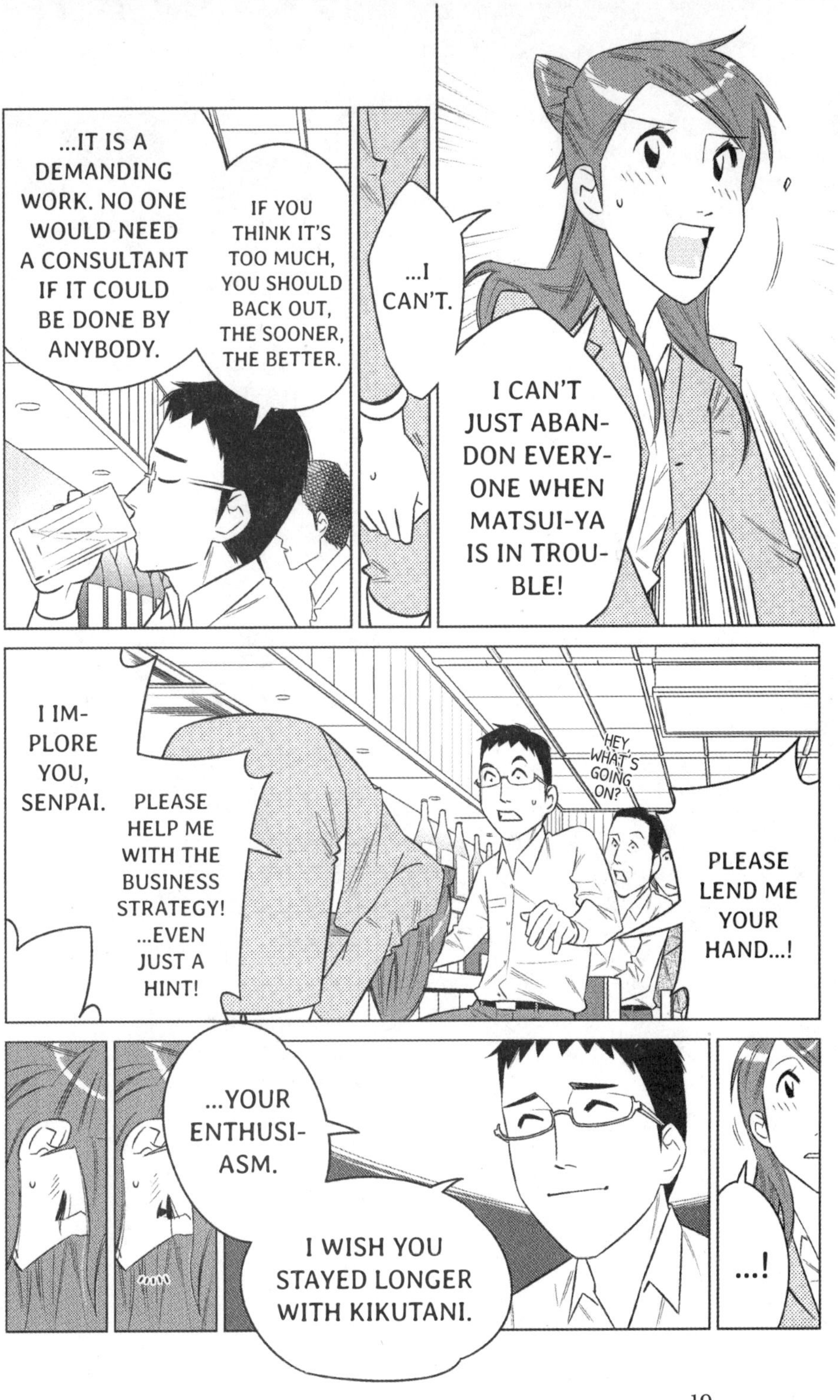
...I CAN'T.
I CAN'T JUST ABANDON EVERYONE WHEN MATSUI-YA IS IN TROUBLE!
IF YOU THINK IT'S TOO MUCH, YOU SHOULD BACK OUT, THE SOONER, THE BETTER.
...IT IS A DEMANDING WORK. NO ONE WOULD NEED A CONSULTANT IF IT COULD BE DONE BY ANYBODY.
PLEASE LEND ME YOUR HAND...!
HEY, WHAT'S GOING ON?
PLEASE HELP ME WITH THE BUSINESS STRATEGY! ...EVEN JUST A HINT!
I IMPLORE YOU, SENPAI.
...!
...YOUR ENTHUSIASM.
I WISH YOU STAYED LONGER WITH KIKUTANI.

ALL RIGHT, THEN. LET'S BREAK DOWN HOW TO CREATE A BUSINESS STRATEGY INTO 4 STEPS.

Y- YES, SIR!

STEP 1

ANALYZE THE SITUATION

SWOT ANALYSIS - OT ANALYSIS (OPPORTUNITIES FOR GROWTH, POSSIBLE THREATS TO GROWTH)

5 FORCES ANALYSIS
• POSITIONING ANALYSIS
• COMPETITION ANALYSIS
• CLIENT (CONSUMERS, CORPORATIONS) ANALYSIS
• SUCCESS ELEMENTS (KSF) ANALYSIS

SWOT ANALYSIS - SW ANALYSIS
• ACHIEVEMENTS AND PERFORMANCE ANALYSIS
• POSITIONING ANALYSIS
• BUSINESS MODEL ANALYSIS
• MARKETING (4P) ANALYSIS
• VALUE CHAIN AND ORGANIZATIONAL ANALYSIS
• TANGIBLE AND INTANGIBLE ASSET ANALYSIS

STEP 2

FORMULATE STRATEGIC OPTIONS

• GOALS AND POINTS OF CONTENTION FOR STRATEGY SELECTION
• GROWTH OPTIONS FOR EXISTING BUSINESSES
• OPTIONS FOR NEWLY ESTABLISHED BUSINESSES
• OPTIONS FOR IMPROVING PROFIT

STEP 3

EVALUATE AND SELECT OPTIONS

• EVALUATE RATIONALITY
• EVALUATE PROBABILITY
• GATHERING INTENSIONS AND ENTHUSIASM OF THE PARTIES INVOLVED

STEP 4

TRANSLATE STRATEGIC OPTIONS INTO PLANS OF ACTION

• TRANSLATING INTO A PLAN
• TRANSLATING INTO ACTION
• ORGANIZING THEM INTO EXECUTABLE PLANS
• BUILD A STRUCTURE TO OVERSEE PROGRESS

UM... SO MANY ITEMS...

SHOCK

YEAH, YOU CAN JUST LOOK AT THEM FOR NOW.

BUT KEEP IT IN MIND AS A WHOLE PICTURE. OTHERWISE, YOU'LL GET LOST IN THE SEA OF STRATEGY CREATION.

WHY AM I ANALYZING THIS...?

THE ULTIMATE GOAL IS MAKING PRIORITIES CLEAR, AND THUS KNOW WHAT TO FOCUS ON.

GOAL

ALWAYS KEEP THAT IN MIND SO YOU DON'T FALL INTO THE TRAP OF OVERANALYZING.

I SEE... I DIDN'T THINK OF IT IN SUCH BROKEN DOWN STEPS...

SOMETIMES PEOPLE PUT TOO MUCH EMPHASIS ON METHODOLOGY AND FRAMEWORK, TURNING THAT INTO A GOAL.

WHY?

FILLING OUT THE FRAMEWORK IS JUST A MEANS. DON'T LOSE SIGHT OF YOUR GOAL.

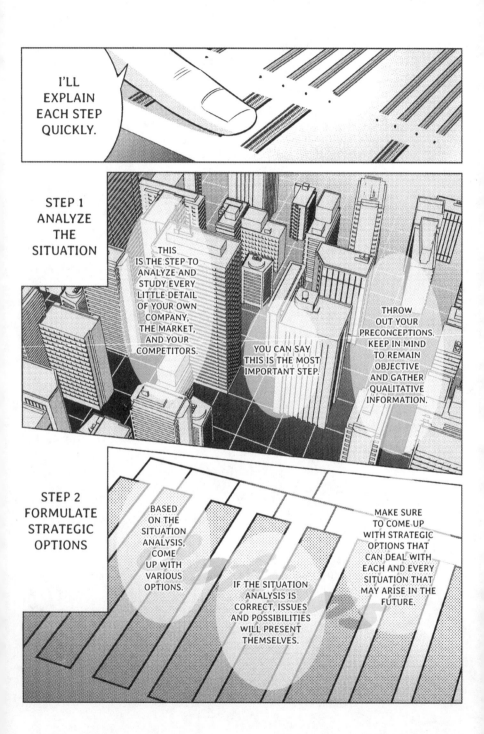

I'LL EXPLAIN EACH STEP QUICKLY.

STEP 1
ANALYZE THE SITUATION

THIS IS THE STEP TO ANALYZE AND STUDY EVERY LITTLE DETAIL OF YOUR OWN COMPANY, THE MARKET, AND YOUR COMPETITORS.

YOU CAN SAY THIS IS THE MOST IMPORTANT STEP.

THROW OUT YOUR PRECONCEPTIONS. KEEP IN MIND TO REMAIN OBJECTIVE AND GATHER QUALITATIVE INFORMATION.

STEP 2
FORMULATE STRATEGIC OPTIONS

BASED ON THE SITUATION ANALYSIS, COME UP WITH VARIOUS OPTIONS.

IF THE SITUATION ANALYSIS IS CORRECT, ISSUES AND POSSIBILITIES WILL PRESENT THEMSELVES.

MAKE SURE TO COME UP WITH STRATEGIC OPTIONS THAT CAN DEAL WITH EACH AND EVERY SITUATION THAT MAY ARISE IN THE FUTURE.

22

STEP 3 EVALUATE AND SELECT OPTIONS

THIS IS WHERE YOU CHOOSE THE MAIN PILLARS OF YOUR STRATEGY FROM VARIOUS OPTIONS YOU'VE COME UP WITH.

BY CREATING AND PRIORITIZING OPTIONS.

KEEP IN MIND, A SITUATION MAY ARISE WHERE YOU MAY NEED AN OPTION THAT YOU DIDN'T CHOOSE.

MAKING CLEAR THE REASON FOR CHOOSING OR NOT CHOOSING IS VERY IMPORTANT.

STEP 4 APPLY THE OPTIONS SELECTED TO THE PLAN AND EXECUTE

Phase 1

Phase 2

Phase 3

HERE YOU HAVE TO APPLY VERY SPECIFIC AND REALISTIC ACTION PLANS BASED ON THE TIME FRAME.

AGAIN, THE FINAL GOAL OF SELECTING A STRATEGY IS THE ACTUAL EXECUTION.

STRATEGY THAT CAN'T BE EXECUTED IS MEANINGLESS.

SO, HOW TO CHOOSE A TOP-NOTCH BUSINESS STRATEGY? HERE'S A QUOTE FROM SUN TZU'S THE ART OF WAR.

"IF YOU KNOW THE ENEMY AND KNOW YOUR-SELF, YOU NEED NOT FEAR THE RESULT OF A HUNDRED BATTLES."

"ENEMY" DOESN'T NECESSARILY MEAN YOUR COMPETITORS. IT CAN INCLUDE ANYTHING FROM THE MARKET TO THE COMPETITORS, BUT ALSO THOSE WHO MAY BE ON YOUR SIDE. CONSIDER IT AS "ALL EXTERNAL ELEMENTS."

"YOURSELF" IS YOUR COMPANY AND FRONT LINE, EVERYTHING THAT PERTAINS TO YOU. HAVE A CLEAR AND REALISTIC UNDER-STANDING OF THE FRONT LINE'S OUT-PUT. OTHERWISE YOU WILL NOT BE ABLE TO OPERATE PROPERLY IN THE EXECUTION STEP.

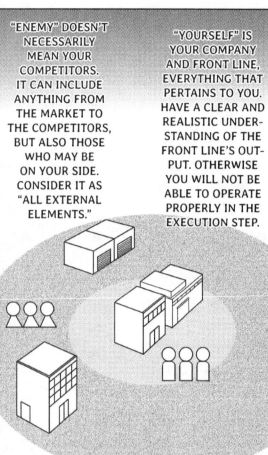

IN MANY CASES, THE COMPANY DOES NOT HAVE AN ACCURATE GRASP OF THE MARKET.

"WE CAN DO IT BECAUSE THEY'VE DONE IT" IS A TRAIN OF THOUGHT YOU HAVE TO WATCH OUT FOR.

BECAUSE SITUATIONS, ISSUES, RESOURCES DIFFER FOR EVERY COMPANY.

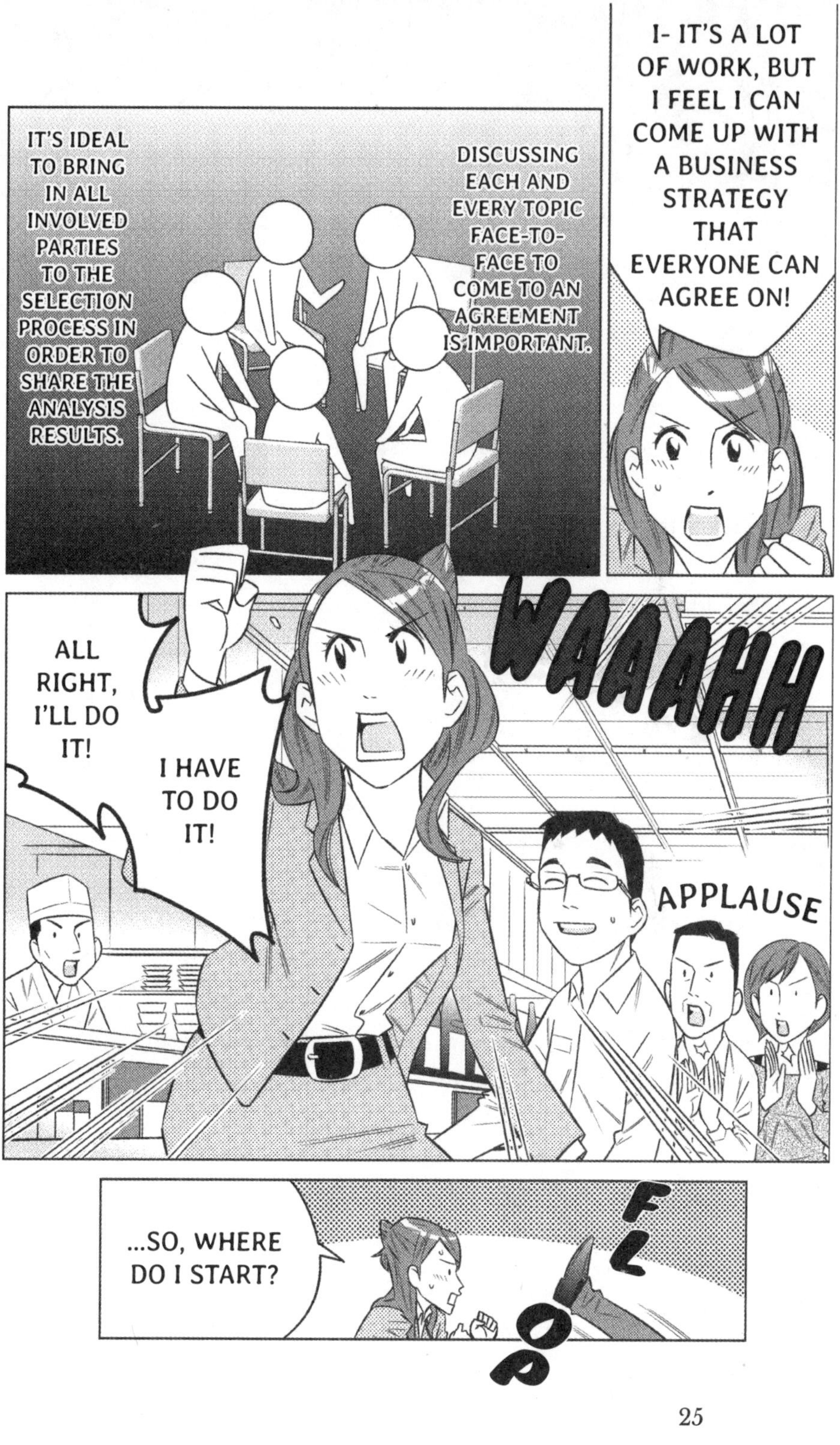
I- IT'S A LOT OF WORK, BUT I FEEL I CAN COME UP WITH A BUSINESS STRATEGY THAT EVERYONE CAN AGREE ON!
DISCUSSING EACH AND EVERY TOPIC FACE-TO-FACE TO COME TO AN AGREEMENT IS IMPORTANT.
IT'S IDEAL TO BRING IN ALL INVOLVED PARTIES TO THE SELECTION PROCESS IN ORDER TO SHARE THE ANALYSIS RESULTS.
WAAAHH
ALL RIGHT, I'LL DO IT!
I HAVE TO DO IT!
APPLAUSE
FLOP
...SO, WHERE DO I START?

1   WHAT IS A "STRATEGY"?

▶ Strategies Are Everywhere

What do you think of when you hear the word "strategy"?

The word "strategy" is ubiquitous. I'm sure you have heard about a lot of different types of strategy, such as business strategy, brand strategy, marketing strategy, sales strategy, organizational strategy, HR strategy, so on and so forth. It is often used as a noun, but it's also common to find it used as an adjective, such as strategic development, strategic employee deployment, and strategic retreat.

When you hear "XX strategy" or "Strategic YY," it gives the impression of something well-thought-out and meticulously planned. Both the noun "strategy" and the adjective "strategic" are often used to cover up a lack of content and depth, causing them to lose their original meaning.

The media such as newspapers and magazines are saturated with the words "strategy" and "strategic," and even the plans revealed by big corporations are peppered with this word. So what exactly is a "strategy"? What is its substance? What does the theme of this book, "Business Strategy," mean?

FIRST, THE DEFINITION OF THE WORD!

▶ Strategy Is a Road Map to Success

Obviously, a company's end goal is to beat its competitors, increase sales and profits, and

26

prove its value to its clients, employees, and stakeholders, and on top of that, to largely contribute to society. In case of a corporation, it is also equally important to distribute profits to its stockholders as a return on their investment.

In order to succeed and increase sales and profit, you will of course have to beat your competitors. In this capitalist society, the free market is full of ever-expanding competitors. The company must first survive in such environment in order to have the possibility to come out on top.

So what do you need to beat your competitors? You need to have a competitive edge over them in your selected market in order to survive and succeed. It sets you apart from your competitors and lets you gain advantage over them.

In order to build your competitive edge, you need to first choose your battlefield (in this case, market) to compete in. Then decide where to focus and distribute your limited resources in order to develop an edge by providing different and/or superior values over your competitors'.

The key essence of a strategy is coming up with a plan and laying down a road map to succeed by choosing your battleground, developing an edge by providing varied and superior values, and deciding how and where to focus your limited resources (see Diagram 1-1). Remember, strategy is all about choices and focus.

▶ Resource Allocation: Decide Where to Focus Your Organizational Resources

When it comes to the term "resource allocation," you probably think of the allocation of the three main resources: manpower,

Diagram 1-1 What Is a Strategy?

The world is full of XX **strategy and strategic** YY...

Management
Strategy

Brand
Strategy

Sales
Strategy

Organizational
Strategy

Strategic
Employee
Deployment

Strategic
Development

Strategic
Retreat

The true essence of strategy

Where to compete?	• Making clear which field (in this case, market) to compete in.
✕	
What edge is necessary to win?	• How to win in the chosen market by developing an edge over the competitors.
✕	
How to distribute resources?	• Coming up with a plan for the most efficient use and directions of your limited resources.

Road map to success

supplies, and funds. Of course, it is very important to consider where and how to distribute these main resources in the strategy. But in order to come up with an actual strategy, you will have to think of the resource allocation in a broader sense. One vital part of resource allocation is coming up with specifics of how and where to focus your organizational power.

For example, a "thorough cost cutting" is one type of a strategy. By focusing your organizational resources to cost cutting, you will come up with the lowest cost, which will provide you with a competitive edge. This is a very valid strategy.

Another example would be if you want to beat the competition by setting your product apart. Therefore, you focus more resources and people to the research and development team. That is also another form of resource allocation.

How about utilizing open innovation knowledge developed by outsiders to set your product apart? This might be different from resource allocation that you have in mind. But this, too, is a strategy. You are enriching your limited internal resources by adding external, oftentimes superior resources. This allows you to keep the resources spent for your own research and development down as you replaced it with external resources.

As you can see, resource allocation, which is a vital part of the strategic framework, is not just about the distribution of your own resources, but also about how to decide where to focus your manpower, as well as coming up with how to supplement resource shortages (see Diagram 1-2).

Diagram 1-2 Resource Allocation

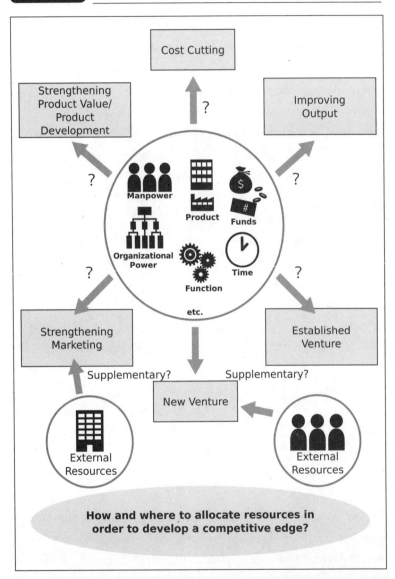

How and where to allocate resources in order to develop a competitive edge?

▶ "Strategy" Is Nothing without Execution

Another key factor when it comes to the core of strategy is this: Even well-thought-out marketing choices, competitive edge, and resource allocation are not enough in building an effective strategy.

Strategy is not only about beating the competition but coming up with a blueprint for execution and actually putting that plan into action. Therefore, a strategy that cannot be executed or put into motion is not a strategy. This is an essential thing to remember.

▶ The Correct Way to Create a Strategy

Keeping these key elements in mind, a business strategy must include: (1) choosing which market/region/clientele to target; (2) comparing and creating an edge over the competition by standing out and offering different/better value; and (3) how best to allocate your resources.

If you think about it, as long as these key factors are kept in mind, you can have a strategy in your everyday life, too. Strategy is an important part of the job-hunting process. You choose your own market, which is the job type or field, and determine how to set yourself apart from your competitors by appealing to companies with your strengths. Managing, or allocating, your limited time efficiently is also a strategy.

An XX strategy or a strategic YY without these essential factors are only incomplete plans that contain the word "strategy" or "strategic" in order to make unfocused or underdeveloped plans look good.

Diagram 1-3 Resource Allocation

	Sales Strategy	Job-hunting Strategy	Golf Strategy
Market	**What is your target clientele?** ○ Attribute ○ Region ○	**What type of company to target?** ○ Industries ○ Job types ○	**What level to aim for?** ○ Competitions, single-digit handicaps ○ Under 100 strokes ○ .....
Competitive Edge & Differentiation	**How to stand out from your competitors?** ○ Flexibility ○ Ideas ○	**How to stand out from other applicants?** ○ Experience ○ Personality ○	**What gives you an edge?** ○ Distance ○ Accuracy ○ Stability ○ .....
Resource Allocation	**How and what to allocate in marketing resources?** ○ Improve training process ○ Review employee allocation ○	**How to use the time most efficiently?** ○ Research and preparation ○ Seek advice ○ Create a checklist ○ Interview ○	**What steps to take in order to improve?** ○ Take lessons ○ Practice ○ Play rounds ○ .....

▶ Business Strategy Is a Blueprint for Your Business Success

Let's go back to this book's theme, business strategy, with those points in mind. Understanding what is the essence of strategy will lead to an understanding of the meaning of business strategy.

In order to beat the competition, you must first select the market; second, create an edge over competitors (by offering better and/or different values); and third, consider how best to allocate limited resources.

You must also consider, fourth, how best to execute the above and put them into motion. This, too, is an essential part of a business strategy.

Diagram 1-4 What Is a Business Strategy?

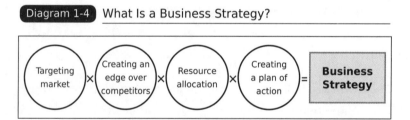

2 The Many Pitfalls of a Business Strategy

▶ Building Strategy the Right Way Is Tough

Sorry to start on a negative note, but building a business strategy is not an easy task. In fact, it is very difficult. That's why I suppose there is such a specialized title as a business strategy consultant.

One of the reasons why it is so difficult to create a strategy lies in its many pitfalls and traps. These pitfalls and traps often result in a strategy that is not efficient or executable. The first "strategic" idea Kazumi created also fell into these pitfalls and traps and was deemed useless by the executives.

Before moving on to the specific steps of building a business strategy, let's look at what kinds of pitfalls and traps are there (Diagram 1-5).

▶ Framework and Concepts: Make or Break the Strategy

There are many frameworks to consider when creating a strategy or strategic concepts that follow certain patterns or formulas. Frameworks such as SWOT, Five Forces, and Positioning are well known, and so are the concepts of the three basic strategies (cost leadership strategy, differentiation strategy, and niche strategy). In addition, there is the dominant strategy, the Lancaster strategy, the Blue Ocean or Red Ocean strategy, etc., There is no end to examples of strategic concepts.

LET'S REVIEW THE COMMON MISTAKES ANYONE CAN MAKE.

These frameworks and concepts can be great tools when utilized correctly. But when applied incorrectly, they can ruin a strategy. Unfortunately, the latter is the case more often than not.

Common mistakes anyone can make are creating a strategy with a skeletal framework and/or borrowing concepts without adapting them. This can never become a fluid, dynamic strategy, and will just be a cookie-cutter strategy. These often do not function properly, either. Each company has its own unique needs, so these frameworks or concepts are not able to meet expectations because they are too standardized.

▶ **Can Looking at the Task at Hand from the Opposite Angle Constitute a "Strategy"?**
You see many "strategies," such as cutting costs because costs are too high, differentiating to create a competitive edge, or strengthening

Diagram 1-5   Strategic Pitfalls and Traps

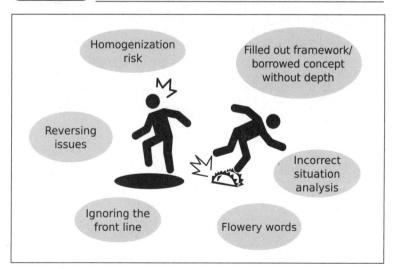

marketing power because it is weak. These initiatives only present the reverse side of the issues and don't present real solutions.

Cutting costs because the costs are too high doesn't delve into the core of the issue, the reason behind the high costs. Without understanding the true reason behind the issue, you can't come up with a realistic solution. You don't know if the high costs are the result of you not having a competitive edge. You can't even tell if the cost cutting is really needed to create a competitive edge.

A business is normally faced with a lot of issues. It is virtually impossible to resolve each and every issue. You have to consider what really needs to be changed or improved in order to create a competitive edge and determine the true cause of the issue. Only when all those factors are thoroughly considered can you create a true strategy. None of these initiatives that attempt to reverse an issue take all these points into consideration and therefore represent a lack of critical thinking.

▶ A Strategy Cannot Ignore the Front Line

A strategy based solely on secondhand information, data, or hearsay will not truly contribute to creating a competitive edge and therefore cannot be considered a true strategy. A strategy like this, or an armchair theory, lacks practical and realistic expectations and fails to rally support from the on-site workers.

A strategy, no matter how great, that can't prompt involved parties to put it into action exists only on paper. A "strategy" that can't be executed is not actually a strategy. A strategy full of borrowed frameworks and concepts often tends to fall into this trap.

▶ A Fake Strategy in Purple Prose

Another popular pitfall is a strategy embellished with trending concepts and keywords, making it look good but lacking depth. The business world comes up with new key phrases and buzzwords all the time. Omnichannel* is a primary example from recent years. Concepts such as SCM, CRM, Web2.0, and freemium are classic examples.

Of course, using these key phrases and buzzwords as hints when building your strategy is not an issue, as long as the true meaning behind them is understood. (In fact, you can use them to your advantage.) But just listing these words causes them to lose their meaning and does not contribute to your strategy.

▶ Failing to Grasp the Current Situation May Lead to Mistakes

Not having an accurate grasp of the situation can also lead to a pitfall or a trap when creating a strategy. An incorrect situation analysis, of course, leads you to an incorrect strategy.

As a case in point, mistakes such as overestimating your strength, incorrect market structure analysis, or underestimating your competitors can be fatal.

Miscalculating issues and organizational structures can also be a fatal mistake. Resolving an issue of habitually high costs can become a point of contention. But misreading the true reason for this habitual spending will result in costs never being lowered and can render the strategy useless.

Another frequent mistake is increasing product quantities in order to increase profit, thus saturating the market. Increased quantity normally results in decreased efficiency and puts a strain on profitability. This could result in a slight increase in sales at the cost of profitability, creating a vicious cycle. This, too, is a result of a strategic mistake stemming from not grasping the situation accurately.

▶ The Risk of Homogenized Strategies

It is true that understanding the situation accurately and thinking logically could lead to a standardized strategy similar to that of others. This is the risk of homogenized strategies. Of course, even with similar strategies, superior execution can give you an edge over the competition, making you come out on top. On the other hand, a homogenized strategy could mean you are competing with similar strategies, which, in the end, becomes all about financial strength and sustainability.

In order for a financially inferior company to come out on top, you must avoid a homogenized strategy at all cost. A financially superior company may still have a chance to beat the competition even with a homogenized strategy. You may consciously choose a similar strategy to that of your financially inferior competitors to drive them out of the market. A leading corporation, such as Toyota, often uses such a strategy.

---

*Omnichannel: Creating and providing a streamlined channel to shop by combining different sales platforms such as brick-and-mortar and online shops, where consumers can seamlessly make purchases without consciously selecting channels.

Preparations to Build the Correct Strategy

▶ Take the Right Steps to Analyze

So how can we avoid these pitfalls and traps? It is important to keep the following six points in mind (Diagram 1-6).

First, take the right steps to accurately analyze the situation. A strategy cannot be built overnight, nor is an idea enough to create a brilliant strategy. Normally, you must consider various elements and follow a complex thought process in order to end up with a functional strategy.

Of course, a standardized process does exist, a formula, if you will. It is important to go through these basic processes with care. Don't expect to get to a strategy by skipping these steps.

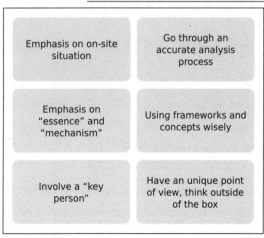

Diagram 1-6 Points in Creating a Functional Strategy

Emphasis on on-site situation	Go through an accurate analysis process
Emphasis on "essence" and "mechanism"	Using frameworks and concepts wisely
Involve a "key person"	Have an unique point of view, think outside of the box

MAKE SURE TO KEEP THESE SIX POINTS IN MIND.

A formula for these processes and proper consideration is exactly what we want you to take away from this book. You can master the basics of strategy building by reading all of this book.

▶ Use Frameworks and Concepts Wisely

We told you that frameworks and concepts can make or break a strategy. Meaning, frameworks and concepts can be great tools when utilized wisely. So how do we use them wisely? The key is to think for yourself by using these as hints.

Filling out a framework or following a concept alone will not do. Frameworks and concepts provide hints but do not do the thinking for you. For example, they can provide a broad point of view when coming up with a strategy. It is hard to create a strategy from scratch. By using frameworks and concepts as stepping stones, you won't have to come up with things to consider or points of contention from scratch.

Frameworks and concepts are the culmination of knowledge from predecessors and can give you a great advantage when applied wisely.

▶Have a Unique Point of View, Think Outside of the Box

It is important to view things from different angles and sometimes even doubt common sense in order to avoid a homogenized strategy. In fact, having a unique point of view and thinking outside of the box can lead to great success.

One example is the "Ore no French"* restaurants, which broke the concept of fine French cuisine being expensive. Breaking such

*Ore no French: A first-class restaurant where top-class chefs serve high-end French cuisine at reasonable prices. Managed by the Ore no Corporation.

preconceived notion and making efforts to do so allow room for a unique strategy and execution.

Uniqlo is another example. At first, it owed its growth to the American apparel company The GAP's SPA model. However, in order to compete with foreign competitions such as ZARA and H&M, Uniqlo shifted its focus onto functionality, which is often overlooked within the apparel industry, thus developing a specific, unique niche market and a competitive edge over its competitors.

The same goes for the grocery chain Oozeki in the Tokyo area. While generally a grocery store operates by hiring part-timers in order to keep the operational cost low, Oozeki mainly operates by hiring full-time employees in order to foster in-depth knowledge of customer needs, improve inventory control and decrease food loss, and generate repeat customers. These allow them to not only cover the higher operational cost but also create surplus profit. Having different points of view and thinking outside of common sense can lead to a unique strategy that actually works. You and your competitors might start from the same starting line, but you can still set yourself apart by thinking and looking at the situations from different angles.

▶Support the Front Line

When building a business strategy, you absolutely need an accurate understanding of the current situation. A situation can include, but is not limited to, the strengths and the weaknesses of your company and how your company is structured, as well as the current market, competitors, and how the industry works.

To understand it correctly, you must not depend on secondhand information and hearsay. You must see, hear, and feel the actual situation on the front line by actually studying the on-site field yourself. Secondhand information can be obtained by just about anyone, but information obtained by being on-site can provide you with vital information other people or companies may have missed. It can also provide you ideas for a unique point of view, or how to think outside of the box.

Sato Camera in Tochigi Prefecture holds the top market share in camera sales in the region, beating electronics giants such as Yamada Electronics and Yodobashi Camera. While it doesn't necessarily offer the lowest price or a strong customer reward program like other big chain stores, 80% of the customers who made a purchase at Sato Camera become repeat customers. Their profit margin increased up to 40% from its previous 25% or so after they eliminated unrealistic discount and point rewards programs. What sets Sato Camera apart is its motto of "Beautifully Preserving Memories," providing very specific customer services tailored to each and every customer's camera needs. They encourage customers to come back anytime even after purchase if they need help operating the camera. Customers coming in to print out photos can wait and relax on comfortable couches as well.

At a glance, Sato Camera's approach seems very inefficient. However, everyone at Sato Camera, from the CEO to the on-site sales clerk, came up with this strategy by interacting directly with customers, learning their needs and issues and what would make them happy. Mr. Sato, the CEO, stated: "We all learn from everyone including complete novices, from the grandma next door to an elementary student."

▶ Emphasis on Essence and Mechanism

It's also important to focus on the essence and the way things work. For example, if restructuring the cost is the key point in strategy, you must have an intimate understanding of what is causing the high cost structure, as well as the issues and reasons for them. You cannot make improvements without accurately understanding the issues at hand.

When we were assisting a food manufacturer with their strategic growth plans, cost rate was a big point of contention. Back then, the company thought the increasing cost was caused by the decreased output and increased ingredient cost. However, our analysis revealed that other factors, such as product selections, also played into the issue. A product with a low cost rate generally has a lower sales ratio. The large increase in product types was causing issues in manufacturing, loss of ingredients, and employees' proficiency, causing the cost rate for each product to increase. The cause of this was their strategy of churning out new products one after another.

As you can see, without truly understanding the essence and mechanism of things, you cannot create a strategy that will trigger a change. In the case of this food manufacturer, lowering ingredient cost and improving production output alone were not enough to turn things around. You need to start by having a clear plan to increase profit with a set number of products and come up with a plan to improve the sales ratio of products with low cost rate. Only then can you lower the cost rate.

Understanding the rules of market competition is also important. There are many frameworks that can help you understand specific markets, such as Five Forces or Advantage Matrix. It is only by using these frameworks wisely on top of understanding the essence and mechanics of the competitive market that you can find an accurate strategy. A prime example of this is how Japanese electronics companies are struggling in certain markets, such as TV and mobile phone markets. The rapid advance of digitalization and the Internet becoming widely available have dramatically changed the industry's structure and its rules of market competition. Their struggle is caused by them not recognizing those changes and consequently being unable to respond to them in time.

▶ Bring in a Key Person

A complete blueprint is not the end of creating a strategy. The ultimate goal is to beat the competition and increase profit, which requires a concrete, executable strategy. It is only when the execution yields the desired result that you can call it a strategy. To do so, of course, a suitable strategy is necessary; however, equally vital is to bring everyone involved (from top management to frontliners) together with a strategy that everyone can agree on and be passionate about. This feeling of togetherness is crucial.

To foster this, in the course of selecting strategy options, you will need to involve a key person from each department in the decision-making process. A strategy that pays no heed to the frontliners' input and suggestions often ends up being ineffective. Of course, you can't let yourself be swayed too much by the reality of the on-site situation. You would end up with a situation similar to the current situation and would not achieve the strategic goal of defeating your competition and increasing profit. The insight of frontliners is important, but sometimes different points of view or out of ordinary measures are needed in order to attain dramatic growth, as we have already discussed.

4

▶ Four Steps in Building a Strategy

Now, how do we create a strategy that is both functional and executable? We've already pointed out that due process is important in creating a strategy. Here are the four key steps in building a strategy:

▶ Step 1 - Analyze the Situation

The first step is situation analysis. This is the starting point and the core of any strategy creation. You can say 70% of strategy building is complete as long as it is based on an accurate situation analysis. That's how important situation analysis is.

In *The Art of War*, Sun Tzu wrote, "If you know the enemy and know yourself, you need not fear the result of a hundred battles." This sums up best how important situation analysis is.

In order to create an effective strategy, you must have a thorough understanding of your company's situation and the external factors, including market structure and rules of competition. The on-site situation can provide you with great clues in coming up with strategic ideas. The core of situation analysis lies in understanding the essence and mechanism of both internal and external situations.

FIRST, UNDERSTAND THE OVERALL FLOW.

Diagram 1-7 Four Steps in Building a Strategy

STEP 1

ANALYZE THE SITUATION

SWOT Analysis - OT Analysis (Opportunities for Growth, Possible Threat to Growth)

5 Forces Analysis
- Positioning Analysis
- Competition Analysis
- Client (Consumers, Corporations) Analysis
- Key Success Factor (KSF) Analysis

SWOT Analysis - SW Analysis
- Achievements and Performance Analysis
- Positioning Analysis
- Business Model Analysis
- Marketing (4P) Analysis
- Value Chain and Organizational Analysis
- Tangible and Intangible Asset Analysis

STEP 2

FORMULATE STRATEGIC OPTIONS

- Goals and points of contention for strategy selection
- Growth options for the preestablished business
- Options for the newly established business
- Options for improving profit

STEP 3

EVALUATE AND SELECT OPTIONS

- Evaluate rationality
- Evaluate probability
- Gathering intents and expectations of the parties involved

STEP 4

TRANSLATE STRATEGIC OPTIONS INTO PLANS OF ACTION

- Translating into a plan
- Translating into action
- Organizing them into executable plans
- Build a structure to oversee progress

You may think situation analysis only applies to the current situation, but that is not true. Your strategy must include how to stay competitive in the future. Considering only the current situation is not enough. You must be especially mindful of the external factors, such as how the market and competitors may expand in the future.

It is crucial for you to have the understanding of not only the current situation, but also foresee how external factors may change in the future by studying the trends, competition strategies, and consumer tendencies in the past.

▶ Step 2 - Formulate Strategic Options

During this step, you will lay out your options based on the situation analysis, which means you will be selecting strategies to win. The goal is to select options that can lead your company to victory with three key factors: the market, competitive edge, and resource allocation.

First, you need to consider each and every possible option. Letting probability and common sense restrict you during this step may hinder you from creating an effective strategy. Worry about them in the next step, and use this opportunity to freely consider options from every possible angle.

▶Step 3 - Review and Select Options

Here is where we take the various options you came up with during Step 2 and evaluate them based on rationality and probability, and start the selection process. The key point is how you think of the selection process.

A selection based on only rational, objective evaluation will most likely end up with an ordinary conclusion. It will not help the company stand out, and even risk it being homogenous.

To avoid this, it is important to keep a different point of view and even question common sense. The intent and expectation of all parties involved are just as important. In the end, what drives people in executing the selected strategy is their will and conviction. You need to take all these into consideration, discuss them with all involved parties, and select strategic options that everyone can agree on.

▶ Step 4 - Translate Strategic Options into Plans of Action

In this step, we will organize and put together selected options into a strategy, draw out a road map needed to execute it, decide on who will execute it and how, as well as come up with a tangible action plan.

The actual execution of the strategy and its result depend on this step. It is crucial that you build a clear plan of action as well as monitor and follow up on its progress.

In other words, build a specific plan plausible for progress monitoring. Your action plan needs to clearly state who will be doing what and until when.

STEP 1

Analyze the Situation

STORY 2 **Knowing Your Enemy Is Knowing Yourself**

FIRST, WE ANALYZE THE CURRENT SITUATION.

AND REMEMBER TO ALWAYS SHARE THE RESULT!

I'VE GOTTEN A LOT OF POSITIVE FEEDBACK ON OUR RED-BEAN PASTE.

BUSINESS PARTNERS AND REPEAT CUSTOMERS ALIKE ALL COMPLIMENTED IT.

IT'S A VERY VALUABLE ASSET.

STORY 2

KNOWING YOUR ENEMY IS KNOWING YOURSELF

50

ALTHOUGH WE CREATED THE BUSINESS PLANNING DEPARTMENT SPECIFICALLY FOR HER JUST AS THE BANK SUGGESTED, I JUST DON'T THINK SHE'LL MAKE IT.

...BUT THE FACT IS THAT WE'VE HAD SALES DECLINING FOR THE PAST FEW YEARS.

WE'VE GOT TO DO SOMETHING ABOUT THAT.

I'VE GOT THAT COVERED.

I'M THE ONE WHO TOOK THE FOUNDER MATSUI'S JAPANESE SWEETS SPECIALTY ALL OVER THE COUNTRY, TURNING IT INTO A 10 BILLION-YEN GIANT.

BUSINESS IN GENERAL IS JUST DOWN RIGHT NOW.

GOODNESS, MATSUI-SAN HAS FALLEN ILL AND RETIRED, AND I'M NOT GETTING ANY YOUNGER.

I'D HAVE BEEN HAPPY TO TEACH THE YOUNGER GENERATION THE ROPES.

I DON'T GET WHY THE BANK INSISTED TO LET HER DO WHATEVER SHE WANTS.

...

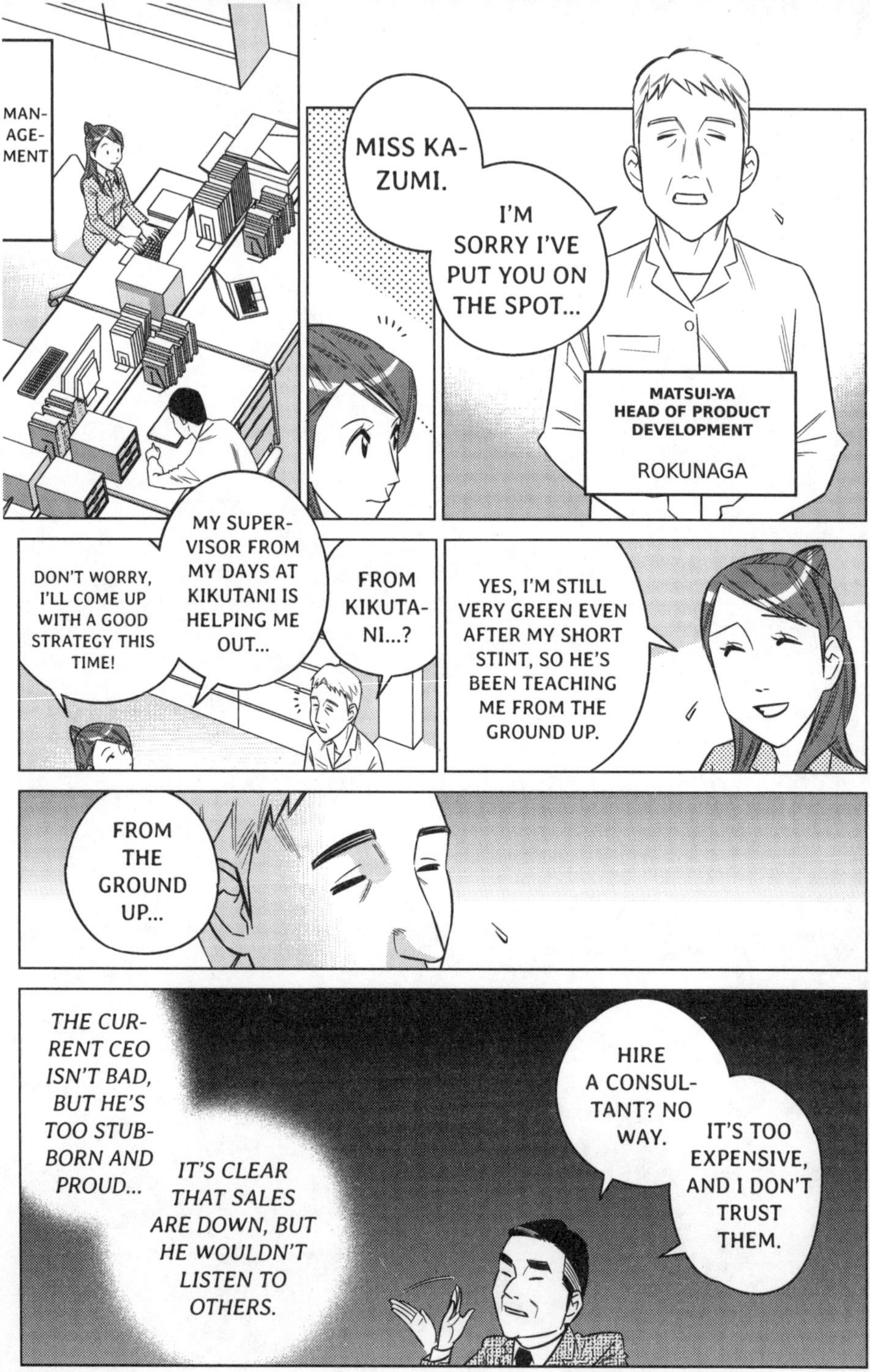
MAN-AGE-MENT
MISS KA-ZUMI.
I'M SORRY I'VE PUT YOU ON THE SPOT...
MATSUI-YA HEAD OF PRODUCT DEVELOPMENT
ROKUNAGA
DON'T WORRY, I'LL COME UP WITH A GOOD STRATEGY THIS TIME!
MY SUPER-VISOR FROM MY DAYS AT KIKUTANI IS HELPING ME OUT...
FROM KIKUTA-NI...?
YES, I'M STILL VERY GREEN EVEN AFTER MY SHORT STINT, SO HE'S BEEN TEACHING ME FROM THE GROUND UP.
FROM THE GROUND UP...
THE CUR-RENT CEO ISN'T BAD, BUT HE'S TOO STUB-BORN AND PROUD...
IT'S CLEAR THAT SALES ARE DOWN, BUT HE WOULDN'T LISTEN TO OTHERS.
HIRE A CONSUL-TANT? NO WAY.
IT'S TOO EXPENSIVE, AND I DON'T TRUST THEM.

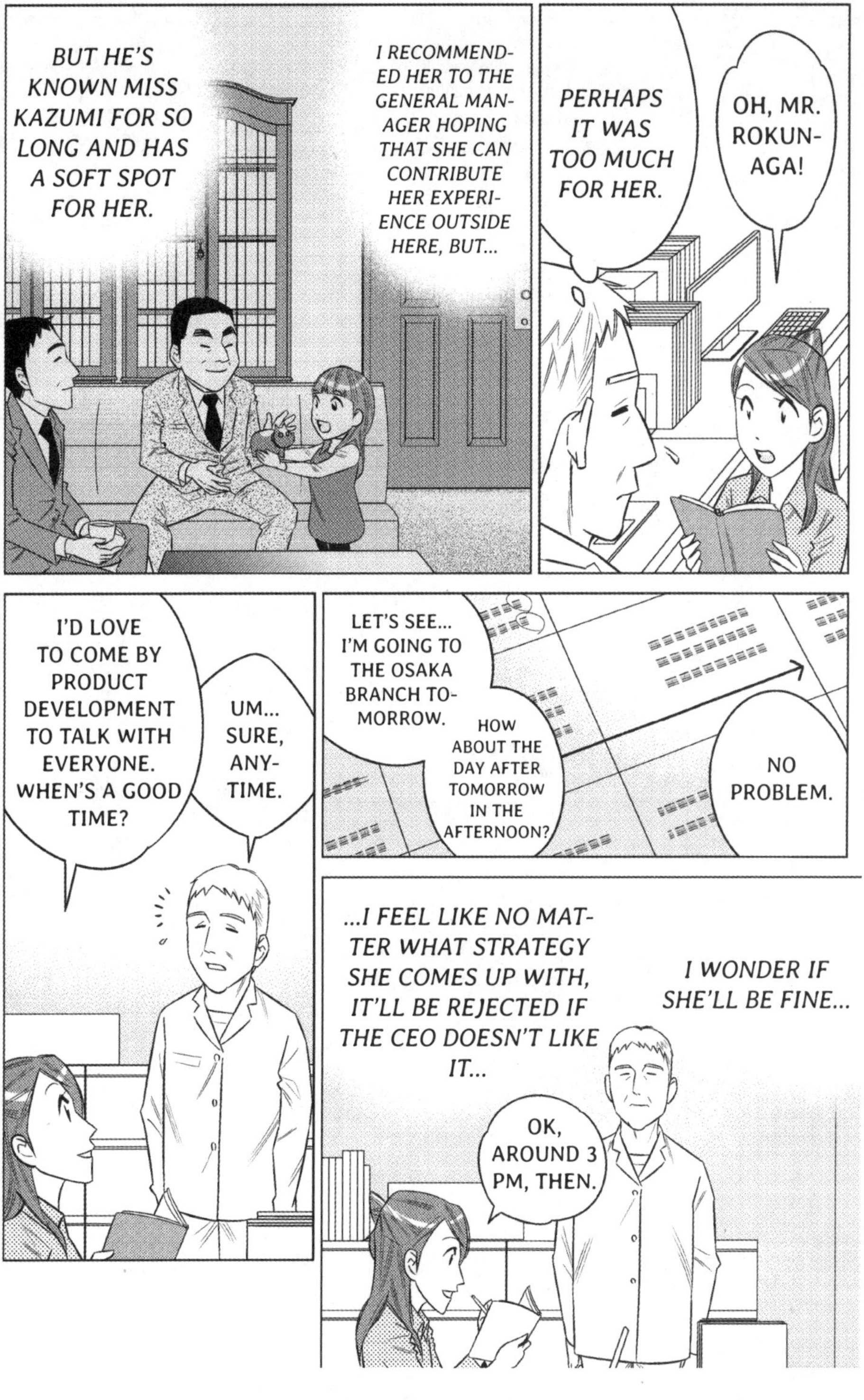
I RECOMMENDED HER TO THE GENERAL MANAGER HOPING THAT SHE CAN CONTRIBUTE HER EXPERIENCE OUTSIDE HERE, BUT...
BUT HE'S KNOWN MISS KAZUMI FOR SO LONG AND HAS A SOFT SPOT FOR HER.
PERHAPS IT WAS TOO MUCH FOR HER.
OH, MR. ROKUNAGA!
I'D LOVE TO COME BY PRODUCT DEVELOPMENT TO TALK WITH EVERYONE. WHEN'S A GOOD TIME?
UM... SURE, ANYTIME.
LET'S SEE... I'M GOING TO THE OSAKA BRANCH TOMORROW.
HOW ABOUT THE DAY AFTER TOMORROW IN THE AFTERNOON?
NO PROBLEM.
...I FEEL LIKE NO MATTER WHAT STRATEGY SHE COMES UP WITH, IT'LL BE REJECTED IF THE CEO DOESN'T LIKE IT...
I WONDER IF SHE'LL BE FINE...
OK, AROUND 3 PM, THEN.

THE FIRST STEP IS ANALYZING THE SITUATION, BUT THERE ARE A LOT OF FRAMEWORKS FOR IT.

THE MOST POPULAR IS THE SWOT ANALYSIS.

IN MOST CASES, AS LONG AS THE SWOT ANALYSIS IS ACCURATE, YOU CAN SAY THAT YOUR SITUATION ANALYSIS IS COMPLETE.

SWOT STANDS FOR THIS, RIGHT?

STRENGTHS	:	COMPANY'S STRENGTHS, EDGE
WEAKNESSES	:	COMPANY'S WEAKNESSES, ISSUES
OPPORTUNITIES	:	OPPORTUNITIES FOR GROWTH
THREATS	:	POSSIBLE THREATS TO THE COMPANY'S GROWTH

I'VE ALREADY FILLED OUT THE MATRIX AND ANALYZED IT!

YOU WENT STRAIGHT TO FILL THEM OUT?

YES! STARTING WITH S.

UM...

WHEN I SAID YOUR ANALYSIS IS COMPLETE IF YOUR SWOT IS DONE PROPERLY, I DIDN'T MEAN JUST FILLING IN THE BLANKS.

FOR EXAMPLE, YOU WROTE "STRENGTH IN PRODUCT DEVELOPMENT" — WHERE DOES THAT STRENGTH COME FROM? HOW STRONG IS IT COMPARED TO OTHER COMPANIES?

? STRENGTH IN PRODUCT DEVELOPMENT

MOREOVER, DOES CUSTOMERS' FEEDBACK SUPPORT THIS?

...YOU NEED TO DO A MORE IN-DEPTH ANALYSIS, OR YOUR STRATEGY WON'T BE PRECISE ENOUGH TO CONVINCE ANYONE.

YEAH, I WAS TOLD IT WAS FULL OF HOLES...

SEE? THAT'S WHY YOU NEED TO ANALYZE FROM EVERY POSSIBLE ANGLE.

ANOTHER IMPORTANT THING.

DIVIDE THE ANALYSIS INTO SW AND OT, AND START WITH OT FIRST.

SW IS ABOUT YOUR OWN COMPANY, WHILE OT IS ALL EXTERNAL FACTORS INCLUDING CONSUMERS, COMPETITORS, AND THE MARKET.

THINK OF IT AS A FISHING TRIP. YOU CHANGE YOUR GEARS AND BAITS DEPENDING ON DIFFERENT FACTORS, RIGHT?

TEMPERATURE?

SEA FISHING? RIVER FISHING?

WEATHER?

TYPES OF FISH AVAILABLE?

TIME OF DAY?

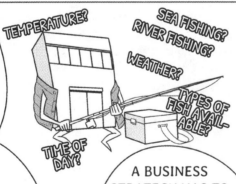

A BUSINESS STRATEGY HAS TO CONSIDER THOSE EXTERNAL FACTORS. COMPARING THEM TO YOUR COMPANY MAKES IT EASY TO SEE YOUR SW TOO.

...HERE'S A MORE IN-DEPTH SWOT ANALYSIS.

OT ANALYSIS

- THE FIVE FORCES ANALYSIS
- POSITIONING ANALYSIS
- COMPETITION ANALYSIS
- CLIENT (CONSUMERS, CORPORATIONS) ANALYSIS
- KEY SUCCESS FACTOR (KSF) ANALYSIS

SW ANALYSIS

- ACHIEVEMENTS AND PERFORMANCE ANALYSIS
- POSITIONING ANALYSIS
- BUSINESS MODEL ANALYSIS
- MARKETING (4P) ANALYSIS
- VALUE CHAIN AND ORGANIZATIONAL ANALYSIS
- TANGIBLE AND INTANGIBLE ASSET ANALYSIS

CHECK AND SEE IF YOU'VE MISSED ANY OF THEM.

OH, AND WHAT'S KNOWN AS 3C ANALYSIS IS ALSO PART OF THIS.

T-THIS MANY?!

YOU DON'T HAVE TO DO AN IN-DEPTH ANALYSIS FOR EACH ONE.

YOU CAN BE MORE EFFICIENT IF YOU USE THE HYPOTHESIS TESTING APPROACH.

THE HYPOTHESIS TESTING APPROACH?

YEAH! GET A BALLPARK BY VIEWING THE WHOLE PICTURE, THEN START ANALYZING IT IN DEPTH.

EVEN IF THE HYPOTHESIS IS WRONG, YOU CAN RESET ITS COURSE AS YOU GO.

SO WE HAVE TO VIEW THE WHOLE INDUSTRY TO ANALYZE IT? THAT REQUIRES A LOT OF RESEARCH MATERIALS...

DON'T WORRY TOO MUCH ABOUT IT FOR NOW.

THE JAPANESE SWEETS MARKET IS NOT EXACTLY BOOMING TO BEGIN WITH, RIGHT?

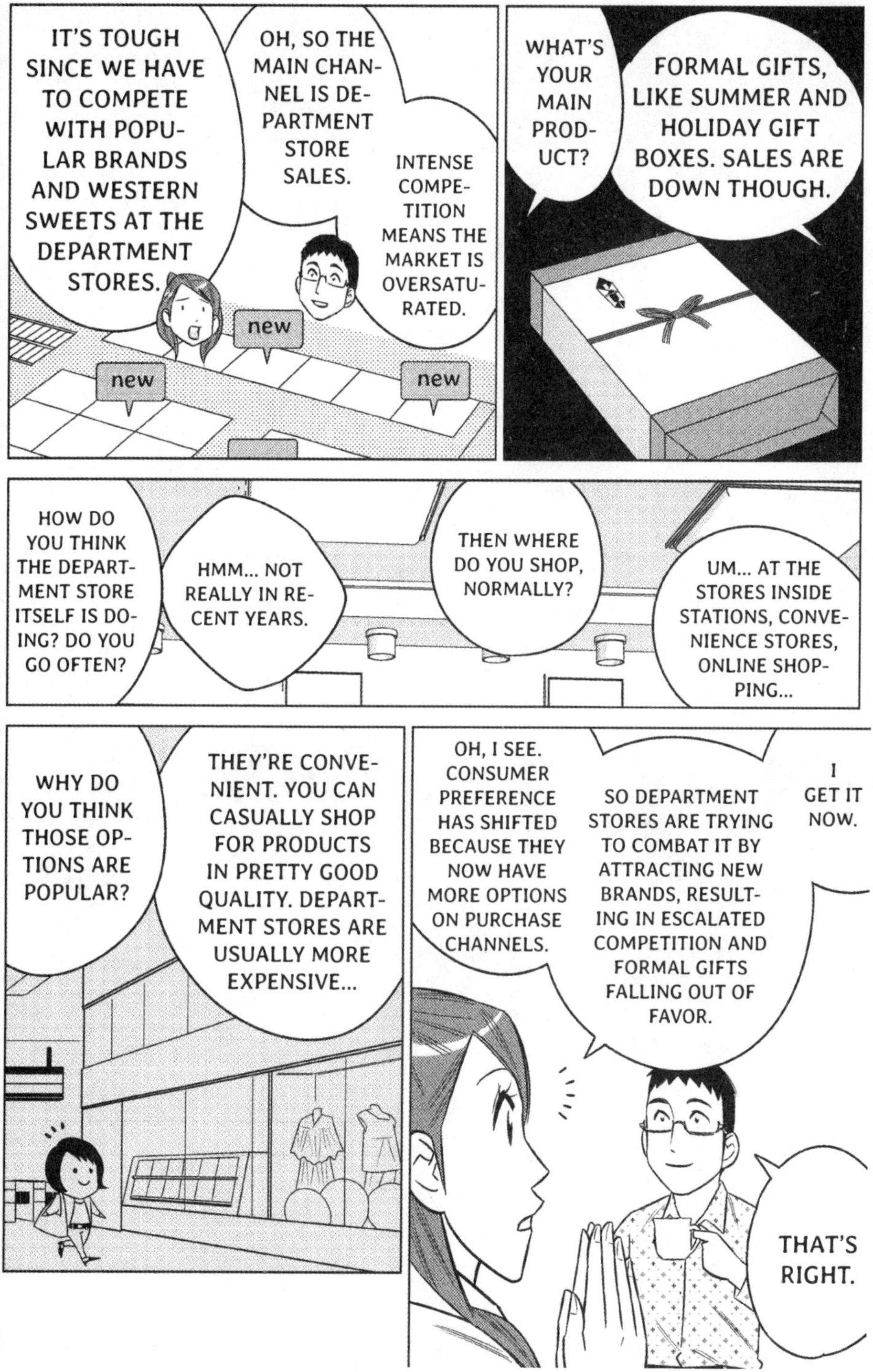

IT'S TOUGH SINCE WE HAVE TO COMPETE WITH POPULAR BRANDS AND WESTERN SWEETS AT THE DEPARTMENT STORES.
OH, SO THE MAIN CHANNEL IS DEPARTMENT STORE SALES.
INTENSE COMPETITION MEANS THE MARKET IS OVERSATURATED.
new
new
new
WHAT'S YOUR MAIN PRODUCT?
FORMAL GIFTS, LIKE SUMMER AND HOLIDAY GIFT BOXES. SALES ARE DOWN THOUGH.
HOW DO YOU THINK THE DEPARTMENT STORE ITSELF IS DOING? DO YOU GO OFTEN?
HMM... NOT REALLY IN RECENT YEARS.
THEN WHERE DO YOU SHOP, NORMALLY?
UM... AT THE STORES INSIDE STATIONS, CONVENIENCE STORES, ONLINE SHOPPING...
WHY DO YOU THINK THOSE OPTIONS ARE POPULAR?
THEY'RE CONVENIENT. YOU CAN CASUALLY SHOP FOR PRODUCTS IN PRETTY GOOD QUALITY. DEPARTMENT STORES ARE USUALLY MORE EXPENSIVE...
OH, I SEE. CONSUMER PREFERENCE HAS SHIFTED BECAUSE THEY NOW HAVE MORE OPTIONS ON PURCHASE CHANNELS.
SO DEPARTMENT STORES ARE TRYING TO COMBAT IT BY ATTRACTING NEW BRANDS, RESULTING IN ESCALATED COMPETITION AND FORMAL GIFTS FALLING OUT OF FAVOR.
I GET IT NOW.
THAT'S RIGHT.

WHAT THAT MEANS IS THAT THE RULES OF COMPETITION HAVE CHANGED DUE TO A SHIFT IN THE MARKET STRUCTURE.

BUT THIS IS OFTENTIMES IGNORED.

EVERY ISSUE HAS ITS CAUSE, SO ALWAYS MAKE SURE TO LOOK INTO WHY IT HAPPENED.

LET'S USE THIS AS A HYPOTHESIS AND DO SOME SUPPORTING ANALYSIS.

- THE JAPANESE SWEETS MARKET HAS LITTLE GROWTH OPPORTUNITY.
- SALES ARE DOWN IN THE MAIN CHANNELS (DEPARTMENT STORES).
- DEPARTMENT STORES SUFFERING FROM THE STRUCTURAL RECESSION.

HAVING A GRASP OF THE MARKET IN GENERAL WILL ALLOW YOU TO KEEP THE WHOLE PICTURE IN MIND AS YOU GO.

OKAY! THEN WE SHOULD DEVELOP A PRODUCT FOR CONVENIENCE STORES—

YOU'RE JUMPING WAY TOO FAR!

TAKE YOUR TIME AND COME UP WITH STRATEGIC PLANS LATER.

FIRST, WE ANALYZE THE CURRENT SITUATION.

AND REMEMBER TO ALWAYS SHARE THE RESULT!

I MEAN, SHARING IT DOESN'T MEAN FORCING IT ONTO OTHERS.

IT'S NORMAL FOR EVERYONE INVOLVED TO UNDERSTAND THE SITUATION A BIT DIFFERENTLY.

MARKETING DEPARTMENT

WHAT BRIDGES THAT GAP IS OBJECTIVE DATA AND THOROUGH DISCUSSIONS.

YOU'LL HAVE TO NOTE DOWN EACH POINT OF VIEW AND OPINION OF THOSE INVOLVED AND ORGANIZE THEM.

AS FOR COMPETITION... MAYBE COMPANY A WITH THEIR CREATIVE JAPANESE SWEETS, COMPANY B, WHICH HAS A STRONG MARKET SHARE IN AIRPORTS, AND COMPANY C WITH ITS FAMED RED-BEAN JELLY?

OH! IT'S NOT SWEETS, BUT HAVE YOU HEARD OF COMPANY D'S RICE SNACKS SPECIALTY?

HUH? WHAT'S THAT?

RICE SNACKS HAVE A HIGH GROSS PROFIT MARGIN.

THE REVENUE PER CUSTOMER IS LOW THOUGH.

TO COVER THAT, THEIR STORES ARE STRUCTURED TO OPERATE AT MINIMUM COST.

THE OPEN STOREFRONT IS DESIGNED SO CUSTOMERS CAN CASUALLY STOP BY.

CUSTOMERS CAN CHOOSE WHAT TO BUY WITHOUT ANY SALES CLERK BOTHERING THEM.

THEIR RICE SNACKS ARE SO VARIED AND THE PACKAGING IS EYE-CATCHING.

HMM... OKAY, I'LL RESEARCH COMPANY D AS WELL!

YEP, THAT'S HOW YOU SHOULD ASK AROUND AND LISTEN. GO ON, JUST LIKE THAT.

YEAH, I WAS TOO FOCUSED ON UNBAKED SWEETS...

THIS REALLY HOOKS YOU, DOESN'T IT?

SO, WE NOW HAVE SOME IDEAS OF OUR COMPETITORS' SUCCESSFUL STRATEGIES.

COMPANY A :	COMPREHENSIVE MODEL WITH A HEAVY FOCUS ON PRODUCT APPEAL
COMPANY B :	OTHER SALES CHANNEL (NO DEPARTMENT STORE) EXPANSION MODEL
COMPANY C :	SPECIALIZATION MODEL FOCUSING ON SIGNATURE PRODUCT
COMPANY D :	LOW-COST MODEL TARGETING PERSONAL CONSUMPTION

➤SUMMARY ON PAGE 91 ONWARDS

COMPANY A RELEASES ATTRACTIVE AND PROFITABLE PRODUCTS. THEIR STOREFRONT KEEPS ITS IMAGE FRESH BY OFFERING SEASONAL ITEMS.

NOT ONLY DO THEY HAVE OUTLETS IN FAMOUS DEPARTMENT STORES, THEIR ONLINE STORE IS ALSO GOING STRONG.

COMPANY B'S STRENGTH IS HAVING OUTLETS OUTSIDE OF DEPARTMENT STORES, LIKE AIRPORTS AND STATIONS. THEY'RE ALSO QUICK TO EXPAND OVERSEAS.

THEY HAVE THEIR GENERAL PRODUCT LINEUP, BUT THEY ALSO SELL AREA OR REGION-LIMITED ITEMS.

COMPANY C FOCUSES ON PUSHING ITS SIGNATURE RED-BEAN JELLY.

BY DOING SO, THEY'VE BRANDED THEMSELVES AS "RED-BEAN JELLY MEANS COMPANY C; COMPANY C MEANS RED-BEAN JELLY."

THEIR PRODUCTS BALANCE TRADITION AND INNOVATION AND ARE POPULAR AS GIFTS, SO THEY GET A LOT OF REPEAT CUSTOMERS.

AND I'VE ALREADY TOLD YOU ABOUT COMPANY D.

EACH COMPANY HAS SOMETHING UNIQUE TO THEM. MATSUI-YA FEELS SO HALF-BAKED IN COMPARISON.

YES, THAT UNIQUE THING THAT SETS THEM APART IS CALLED POSITIONING.

BUT, HOW COULD THEY FEATURE IT SO CLEARLY?

THAT'S A GOOD WAY OF LOOKING AT IT. IT'S SOMETHING YOU SHOULD ALWAYS THINK ABOUT. "HOW IS THAT POSSIBLE?"

FOR EXAMPLE, I'VE HEARD COMPANY A'S ATTRACTIVE PRODUCTS ARE THE RESULT OF THE CEO PERSONALLY OVERSEEING THE PRODUCT DEVELOPMENT.

THEY MIGHT ALSO HAVE OUTSTANDING EMPLOYEES, A GOOD TRAINING PROCESS, OR TANGIBLE ASSETS. IT COULD BE ANYTHING.

REALIZING THAT YOU ARE HALF-BAKED IS PROGRESS IN ITSELF.

Y-YOU'RE RIGHT!

KEEPING ALL THESE IN MIND... LET'S ANALYZE THE SUCCESS FACTORS, OR KSF.

KSF STANDS FOR THESE.

WE'RE TALKING ABOUT FACTORS LEADING TO A VICTORY IN THE INDUSTRY, OR A KEY TO SUCCESS.

KEY SUCCESS FACTOR

IDENTIFYING THESE IS REALLY DIFFICULT.

BUT WE ALREADY HAVE SOME CLUES FROM ANALYZING THE CHANGE IN THE MARKET AND COMPETITION.

FIRST, WE NEED TO MAKE A CLEAR BUSINESS MODEL.

EACH COMPANY FOLLOWS ITS OWN, SPECIFIC BUSINESS MODEL.

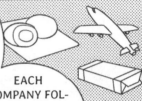

DEVELOPMENT OF THE SIGNATURE PRODUCT IS ONE OF THEM.

A SUCCESSFUL PRODUCT BRANDING SUCH AS "XX MEANS YY" IS A STRONG CONTENDER.

I SEE. A KEY TO SUCCESS...

ANOTHER ONE MAY BE BRAND REVITALIZATION.

ESTABLISHED BRANDS CAN'T JUST RELAX, THEY'LL NEED TO CONTINUOUSLY COME UP WITH NEW CONCEPTS AND PRODUCTS.

THERE'S MORE.

DEVELOPING OTHER SALES CHANNELS OUTSIDE OF THE DEPARTMENT STORES SEEMS IMPORTANT, AS WELL.

WITH THE DECLINING SALES AT DEPARTMENT STORES, WE'LL NEED NEW SALES CHANNELS SUCH AS ONLINE SHOPS AND STORES WITHIN STATION BUILDINGS.

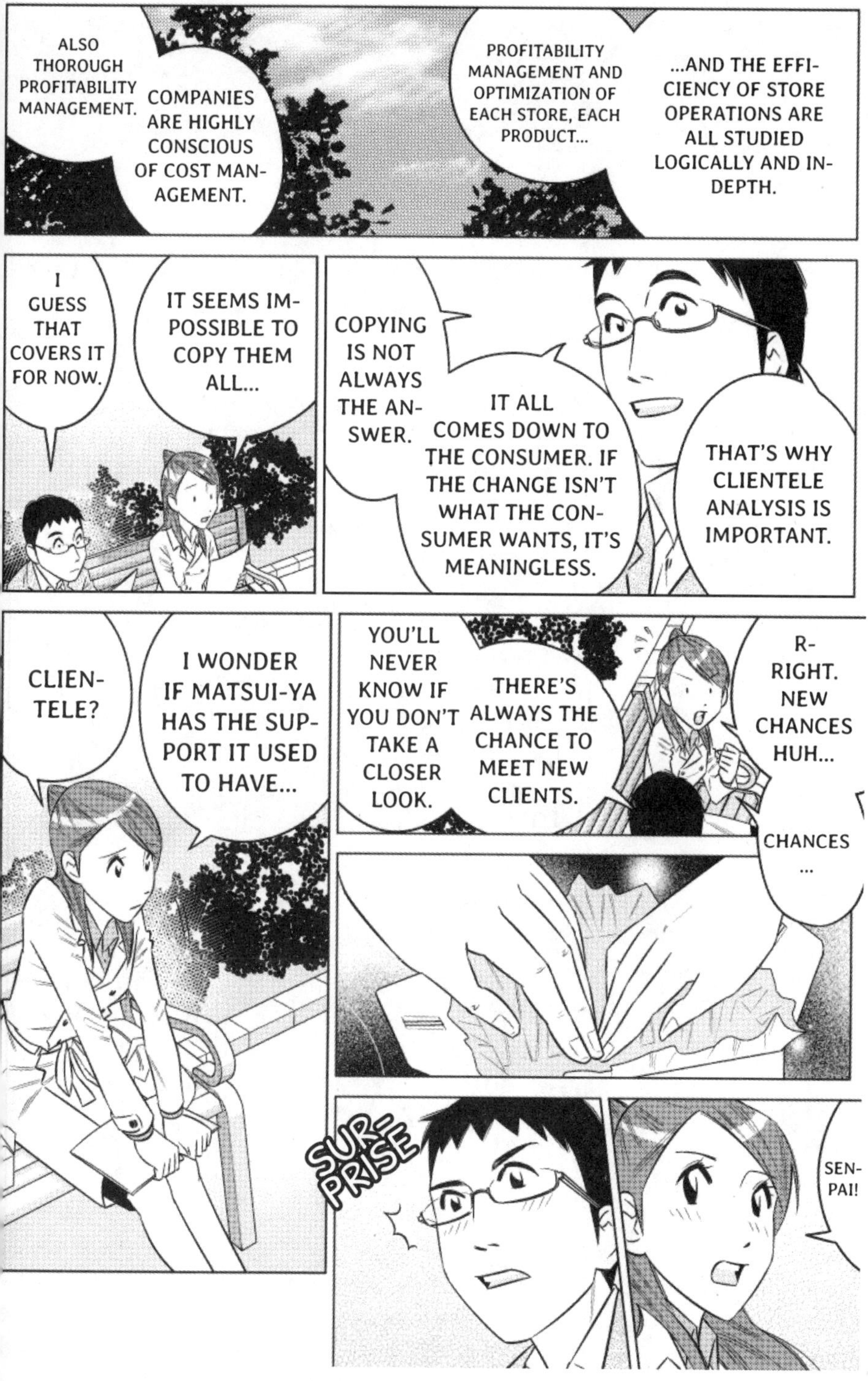
ALSO THOROUGH PROFITABILITY MANAGEMENT.
COMPANIES ARE HIGHLY CONSCIOUS OF COST MAN-AGEMENT.
PROFITABILITY MANAGEMENT AND OPTIMIZATION OF EACH STORE, EACH PRODUCT...
...AND THE EFFI-CIENCY OF STORE OPERATIONS ARE ALL STUDIED LOGICALLY AND IN-DEPTH.
I GUESS THAT COVERS IT FOR NOW.
IT SEEMS IM-POSSIBLE TO COPY THEM ALL...
COPYING IS NOT ALWAYS THE AN-SWER.
IT ALL COMES DOWN TO THE CONSUMER. IF THE CHANGE ISN'T WHAT THE CON-SUMER WANTS, IT'S MEANINGLESS.
THAT'S WHY CLIENTELE ANALYSIS IS IMPORTANT.
CLIEN-TELE?
I WONDER IF MATSUI-YA HAS THE SUP-PORT IT USED TO HAVE...
YOU'LL NEVER KNOW IF YOU DON'T TAKE A CLOSER LOOK.
THERE'S ALWAYS THE CHANCE TO MEET NEW CLIENTS.
R-RIGHT. NEW CHANCES HUH...
CHANCES ...
SUR-PRISE
SEN-PAI!

I GOT IT FIRST RIGHT?!

THE LAST ONE.

GO AHEAD.

YUMMY.

INTERVIEWING DEPARTMENT STORE CLERKS

THANK YOU FOR YOUR TIME.

YOU'RE RIGHT. WE'RE RARELY THE CUSTOMER'S FIRST STOP.

THOSE WHO DO COME TO US FIRST ARE MOSTLY ELDERLY.

A MAJORITY OF THEM ARE LOOKING FOR FORMAL GIFTS.

LOOKING AT THE CUSTOMER FLOW, I FEEL IT'S BECOME INCONSISTENT OR MAYBE MORE DIVERSE.

MANY OF THEM LOOK AT BOTH JAPANESE AND WESTERN SWEETS AND PURCHASE THEM ON A WHIM.

BUT THOSE CUSTOMERS DON'T STAY LONG AT OUR STORE.

THEY DON'T STAY LONG?

THAT'S RIGHT.

...

DO YOU HAVE ANY INPUT FROM A PART-TIMER'S POINT OF VIEW?

ACTUALLY, I WANTED TO WORK AT HIVER COFFEE.

BUT THEY WEREN'T HIRING...

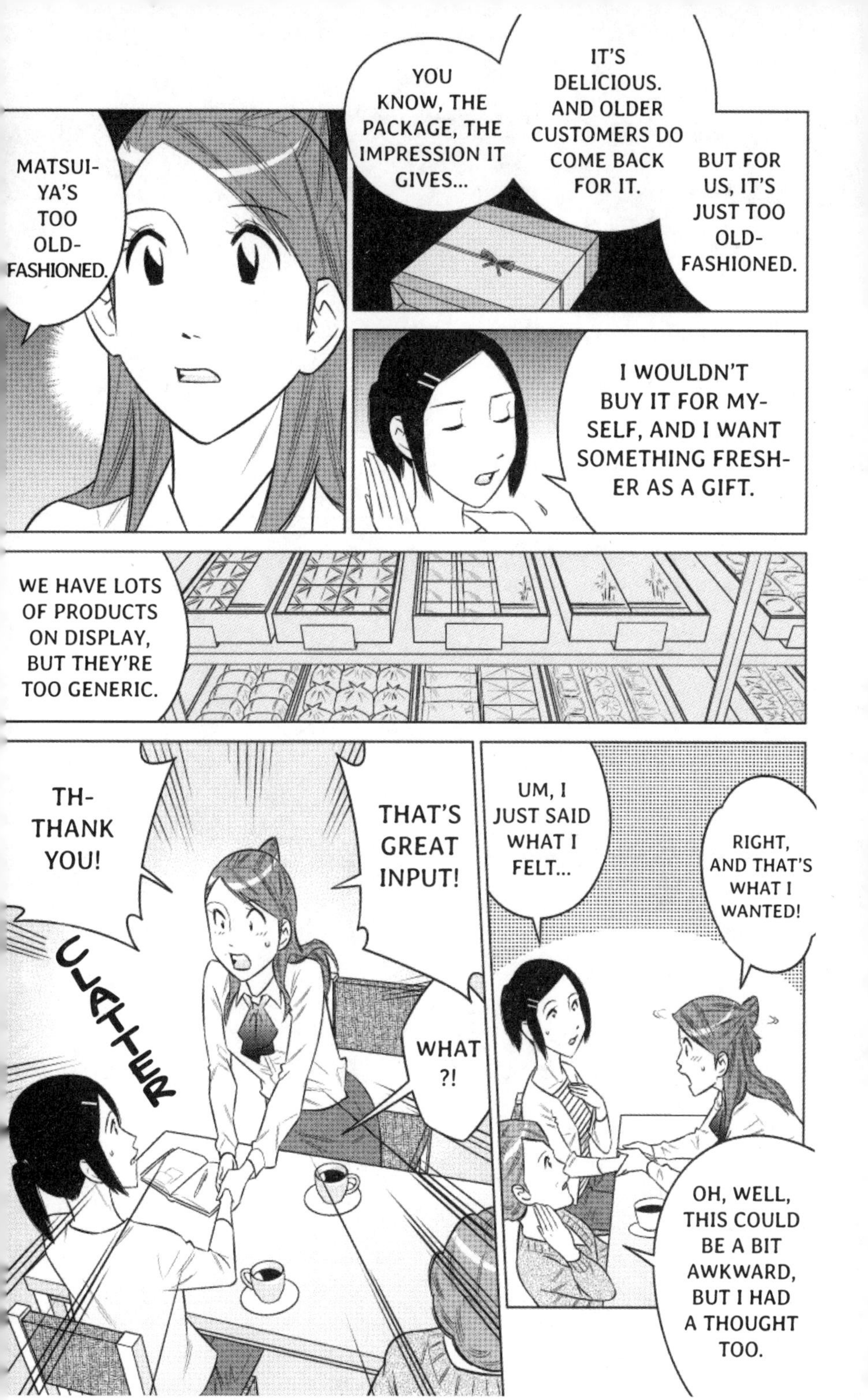
MATSUI-YA'S TOO OLD-FASHIONED.
YOU KNOW, THE PACKAGE, THE IMPRESSION IT GIVES...
IT'S DELICIOUS. AND OLDER CUSTOMERS DO COME BACK FOR IT.
BUT FOR US, IT'S JUST TOO OLD-FASHIONED.
I WOULDN'T BUY IT FOR MY-SELF, AND I WANT SOMETHING FRESH-ER AS A GIFT.
WE HAVE LOTS OF PRODUCTS ON DISPLAY, BUT THEY'RE TOO GENERIC.
CLATTER
TH-THANK YOU!
THAT'S GREAT INPUT!
WHAT?!
UM, I JUST SAID WHAT I FELT...
RIGHT, AND THAT'S WHAT I WANTED!
OH, WELL, THIS COULD BE A BIT AWKWARD, BUT I HAD A THOUGHT TOO.

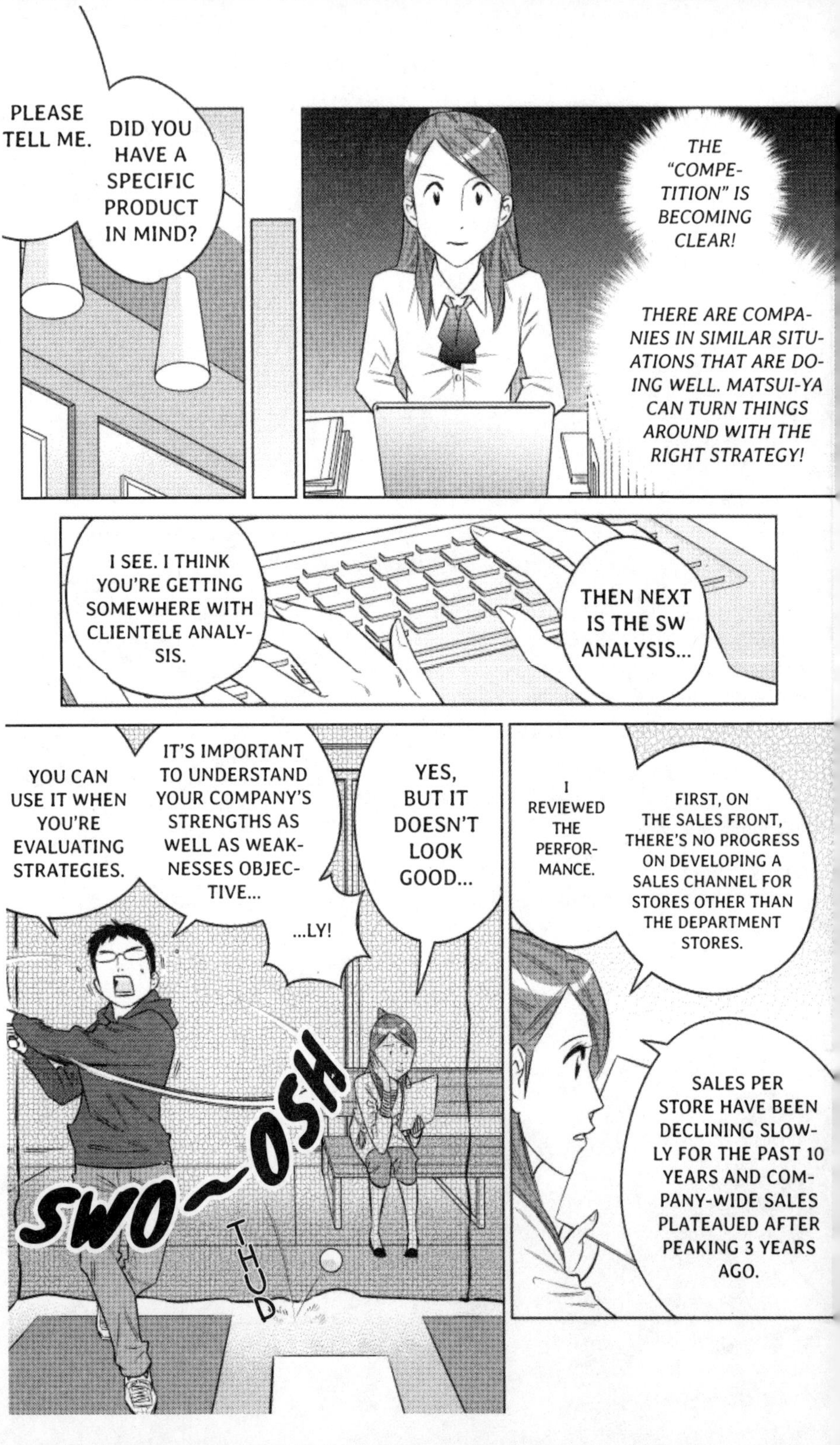

PLEASE TELL ME.
DID YOU HAVE A SPECIFIC PRODUCT IN MIND?
THE "COMPETITION" IS BECOMING CLEAR!
THERE ARE COMPANIES IN SIMILAR SITUATIONS THAT ARE DOING WELL. MATSUI-YA CAN TURN THINGS AROUND WITH THE RIGHT STRATEGY!
I SEE. I THINK YOU'RE GETTING SOMEWHERE WITH CLIENTELE ANALYSIS.
THEN NEXT IS THE SW ANALYSIS...
YOU CAN USE IT WHEN YOU'RE EVALUATING STRATEGIES.
IT'S IMPORTANT TO UNDERSTAND YOUR COMPANY'S STRENGTHS AS WELL AS WEAKNESSES OBJECTIVE...
...LY!
YES, BUT IT DOESN'T LOOK GOOD...
SWO~OSH
THUD
I REVIEWED THE PERFORMANCE.
FIRST, ON THE SALES FRONT, THERE'S NO PROGRESS ON DEVELOPING A SALES CHANNEL FOR STORES OTHER THAN THE DEPARTMENT STORES.
SALES PER STORE HAVE BEEN DECLINING SLOWLY FOR THE PAST 10 YEARS AND COMPANY-WIDE SALES PLATEAUED AFTER PEAKING 3 YEARS AGO.

INDIVIDUAL STORE SALES ARE DECLINING MORE THAN THE DEPARTMENT STORES. BRAND RECOGNITION CONTINUES TO BE HIGH, BUT IT'S NOT RESULTING IN ACTUAL SALES.

AS FOR PROFIT... PROFIT HAS BEEN DOWN FOR THE PAST 5 YEARS, BUT WE FINALLY ENDED UP IN THE RED LAST YEAR.

THE REASON IS THAT UNDER-PERFORMING STORES WERE NEGLECTED, AND UNPROFITABLE PRODUCTS WERE INTRODUCED CONTINUOUSLY ...

WE HAVE TOO MANY PRODUCTS, BUT PROFIT IS DEPENDENT ON ONE PRODUCT THAT HAS THE HIGHEST RETURN.

OTHER CONTRIBUTORS INCLUDE DECREASED GIFT SALES AND THE HIGH-COST RATES FOR UNBAKED SWEETS. OUR OPERATIONAL AND MANUFACTURING COSTS ARE ALSO HIGHER THAN THE COMPETITION'S.

WE EXPANDED OUR MANUFACTURING LINE THREE YEARS AGO AT RECORD HIGH SALES. BUT THE CURRENT UTILIZATION RATE IS ONLY 55%. IT'S CLEAR WE'RE OVER CAPACITY.

WE'RE INCREASING PRODUCTIVITY BY TAKING ORDERS FROM OTHER COMPANIES IN THE SAME BUSINESS, BUT IT'S BARELY CONTRIBUTING TO PROFITS.

I SEE. THAT'S A TOUGH SITUATION.

HOW ABOUT THE MARKETING (4P) ANALYSIS?

OH YES, LET'S SEE...

COMPARED TO THE COMPETITION WE'RE BEHIND ON PROMOTION.

COMPETITORS ARE COLLABORATING WITH FASHION AND LIFESTYLE MAGAZINES ON AD CAMPAIGNS.

IT'S BOTH BRANDING AND AN EFFECTIVE WAY TO GET EXPOSURE.

SOCIAL MEDIA MARKETING IS ALSO HUGE, BUT WE'RE NOT DOING THAT EITHER.

PRODUCT APPEAL AT THE STORE FRONT IS WEAK TOO.

STORE STRUCTURES, DISPLAYS, STORE GREETINGS...

HONESTLY, THERE ARE TOO MANY ISSUES TO LIST.

I SEE.

BUT THAT'S HOW IT IS.

NO ONE ANALYZES THE SITUATION WHEN THINGS ARE GOOD. THEY DON'T CATCH ISSUES UNTIL IT'S TOO LATE.

THIS GOES FOR OT ANALYSIS TOO. THE MAIN GOAL IS NOT TO BRING YOU DOWN.

THREATS AND WEAKNESSES ARE EYE-CATCHING.

HOW CAN WE TURN THREATS INTO OPPORTUNITIES? HOW CAN WE STRENGTHEN WEAKNESSES AND DEVELOP STRENGTHS? VIEWPOINTS LIKE THOSE ARE THE...

...KEY!!

WHO~OSH

I'M MISSING AND I'M EXHAUSTED.

YOU'RE NOT LOOKING AT THE BALL.

YOUR FORM TOO...

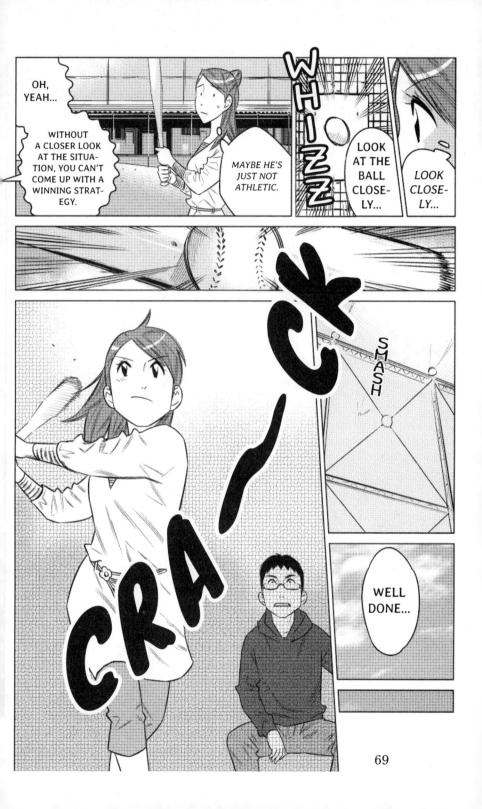

OH, YEAH...

WITHOUT A CLOSER LOOK AT THE SITUATION, YOU CAN'T COME UP WITH A WINNING STRATEGY.

MAYBE HE'S JUST NOT ATHLETIC.

WHIZZ

LOOK AT THE BALL CLOSELY...

LOOK CLOSELY...

CRA-CK

SMASH

WELL DONE...

THE SWOT ANALYSIS IS FINALLY COMPLETE!

THE KEY TO SUMMARIZING THE SWOT ANALYSIS IS...

...TO QUESTION ALL ANALYTIC RESULTS WITH THE POINT OF VIEW OF "HOW WILL THAT SPECIFICALLY AFFECT OUR COMPANY?"

...I HOPE THIS IS ACTUALLY RIGHT.

YEAH, I THINK THIS IS FINE.

PRODUCT DEVELOPMENT DEPARTMENT

GOOD EVENING. YOU'RE STILL HERE?

...AH, MISS KAZUMI.

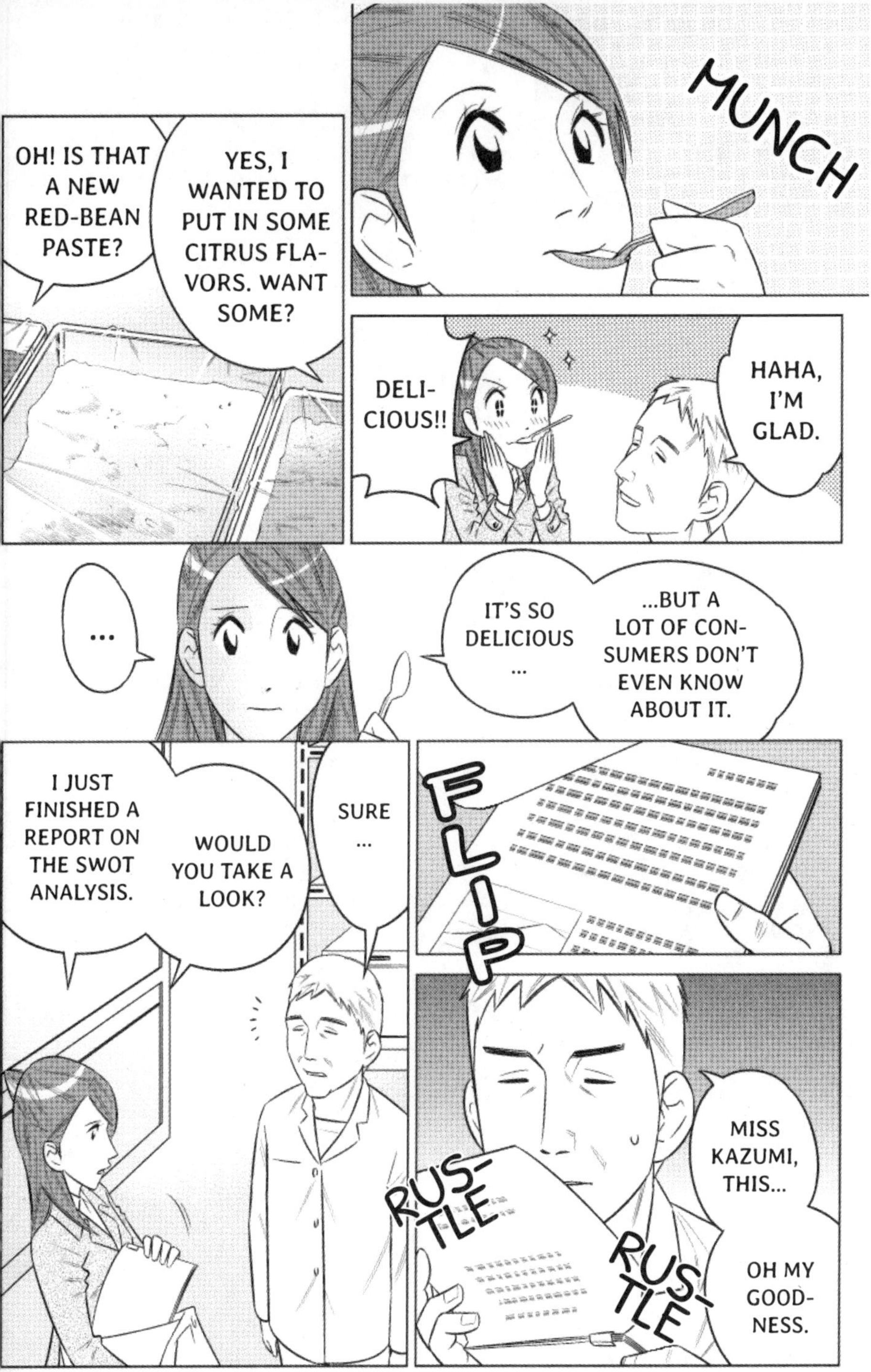
MUNCH
OH! IS THAT A NEW RED-BEAN PASTE?
YES, I WANTED TO PUT IN SOME CITRUS FLA-VORS. WANT SOME?
DELI-CIOUS!!
HAHA, I'M GLAD.
...
IT'S SO DELICIOUS ...
...BUT A LOT OF CON-SUMERS DON'T EVEN KNOW ABOUT IT.
I JUST FINISHED A REPORT ON THE SWOT ANALYSIS.
WOULD YOU TAKE A LOOK?
SURE ...
FLIP
RUS-TLE
RUS-TLE
MISS KAZUMI, THIS...
OH MY GOOD-NESS.

THIS IS EXACTLY IT. THIS SUMS UP MY VAGUE WORRIES IN SUCH A LOGICAL MANNER!

GREAT! I'LL PRESENT IT TO EACH DEPARTMENT HEAD TOMORROW THEN.

YES, PLEASE. BUT...

THERE'S NOTHING BUT ISSUES...

YES, BUT...

PLEASE LOOK AT THE ASSET ANALYSIS AT THE END.

≪ASSET ANALYSIS≫

COMPANY ASSETS ARE TANGIBLE...AS SEEN BELOW

I'VE GOTTEN A LOT OF POSITIVE FEEDBACK ON OUR RED-BEAN PASTE.

BUSINESS PARTNERS AND REPEAT CUSTOMERS ALIKE ALL COMPLIMENTED IT.

IT'S A VERY VALUABLE ASSET.

MATSUI-YA IS WELL RECOGNIZED.

THE ISSUE IS THAT OUR IMAGE IS STUCK AS BEING OLD-FASHIONED.

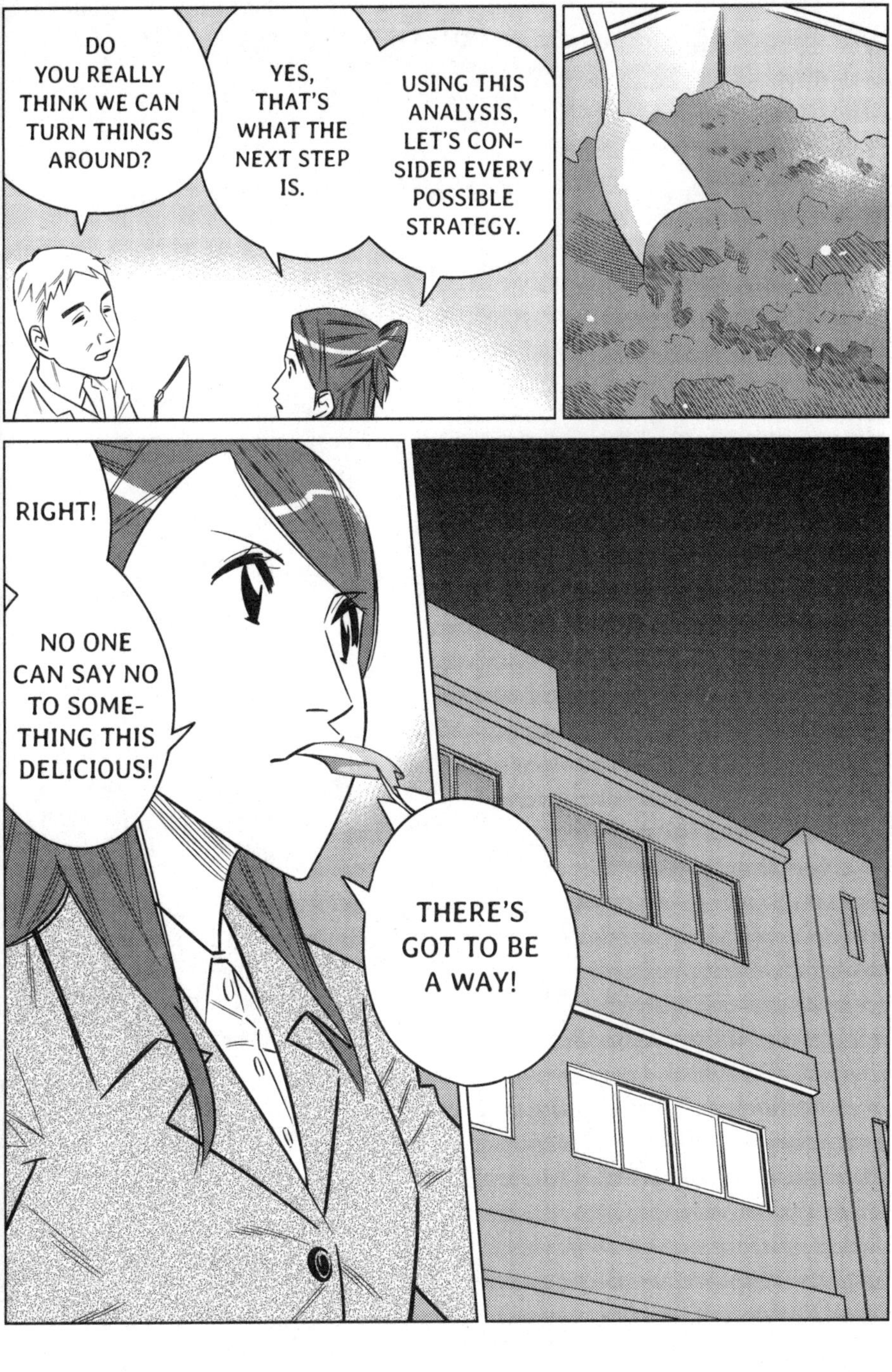
DO YOU REALLY THINK WE CAN TURN THINGS AROUND?
YES, THAT'S WHAT THE NEXT STEP IS.
USING THIS ANALYSIS, LET'S CONSIDER EVERY POSSIBLE STRATEGY.
RIGHT!
NO ONE CAN SAY NO TO SOMETHING THIS DELICIOUS!
THERE'S GOT TO BE A WAY!

1   The Essentials of Situation Analysis

▶ Analyzing the Situation Is The First Step in Building a Strategy

As explained in the prologue, the most important point in building a strategy is the present. This means having a clear and accurate grasp of the current situation surrounding the company, industry, and everything around it. When building a strategy, you must select the target market and decide how and where to allocate your limited resources in order to create an edge over your competition. Your strategy is a culmination of multiple decisions, which you can't do without an accurate understanding of the current situation.

However, in analyzing the situation, you need to not only think about the present but also work on your prediction for the future. Your strategy will soon turn obsolete if you focus too much on the future, especially in the current ever-changing market. Keep in mind to observe the external factors closely in order to foresee the future. You'll end up with an invalid strategy if the situation analysis you base it on is inaccurate. This is why situation analysis is such an important task.

INCORRECT ANALYSIS CAN LEAD TO A MISGUIDED STRATEGY...

▶ Only a Handful of Corporations Truly Understand the Current Situation

Even though it is an integral step, the fact is there are not many companies that accurately and thoroughly understand their situation. A lot of them draw conclusions and build strategies based on past experiences and assumptions, which they believe to be true. This is why they also believe that their strategies are accurate, and often end up turning a blind eye until it is too late.

A correct strategy will grow obsolete as time passes by. All factors including the market, your company's position in it, the edge and strengths relative to the environment are subject to change. What might have started out as an accurate strategy based on a precise situation analysis might turn irrelevant if you don't anticipate changes over time or make an error in judging them. An example of this would be how Japanese electronics manufacturers are now struggling due to the error in judging the situation surrounding digitalization and emerging new markets.

Typically, executives and employees have knowledge and expertise resulting from their experience in the industries they are in. However, this can turn into a pitfall. Depending too much on past experience and knowledge can lead to incorrect assumptions, keeping them from realizing that there is a shift in the situation. Previously successful companies are more prone to fall into this trap.

Matsui-ya's CEO, Umesawa, is a prime example of this (see page 51). Even though the industry and the market surrounding Japanese sweets are changing dramatically, he keeps following the same old strategy simply because it worked before, blaming the declining sales on the general business climate.

A misaligned situation analysis among involved parties is another issue faced by a lot of companies. The sales department may claim that a product is not selling because it is not good enough, while the product development team might say it is not selling because the sales and marketing are not working properly. This shows that there is a "gap in the grasp" of the situation among involved parties. Such a gap will not entail any agreement or correct decision-making, and therefore cannot lead to an accurate strategy either.

▶ Methodology and Frameworks: A False Sense of Completing the Situation Analysis

Various books on methodology and frameworks of situation analysis are widely published today and are used by companies. However, many still do not have an accurate grasp of the situation. Why is that?

One reason is because of the lack of analysis about the change in market structure and rules of competition. Or it could be because they may have identified the issues but had not done in-depth analysis of the actual cause. Many seem to think that filling in the blanks within the framework means that the situation analysis is complete.

Matsui-ya's Kazumi, too, thought she completed the SWOT (Strengths, Weaknesses, Opportunities, Threats) analysis simply by filling in the blanks. But this alone is not enough to build a strategy. The key here is to grasp the causal effect through in-depth situation analysis based on accurate information. Finding the core cause of the problem to reveal the true situation is vital.

▶ Three Keys in Understanding the True Situation

What should you do to avoid falling into the trap of superficial situation analysis? Here are three important points you should keep in mind.

First of all, you need to thoroughly collect objective, accurate facts. This is your starting point. Facts are the information you will base your analysis on, including information backed with quantitative data, qualitative data of the actual condition of the market, and on-site frontline, consumer demands, and competitor trends. Without the facts, you cannot analyze the situation. Do on-site fieldwork so you can gather these facts and experience them firsthand.

Secondly, you must analyze these facts structurally to understand the essence of the situation. Many often present a "situation analysis," but it is really just a well-organized, but superficial, list of issues (Diagram 2-1). An example of this can be seen on page 78, which is merely a list of circumstances and cannot be called a situation analysis. It only contains circumstances and results, and does not look into actual causes or the mechanics of the situation. There is no structured analysis that can give you an insight of why this circumstance happened, or what is the actual issue, or what sort of mechanism might have contributed to this circumstance. Try comparing it to the example of a proper situation analysis on pages 80–81 (Diagram 2-2).

Thirdly, it is essential to discuss and share the results with all parties involved. Simply analyzing the facts and writing the report will not change anything. The true meaning of situation analysis lies in sharing the result and coming to a general consensus. The original aim of strategic planning is to bridge the gap in each party's grasp on the situation. Not only do you need to have both objective data and accurate analysis, a thorough discussion based on those is also necessary. Listen to everyone's opinions and points of view in order to build the whole picture of the situation analysis.

▶ The Basics of Situation Analysis: SWOT Analysis

To review, the point of the situation analysis is finding ideas for

Diagram 2-1 Example of Incorrect Situation Analysis

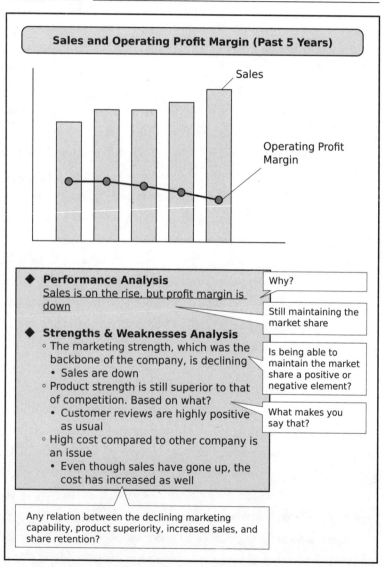

Sales and Operating Profit Margin (Past 5 Years)

Sales

Operating Profit Margin

◆ **Performance Analysis**
Sales is on the rise, but profit margin is down

Why?

Still maintaining the market share

◆ **Strengths & Weaknesses Analysis**
○ The marketing strength, which was the backbone of the company, is declining
 • Sales are down
○ Product strength is still superior to that of competition. Based on what?
 • Customer reviews are highly positive as usual
○ High cost compared to other company is an issue
 • Even though sales have gone up, the cost has increased as well

Is being able to maintain the market share a positive or negative element?

What makes you say that?

Any relation between the declining marketing capability, product superiority, increased sales, and share retention?

building and strengthening a strategy or competitive edge. The most famous framework used to do so is the SWOT analysis. SWOT stands for your company's strengths and competitive edge (Strengths), your company's weaknesses and issues (Weaknesses), opportunities for growth (Opportunities), and possible threats to your company's growth (Threats). In most cases, an accurate SWOT analysis generally means the situation analysis is complete.

So what needs to be analyzed specifically? Depending on situations and targets, the answer varies and there is not a single correct answer. However, generally the following methodology is used to do a SWOT analysis.

First, OT (opportunities for growth and possible threats to your company's growth) are based on the Five Forces analysis (industry structure analysis), positioning analysis, competition analysis, client (consumers and corporations) analysis, and key success factor (KSF) analysis. SW (company strengths, edge, weaknesses and issues), on the other hand, are based on achievements and performance analysis, positioning analysis, business model analysis, marketing (4P) analysis, value chain and organizational analysis, and tangible and intangible asset analysis. Of course, there are many other frameworks and methods to analyze the external factors and the company's current situation. We won't be able to cover them all here, but please take up other related books if you are interested.

Why are we starting with OT analysis before going to SW, even though it is called SWOT analysis? There's a reason behind it. SW normally pertains to your own company and situation while OT is all about external factors such as the market, competition, and clients. To understand yourself, you must first have a clear grasp of all external influences.

Please recall the quote from Sun Tzu's *The Art of War*: "If you know the enemy and know yourself, you need not fear the result of a

Diagram 2-2 Example of Company Analysis

Structured, logical in-depth analysis to find the causal effect

○ The two main reasons for the market share retention are high customer approval and the strong marketing
  • Product strength lies in its functionality and balanced pricing point, making it superior to that of the competitors
  • High approval resulting from frequent visits and in-depth product knowledge of the marketing personnel

Top 5 Reasons Why Customers Choose Our Company

Confirming cause based on objective, quantitative data

Customer Satisfaction Based on Marketing Personnel's Age

○ Our marketing strength lies in having experienced and skilled marketing personnel
  • However, many are approaching the retirement age, while the next generation's experience and skill level are declining
  • Low customer satisfaction toward mid-level employees
  • Mid-level employees have the lowest sales per person and number of clients per person (based on company data)
  • As a result, marketing strength is taking a hit

Confirming cause based on objective, quantitative data

○ One of the factors contributing in the decrease of profitability is the company's countermeasure of increasing on-site marketing personnel. This resulted in an increase of labor costs.
  • Marketing productivity (sales per person) has dipped dramatically compared to 5 years ago (based on company data)

Number of Marketing Personnel vs Labor Cost Rate
(5-year comparison)

Confirming cause based on objective, quantitative data

Number of Marketing Personnel

Labor Cost & Labor Cost Rate

hundred battles." Just as Sun Tzu preached to "know the enemy" first, and then to "know yourself," it is ideal to start with OT analysis before moving on to SW when doing the SWOT analysis. But, as we mentioned before, covering these points alone does not automatically mean that you correctly understand the situation.

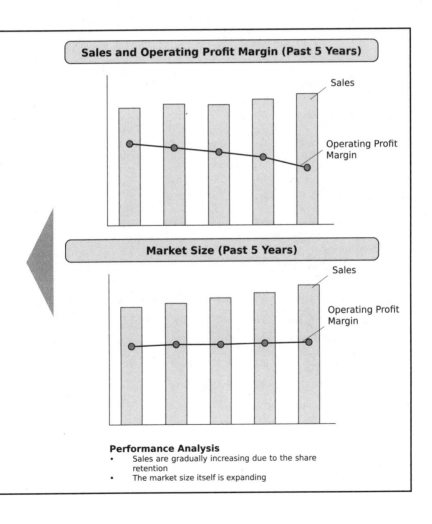

Sales and Operating Profit Margin (Past 5 Years)

Sales

Operating Profit Margin

Market Size (Past 5 Years)

Sales

Operating Profit Margin

Performance Analysis
- Sales are gradually increasing due to the share retention
- The market size itself is expanding

Diagram 2-3 Goal of Situation Analysis and SWOT Analysis

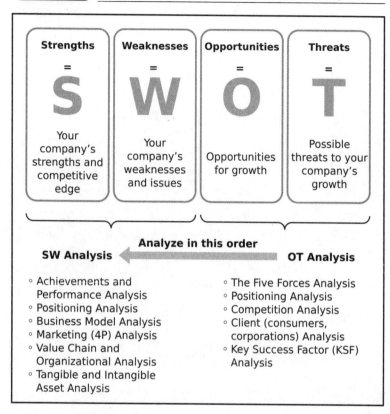

Strengths = **S**
Your company's strengths and competitive edge

Weaknesses = **W**
Your company's weaknesses and issues

Opportunities = **O**
Opportunities for growth

Threats = **T**
Possible threats to your company's growth

Analyze in this order

SW Analysis ← **OT Analysis**

- Achievements and Performance Analysis
- Positioning Analysis
- Business Model Analysis
- Marketing (4P) Analysis
- Value Chain and Organizational Analysis
- Tangible and Intangible Asset Analysis

- The Five Forces Analysis
- Positioning Analysis
- Competition Analysis
- Client (consumers, corporations) Analysis
- Key Success Factor (KSF) Analysis

Again, these are merely a methodology on point of view, way of thinking, and analysis. You must keep the goal in mind as you continue with the analysis. Additionally, it may not be necessary to do an in-depth analysis for each and every point listed here. In order to come to an accurate analysis result efficiently, you will need to do a hypothesis testing.

▶ OT Analysis: Three Core Elements

The goal of OT analysis is to identify the key points in strategy building, namely opportunities for growth and possible threats. Keep these three core elements in mind when proceeding with OT analysis (Diagram 2-4). First, visualize the market and the consumers. You need to visualize it through a realistic analysis of the current market as well as objective and logical analysis backed up by quantitative data.

Secondly, get a grasp of the current industry structure. You can utilize the Five Forces analysis to look into the structure, and then sort out various viewpoints on the flow of products, money, and service (such as the value chain, distribution, and manufacturing process). Segmenting the market size, the positioning of your company as well, as the competitors (by region, product types, price range, channels, etc.) can also provide you with valuable insights.

Lastly, you must understand that the industry structure could change at any time, now or in the near future, which will present you with business opportunities and risk factors. Among these are the increase of income level, lifestyle changes, shifts in consumers' choice of place and way of purchase, competitors entering or exiting the market, market structure turning exclusive due to M&As, change in market

GOTTA UN-
DERSTAND
THE CORE
ELEMENTS
FIRST!

players due to globalization, reduced regulations, improved infrastructures and distribution lines, as well as changes in the industry resulting from advances in technology.

You must especially pay close attention to changes that can rewrite the rules of the entire industry. Global markets for mobile phones and television have reshaped their structures drastically in a very short time, consequently changing their rules as well. The same happened to the PC and mobile app market, which had to catch up with the speed of expansion and advances of mobile devices and apps. It has revolutionized the market structures so much, even Microsoft, once considered to have a near monopoly of the market, is forced to change its strategies.

As you can see, it is essential to assess the changes in market structures and rules of the competition by taking both business opportunities and risks into consideration.

Diagram 2-4 Three Core Elements of OT Analysis

① **Visualize the market and the consumers**
  • Realistic analysis of the current market
  • Objective and logical analysis backed by quantitative data

② **Understanding the industry's structure**
  • Utilize the Five Forces analysis to grasp the competitive environment of the industry
  • Sort out various viewpoints on the flow of products, money, and service (including value chain, distribution, and manufacturing process)
  • Segmenting the market size, the positioning of your company as well as the competitors (by region, product types, price range, channels, etc.)

③ **Attention to ongoing and possible changes in the industry structure (presenting business opportunities and risk factors)**
  • Change in consumers (income level increase, lifestyle changes, shifts in consumers' choice of place and way of purchase)
  • Change in competition (competitors entering or exiting the market, market exclusivization due to M&As, change in market players due to globalization)
  • Change in industrial environment (reduced regulations, improved infrastructures and distribution lines, changes in the industry resulting from advances in technology)

▶ The Five Forces Analysis

The Five Forces analysis is a well-known framework for analyzing the industry's competitive environment and the basis for identifying opportunities and risks. According to the Five Forces analysis, the competitive environment of any industry is influenced by five factors: intensity of rivalry among competitors, threat of new entrants, threat of substitute products, buyer bargaining skill, and supplier power.

The company that surpasses the competition in any of these elements will come out on top. Therefore, the following three strategies become imperative: a differentiation strategy to set your company apart from others, a cost leadership strategy that focuses on providing high-quality products at a low price, and a niche strategy, which aims to dominate a very specific field. Of course, in today's diverse market, these three strategies alone may not be enough to create a winning strategy. Still, keep them in mind as the most essential concepts in business strategy.

In the Five Forces analysis, you must consider your current company situation, as well as the future outlook, in relation to each factor. Doing so will help in revealing what the opportunities and threats to your company are.

Before you start analyzing the five factors, you must get an overview of the target industry. Otherwise, you won't be able to see the big picture and may not be able to read the market flow. To get a good overview, you need to grasp the change in market size, the industry's value chain and business model, key players, and the main clientele.

Understand the market tendency by paying close attention to the target market of your chosen field (or the target market of the new industry you are entering): Is it expanding, holding steady, or declining? Normally, the market size is judged by the monetary value, but in this case, separating the unit price and the quantity can provide a valuable point of view.

Superficial rise or decline are not the important points in market size analysis. What is vital are the causes and effects that play behind that rise or decline. Let's take a look at the Japanese sweets market Matsui-ya is in, specifically the department store Japanese sweets market.

The Japanese sweets market in general is suffering from stagnation, and the department store Japanese sweets market specifically is in a slump. The cause behind it is the dropping sales in formal gifts for summer and holidays at the department stores, which, when we delve even deeper, is caused by the decline in the tradition of seasonal gift giving in the general public. This means that there is a shift in consumers' lifestyle.

The line between the Japanese and Western sweets has blurred in recent years, sparking a competition among different genres. This, too is a big stagnation factor. On top of that, the development of various other sales channels such as station buildings, convenience stores, and online stores is contributing to the decline of the department store sales, including the sweets market.

As you can see, "Analysis" is not simply reviewing the result of market change, but also getting an in-depth understanding of the market's mechanism and causal effects behind that result.

▶Analyzing the Five Points

Now that we have the market overview, let's proceed with the Five Forces analysis. Each of the five forces is explained in Diagram 2-5. There are many publications that cover the Five Forces elements in depth that you can refer to, should you wish to learn more. This book will go over what you should keep in mind when identifying the opportunities and threats.

There are three things to consider when analyzing the opportunities and threats. First, remember that opportunities and threats are two sides of the same coin. For example, an escalating buyer bargaining power is generally considered a threat. However, if you think of it as an opportunity to create a stronger bond with that consumer, it might lead to stabilization and expansion of the business.

Procter & Gamble, a major American daily necessities manufacturer with strong ties with retail giants such as Walmart, is a good example of this. Through its close relationship with large retailers, P&G is able to obtain various sales data that they can apply to their product development and marketing.

Next, you should always try to seek new opportunities to counter the threats. Take Fujifilm as an example. As a company specializing in film photography, the rising market of digital cameras is a very clear threat toward their company's declining business. However, they used that very threat to look into and develop new ventures. As a result, with their years of knowledge and skills, they have successfully developed growing ventures in medical equipment and cosmetics. The material manufacturer Toray Industries is another example of this. By changing your viewpoint and way

Diagram 2-5 The Five Forces and Their Analytical Points

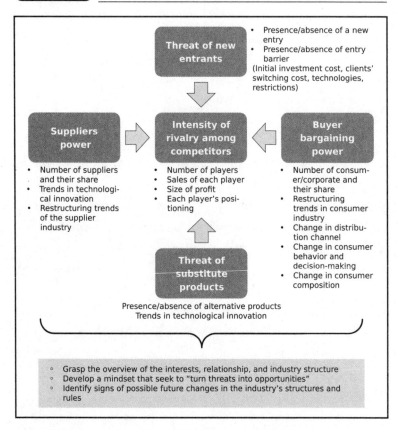

Threat of new entrants
- Presence/absence of a new entry
- Presence/absence of entry barrier
(Initial investment cost, clients' switching cost, technologies, restrictions)

Suppliers power
- Number of suppliers and their share
- Trends in technological innovation
- Restructuring trends of the supplier industry

Intensity of rivalry among competitors
- Number of players
- Sales of each player
- Size of profit
- Each player's positioning

Buyer bargaining power
- Number of consumer/corporate and their share
- Restructuring trends in consumer industry
- Change in distribution channel
- Change in consumer behavior and decision-making
- Change in consumer composition

Threat of substitute products
Presence/absence of alternative products
Trends in technological innovation

- Grasp the overview of the interests, relationship, and industry structure
- Develop a mindset that seek to "turn threats into opportunities"
- Identify signs of possible future changes in the industry's structures and rules

of thinking, a threat can turn into an opportunity, or vice versa. In many cases, by doing the Five Forces analysis, you will discover way more threats than opportunities. This is why having an opportunistic mindset is crucial.

Lastly, in addition to the current opportunities and threats, you must also speculate on future opportunities and threats. Of course, it's not easy to predict the future. But without considering what opportunities and threats might come in the future, you cannot build an outstanding strategy.

Clear and present opportunities and threats are obvious to anyone and not enough to create a strategy that stands out. You must let your imagination go wild and predict future opportunities and threats that your competitors can't think of. This will lead you to a winning strategy. The rapid growth of IT companies such as Apple and Google can be attributed to their management, who could sniff out these future opportunities before the competitors.

▶Positioning Analysis and Competition Analysis

The next and of equal importance in OT analysis is positioning analysis/competition analysis. Positioning analysis aims to see where you and your competitors stand within the market. On top of that, you will be able to see the competitive patterns in the market by looking into your competitor's strengths and weaknesses. The key in positioning and competition analysis is to find out "what area in the market does each player focus on?" and "what is each player's approach?" In consideration of opportunities and threats, you will need to analyze the following issues.

◎ Is there any new, opportune market (undeveloped, or market with less competition) or not?

◎ Is the new market really an opportunity? (Undeveloped market may not have any consumers.)

◎ Are there any newcomers/competitors threatening your company's position?

◎ Can the strengths and weaknesses of the competitor become your own?

◎ Are there any patterns in the competition within the market? Can a strategy used by another company create business opportunities for your company?

◎ What are the possible changes in positioning and competitive environment in the future?

Using your competitor as a benchmark is very effective and indispensable in deciding your strategy. Analyzing your competitors' positioning and strategies allows you to determine survival and growth directions (business opportunity) in the industry.

Keep in mind, these patterns in strategies only apply to current strategies. Following that pattern too closely will not necessarily lead to success. It is better to build an innovative strategy that sets you apart from the strategies used by your competitors and create a competitive edge over them.

LCC (low-cost carrier company) and "Ore no French" (see page 40) are great examples of innovative and brand-new strategies. You

Diagram 2-6 Example of Strategy Patterns Used by Grocery Chains

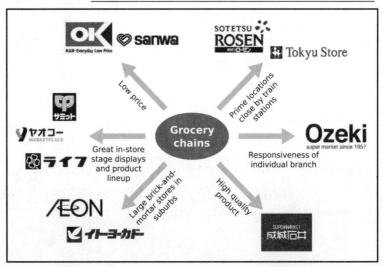

can refer to your competitors' strategies when building your own, but you must analyze and consider whether your company can come out on top by utilizing a similar strategy, or if you should engage with an entirely different strategy.

To continue with our case in hand with Matsui-ya, in their department store Japanese sweets market, four strategic patterns have emerged after analyzing the competitors and their success.

As you can see, each successful competitor has a different approach. These differences and individuality are each company's positioning in the market. It is important to delve into how they were able to make this work, and what their competitive strength is.

To figure out the source of each competitor's strengths, you need to examine not only their performance, but also the 4 Ps of their marketing (product, price, place, and promotion),

---

Competitor Company A: Comprehensive model with a heavy focus on product appeal

- Attractive and profitable product lineup
  - Sustaining the store appeal by concentrating on both traditional and limited, seasonal products
  - Focusing on developing products that are both popular and profitable, such as the red-bean jelly, wafer cake filled with red-bean paste, and baked goods. The less profitable unbaked sweets are used to attract customers.
- Product development department overseen directly by the CEO to develop new, innovative products
- Expanding business opportunities by strengthening new sales channel and introducing new brands
  - 10% increase in online sales channel
  - Successfully introducing new Western sweets brand to keep up with the trend in department stores

---

- Reducing outlets in department stores to focus on stores with top sales only
  - Selecting the outlets with top sales only in department stores in metro and urban areas
  - Reaching out to the suburbs by festival booths requiring no fixed cost
- Aggressive implementation of IT technology to improve sales floor efficiency and effective product deployment
  - First implementation of POS system in the industry

Competitor Company B: Other sales channel (no department store) expansion model

- Accelerating growth by expanding to various sales channels
  - Approximately 150 stores countrywide, including both company-operated stores and pop-up stores within department stores, station buildings, and airports
  - Concentrating on storefronts within public transportation system buildings to lessen dependance on department stores
- Aggressive development of overseas market to combat the shrinking domestic market
  - Currently operating 15 branch stores overseas in the United Stattes, the UK, and Asia
- Has a generalized product lineup, but also sells specialized area or region-limited items

Competitor Company C: Specialization model focusing on signature product

- **Focusing on their signature product, red-bean jelly. Product portfolio is full of varieties of red-bean jelly.**
  - Holds 70% share in red-bean jelly sales
  - Offering various flavors and sizes
- **Successfully branded itself as "red-bean jelly means Company C; Company C means red-bean jelly"**
- **Pursuing both "traditional" and "innovative" red-bean jelly in product development**

- Has a loyal clientele supporting the sales centering on formal gifts

---

Competitor Company D: Low-cost model targeting personal consumption

- Has store outlets designed to attract customers and targeting personal consumption
  - Open storefront with wide variety displays, enabling customers to shop without being bothered by sales clerks
- Focusing on low-cost operation to maintain profitability due to low revenue per customer
  - Designed setting in which customers can choose what to purchase themselves (lower customer service cost)
  - Minimizing flowline and employees space
  - Simplifying indirect operations
- Specializing in products with high gross profit to counter the low revenue per customer
  - Offering only high gross profit rate products such as rice crackers
  - Compensating fewer product assortment with more variations

---

value chain, business model, tangible and intangible assets, and their organizational structure. As you go, you will also need to analyze which competitor's strength might be a threat, and which competitor's weakness might turn into your opportunity, as well as which strength your company can learn from.

▶Client Analysis

"Client" is another key point in analyzing opportunities and threats. This viewpoint consists of four core elements, which can then be further divided into nine points. Always keep these nine points in mind as the basic principles in order to effectively analyze the current situation and changes in your clientele (Diagram 2-7).

Diagram 2-7 Viewpoint for Client Analysis

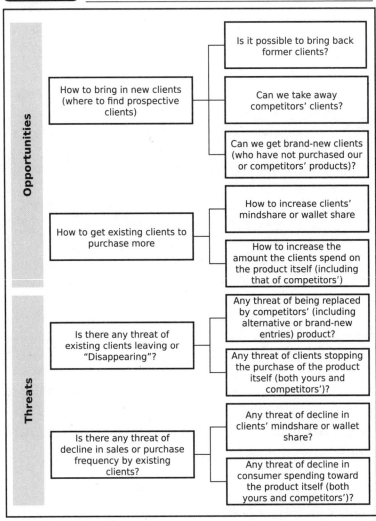

Start with analyzing the clientele structure. In the targeted market, generally you have your existing clients and your competitors' clients, as well as potential clients, who are not yours or your competitors' but have a potential to be, and non-target clients, who are not even the target of your market. You may also want to take

Diagram 2-8 **Putting Consumers and the Market in a Whole Perspective**

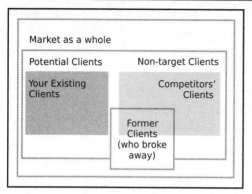

your former clients into consideration (Diagram 2-8).

In order to see the opportunities and threats in relation to clients, you need to look at any change in values, needs, purchase priorities and decision factors, and buying behavior. Keep in mind to not only look at the current changes, but also anticipate possible changes in the future. For example, in Matsui-ya's case, the following circumstances and changes in consumers were discovered. How should Matsui-ya perceive and utilize these changes?

▶Key Success Factor (KSF) Analysis

As the last viewpoint of OT analysis, we'd like to go over success factor (KSF) analysis. Companies that are growing rapidly or

Japanese sweets consumers are diversifying
- ● Traditional, formal gifts consumers (elderly population)
- ● Those interested in innovative and new formal gifts
- ● Those looking for more casual, personal gifts
- ● Consumers who enjoy Japanese sweets for personal consumption
- ● Consumers who consider both Western and Japanese sweets before purchasing on a whim

Decrease in brand appeal toward new customers
- ● Company recognition is down among targeted consumers
  - • No features to stand out

95

- Considered old-fashioned, especially the storefront, products, and packaging
● Especially low recognition, satisfaction, and comparison rate among the younger generation

Weakening clientele foundation
● Current customers are aging
● Low rate of acquisition of new customers
● Decrease in sales per customer

However, the rate of returning customers is high
● More likely for a customer who has once made a purchase to return
● Customer satisfaction for taste among purchasing customers is high

sustaining their lead for an extended period always have success factors. Factors that lead them to come out on top in the industry are referred to as success factors. Successful companies all have an edge over the competition or a successful mechanism, but the source of that edge and strategic tricks are what make their KSF work. Therefore, you could say they are the KSF of the industry itself.

It is important not only to understand the current KSFs but also to anticipate changes in industry structures and how changes in competitive rules can influence them. Foresight into the future can reveal future opportunities and threats and is essential to build an effective business strategy.

KFS factors change as the rules of competition change. These pivot points can become either a new opportunity or a new threat. Take the Korean electronics company Samsung. They have beaten world-famous Japanese electronics manufacturers and become a global leader in the industry. This is due to their prediction of oncoming change. The former chairman of Samsung, Lee Kun-hee, got wind of the advancement in digitalization and its influence over home electronics back in the 1990s. His vision was clear: It would become harder and harder to differentiate themselves by function, performance, or quality. The key to success will be the design of the product, and Samsung proceeded to hire leading designers from all over the world. Foresights like those led to the great success of the Galaxy series. Quite the opposite of Japanese electronics manufacturers, who are suffering because of the failure to anticipate such a pivotal change.

You can also use KSF analysis to analyze the strengths and weaknesses of your company. To determine whether your company has enough success factors, you must review your strengths, weaknesses, and issues.

Keeping these in mind, let's take a look at Matsui-ya's situation. By analyzing the KSFs of department store Japanese sweets manufacturers, these five points become clear based on changes in market structure and examples of success.

① Clarifying the business model
  ● In the Japanese sweets market, there are various strategies (business models) to win
  ● By viewing successful companies we can determine specific business models
② Developing a flagship product
  ● No matter the type of product, a brand with a strong flagship product that has the "X product means Y Company" product image has a great advantage. Those are the brands that are chosen in the department store market.

③ Vitalization of the brand (fresh products and spreading the message)
- Even a traditional company is mindful of sustaining a fresh brand image
- Coming up with new concepts and products while honoring traditions

④ Diversifying sales channels other than department stores
- Developing new sales channels such as online storefronts, stations, and fashion malls is a must

⑤ Thorough management of profit
- Optimizing the profit management per store and per product
- Lowering the cost price of the products with a low profit ratio
- Maximizing the store operational efficiency

Diagram 2-9 Three Elements of SW Analysis

Using superior/successful companies as a benchmark
- What strengths are supporting the success
- What is the fundamental value of the product offered
- What profit structure or winning strategies are used

Analyzing consumer needs
- What are the fundamental needs of the consumers?
- What plays into the consumers' decision-making when purchasing a product

Industry structure and its changes
- How is the industry structured?
- What influence can changes in competition rules have over KSF?

Taking foundation and mechanism apart
- Identifying the foundational factors in value and mechanism

Identifying the success elements

▶Deciding Pros and Cons Based on Relativity

After the OT analysis comes the SW analysis. We will cover ways, concepts, and key points to analyzing your company's strengths and weaknesses.

First, remember that your company's strengths and weaknesses are relative to those of your competitors and that there is no golden standard. This is also true when analyzing competitors' strengths and weaknesses. In a competitive environment, everything is judged by relative evaluation.

Moreover, strength doesn't always lead you to success. Just as weakness may not be the decisive factor for your loss. Because if your strength is not connected to the element that could make or break the competitive edge, or the industry-wide success factor (KSF), it is not very useful. On the other hand, a grave weakness that is not related to the KSF may not directly lead to a disaster. The opposite is true as well. A weakness that is linked to the KSF can make you fail, while a strength that is directly connected to the KSF can provide you with a great advantage.

DETERMINE THE TRUE STATE OF YOUR COMPANY IN RELATION TO THE MARKET!

Here's an example: Many Japanese companies are faced with the issue of "excessive quality" in emerging countries. The quality of Japanese manufactured goods is top-notch, and in that sense, this is a strength. However, the KSF of those emerging markets are products with so-so quality but with decent design and an affordable price, not overwhelming quality. So here, the quality of Japanese manufactured goods is actually a weakness. High quality means higher prices, which cannot gain enough support in those markets.

Now you understand why strengths and weaknesses cannot be judged by a standard, and differ from market to market. You must always consider strengths and weaknesses relative to the market. Many consider superiority as a "strength," but that notion can make them blind to true strengths and weaknesses.

▶Achievements and Performance Analysis

The first step in analyzing your company's strengths and weaknesses is identifying performance transition and understanding each performance benchmark. A company's strengths, weaknesses, and character can be interpreted in numerical values.

Diagram 2-10 How to Identify KSF

---

① **First, take inventory of your company's performance and function**
- Have a thorough grasp of your company's resources (tangible assets such as funds and employees, intangible assets such as brand and network)
- Identify your company's value from the client's and competitors' points of view (quality, service level, price, speed)

② **Identify your company's strengths and weaknesses in relation to the competitors based on KSF**
- How does your company's value compare to that of the competitors in relation to the KSF of the industry or market in which you are competing?
- Keep in mind that KSFs and the competitors can differ depending on the market (strength in market A can be a weakness in market B)

③ **Look for ways to increase your competitive edge**
- Possibility of reinforcing your strength (possibility of expanding profit by creating an overwhelming edge over the competitors)
- Possibility of supplementing your weakness (possibility of expanding the profit by inching closer to the competitors)

There are different numerical values and benchmarks that reveal a company's performance and situation. Diagram 2-11 lists the main points used in identifying a company's strengths and weaknesses.

Diagram 2-11	Examples of Benchmarks Often Used in Achievements and Performance Analysis

Benchmark to review performance bottom line	• Sales • Operating profit and operating profit margin • Cost price and cost price margin • Managing cost and managing cost ratio	
Benchmark to review the cost structure	• Cost price and cost price margin • Managing cost and managing cost ratio • Breakdown of cost-to-profit margin ratio • Per unit cost, etc.	**Compare with the numerical values below and not just a standard value**
Benchmark to review efficiency and productivity	• Sales and gross profit margin per person • Amount processed per person (man-hours per unit) • Inventory turnover rate and period in days • Sales per store • Sales per square foot • Sales per customer • Return on equity, return on investment, etc.	• Industry average • Best practice • Competitor average • Your company's past performance data and progress
Benchmark to review profit structure	• Unit price, number of customers • Sales and profit per product/division/area • Sales and profit structure (percentage of sales and profit per consumer)	

101

Diagram 2-12 Example of Matsui-ya's Performance Analysis

Profit and Cost Side

- Profit has been on the decline for the past 5 years and went into the red last year
- Neglecting stores in the red
  - 1/3 of the stores, centered on relatively new stores, are in the red
- Too many products and excessive deployment of products in the red
  - Ended up with over 100 product types due to the lack of careful selection (double the product types compared to the competitors)
  - 1/3 of the products, centered on unbaked sweets, are in the red
  - Profit structure is too too dependent on the select high-profit product (wafer cake filled with red-bean paste)
- Profit in the formal gift segment is down
  - Historical revenue source was assortment boxes targeted toward the formal gift segment but is declining in relation to the decline in wafer cake filled red-bean paste sales
- High cost-price ratio
  - High cost-price ratio especially in unbaked sweets
- Distribution costs remain high
  - The labor cost rate is high, while productivity per employee is extremely low compared to the competition (operation too reliant on personnel)
- Expensive manufacturing facility cost (excessive output)
  - Went through a major renovation during the sales peak 3 years ago. Depreciation is weighing the company down. Facilities are over capacity with the utilization rate only at 55%
  - Taking orders at a lower price from other companies in the same business, but its contribution to the revenue is meager at best

Sales side

■ Dependency on the department stores is limiting growth
- ○ After record high sales 3 years ago, sales have plateaued due to the decline in fundamental department store sales
- ○ Was able to increase sales by branching out to new department stores up until 3 years ago (continuous growth)
- ○ Limited growth opportunity by branching out further in the department store market, which has become stagnant (this business model has reached its limit)

■ Decreased sales in current stores
- ○ Per store, sales have been gradually declining for 10 years
- ○ The decrease rate of the per store sale is greater than that of the department store market in general
- ○ Market share among the department stores is down

■ Delay in developing sales channels other than department stores
- ○ Sales ratio through sales channels other than the department stores is under 5% (major competitors are developing alternate sales channels aggressively)

■ Consumer recognition continues to be high, but the rate of products being considered for purchase has dropped dramatically

ANALYZE THE SITUATION IN DEPTH USING OBJECTIVE FACTS BASED ON NUMBERS!

When analyzing these, make sure to look at not only the golden standard and your company's progress but also the industry average, best practices, and competitors' numbers. Also, don't get too caught up in numbers alone. It is important to understand and interpret what those numbers reveal and what they mean. Numbers show the result of the company's activities. Understanding the meaning behind them can provide you with various clues about the strengths, weaknesses, and issues.

▶Positioning Analysis

We've mentioned this during the OT analysis, but it is vital to analyze your company's position in relation to your competitors and have a clear understanding of your position within the market. If you can position yourself differently than your competitors and be supported by clients, that can be considered a strength or an edge. But if your position is similar to your competitors and

Matsui-ya's Positioning
- Half-baked positioning not following any of the winning patterns
- Half-baked business model not following the four strategic patterns that emerged from competition analysis

Considered as an "old-fashioned, average Japanese sweets maker" by consumers
- Competitors are pushing innovative and distinctive business models
- A decline in customers who come specifically to visit Matsui-ya

Positioning within the department store market has declined
- Considered an underperforming brand, resulting in reduced sales floor footage and placement away from the major customer flow (no longer being asked by department stores to operate a branch within their stores)

sales and profits are declining in a competitive market, that issue needs to be addressed.

Positioning analysis is about determining whether or not your company manages to establish a unique position in the market, creating a competitive edge. If your positioning advantage is on

| Diagram 2-13 | Example of Matsui-ya's Marketing 4P Analysis (weakness) |

Product	• Lack of new products that can attract new customers • Products for personal consumption were developed, but their recognition is low and they are buried among the formal gift lineup • Weak flagship product (used to be wafer cake with red-bean paste, but its appeal is on the decline) • A large number of products, but the brand value is ambiguous • Packaging appeal is also declining
Pricing	• Pricing is equivalent to that of the competitors in the department store Japanese sweets market • Pricing is higher when compared to the competitors in the personal consumption market
Promotion	• Low exposure compared to competitors, which are deploying ad campaigns by collaborating with fashion and lifestyle magazines • No presence on social media, compared to competitors with aggressive campaigns to create popularity • Low storefront appeal (storefront design, POP advertising, outreach to customers, etc.)
Channels	• Behind in developing markets other than the department stores • Widespread deployment in the department store market, but neglect of low-performance stores • Weak negotiation skills compared to competitors (competitors are negotiating to gain better deals while our company remains passive)

the decline in relation to the competitors, it could mean the degree of differentiation is decreasing and could become a big issue.

Another potential issue is when your current positioning is not supported by your clients, meaning the way you differentiate from other companies is not connected to creating an edge over them. In Matsui-ya's case, the following factors became apparent: From a positioning point of view, there are many large issues to be overcome.

▶Business Model Analysis

A business model is a model of how to be profitable. Even in the same market, it is common to take different approaches. Take razors, for example. There are different types of razors, such as disposable and replaceable blade models. The former profits from the razor itself, but the latter's profit comes from replacement blades.

Another example: Previously, home espresso machines were divided into two separate suppliers. Meaning, machine manufacturers sold the machines, while the coffee suppliers profited from coffee beans. But Nespresso developed a brand-new business model. The machine itself is provided at a lower cost, while the consumer must purchase specialized pods filled with ground coffee beans. Nespresso is making a profit not from the sale of the machine but the sale of coffee capsules. This is similar to the makers of copy machines profiting from expendables such as paper and toner.

So the same market can have different business models, and they are often connected to differentiation and competitive edge and contribute to establishing a unique positioning.

A prime example of a business model creating different positioning is perhaps the airline industry. There are different types of air carriers, such as FSC, full-service carriers (e.g., JAL and ANA), and LCC, which stands for low-cost carrier (e.g., Air Asia, Jetstar, and Vanilla Air). They are all air carriers, but the business models for FSC and LCC differ greatly. FSC's main source of revenue is the profit from the premier seating classes such as business and first classes. On the other hand, LCCs profit from their firm's low-cost model and high rate of operation.

LCCs don't just try to pack their aircraft by increasing the number of seats; they also focus on lessening the time spent at the airport by increasing efficiency to fly more customers. They lower the cost by removing non-essential services and increasing operational efficiency.

Similarly, fine French cuisine profits from a high unit price per customer, while "Ore no French" depends on the turnover rate of the casual customers or a low-profit, high sales model.

The market is full of many players following different business models, which in turn establishes differentiation, competitive edge, and unique positioning. From a business model point of view, you must analyze the difference between your company and the competitors and study each strength, weakness, and issue to be overcome.

► **Marketing, Value Chain, and Organizational Analysis**

When considering the causes of strength and weakness, start by analyzing the competitiveness of business necessities by each element and function. What to consider depends on the industry's type or specialty, but the most efficient analysis method is to evaluate the business from each of the 4Ps of marketing elements and each function of the value chain.

The 4Ps of marketing stand for product, price, promotion, and place (or channel). The value chain is the overall flow of business activities providing value (product or service) to consumers. Everything from research and development, procurement, manufacturing, marketing, distribution, sales, service, and after-sales service is part of the value chain.

In order to provide unique value, you must consider how best to match the four elements of marketing and build an efficient value chain, which can create a competitive edge in the market. A comparison of the four elements of marketing and each function of the value chain between your company and its competitors can bring your strengths and weaknesses to light.

Key success factor (or KSF) becomes extremely important here. As stated before, if you have elements or functions that are directly connected to the industry KSF, it becomes a great advantage. If not, you'll have to consider it a critical issue.

Let's take a look at Matsui-ya's case. Matsui-ya's 4Ps are summarized in Diagram 2-13, with a heavy focus on weakness. What KSFs were critical to the survival of department store Japanese sweets

Diagram 2-14 Example of Matsui-ya's Asset Analysis

- ■ Widespread recognition
- ■ The biggest assets are the company's history and tradition, which are highly recognized by consumers
- ■ High praise for the red-bean paste from customers and industry professionals
  - ○ Commitment and skills in red-bean paste creation are highly reputed
  - ○ Zero recognition among new and potential clientele
- ■ On the other hand, the brand image lacks innovation and fun. The brand itself has aged and is losing the strength it used to have
  - ○ History and tradition are associated with an old-fashioned image
  - ○ Not known as an eye-catching, innovative product
  - ○ No features that stand out

---

manufacturers (see page 97)? Which issues are the most crucial to Matsui-ya?

A similar evaluation of organizational systems and structure is needed in order to execute business operations. No matter how great a strategy is, it will not function properly without the right personnel and organizational structure. In order to build a functional strategy, we must identify strengths, weaknesses, and issues from the management infrastructure point of view, such as organizational structure and personnel, business administration, and IT systems.

▶ Tangible and Intangible Asset Analysis

The final points to consider when analyzing your company's strengths and weaknesses are the tangible and intangible assets. A company can hold various assets that are both tangible and intangible. Tangible assets refer to tangible resources from funds, real estate, and facilities. Brand power, network, clientele, intellectual property, and personnel are examples of intangible assets.

Comparing each in relation to your competitors can clarify whether you are superior or inferior. Also, keep an eye out for "dormant" assets that can be utilized. Indeed, a lot of useful assets are not utilized properly or remain dormant in many cases.

If you can make good use of your assets, it will broaden your opportunities. Seven Bank succeeded by emphasizing the installation of ATMs in many of their branches country-wide. Fujifilm and Toray are expanding their business opportunities by applying their skills to new ventures.

What about Matsui-ya? As far as brand asset goes, which is essential in the department store brand, Matsui-ya has some useful assets, such as a high recognition rate, history, tradition, and high praise toward their red-bean paste. However, an "old-fashioned" image is fatal to a department store channel, which focuses heavily on brand freshness.

▶ Understanding the Structures of the Issue at Hand
You should always keep the overview and cause and effect in mind when analyzing performance, positioning, business model, marketing/value chain/organization, and assets, instead of analyzing each of them separately. By doing so, you will begin to see the fundamental issues at hand.

Normally, you begin with performance analysis, which allows you to sort out your advantages and/or disadvantages relative to your competition, increase and/or decrease in sales and profit, company management style, and the "result" of the current state of business.

Next, you must consider the cause and the mechanism behind what led your company to that result. For example, if you are faced with results such as "sales are down" and "profit ratio is also down," you will have to analyze the reason behind them. Analyzing the positioning, business model, marketing, value chain, organization, and assets all leads to the clarification of the reason behind the result of the performance analysis.

If sales continue to be down, you must determine if it is the result of a decrease in the number of customers, a decrease in unit price, or perhaps both. If the number of customers is down, is the decrease in the new customer base or in the established clientele? You have to dissect the result and analyze in depth where the issues may lie.

It is important to analyze the cause in depth by backtracking from the result. But don't focus on any one individual analysis. That could make you lose sight of the whole picture, which is the same as losing sight of the essence. It is crucial to determine the true cause of why problems were discovered individually in the first place.

The same goes for cost. If costs are high, what area is driving it up? Take each possibility apart, one by one.

It is important to analyze the cause in depth by backtracking from the result. But again, don't focus on any one individual analysis. That could make you lose sight of the whole picture, which is the same as losing sight of the essence. It is crucial to determine the true cause of why problems were discovered individually in the first place.

One of the issues Matsui-ya has is not meeting the industry's success factors. They did not have a clear business model, resulting in their position in the market without any innovation. This was the core of Matsui-ya's distress.

Symptomatic treatments such as product improvement and strengthening of the marketing power alone will not contribute to differentiation and establishing a competitive edge. Such was Matsui-ya's case. You cannot sustain growth without advantageous positioning and a business model. You will not be able to build a true strategy with an analysis based on superficial issues.

This is true even when business growth is on track. You must consider the true cause behind the growth thus far and analyze whether or not it can be sustained. And that requires accurate situation analysis and a true understanding of the cause and structure.

4

▶Keeping the Impact on Your Business in Mind

Once you have finished analyzing each element, it is time to organize them into SWOT. When summarizing, you must specifically think of how the results of each analysis could influence your business. Remember: analysis is a tool, not a goal.

In regards to opportunities and threats, consider the following:
- Room and potential for growth in sales
- Room for improvement in profit
- Possible risk of decreased sales
- Possible risk of decrease in profitability

In regards to strengths and weaknesses, consider the following:
- Are the strengths you have now enough to contribute to business growth?
- Can the strengths you have be applied to a new venture?
- Can the weaknesses you have now hinder your business growth in the future?
- Can the weaknesses you have now kill your business?

LET'S RE-VIEW THE GOAL OF THE ANALYSIS AGAIN!

Summarize in a way that can provide direction to some extent. Let's take a look at the SWOT Analysis summary compiled by Kazumi.

Finally, let's go over things to keep in mind when analyzing the situation.

Diagram 2-15 Matsui-ya's SWOT Summary

Opportunities

- Potential to develop new sales channels other than department stores
- Potential in new Japanese sweets consumers
- Room for growth in sales per store
- Room for improvement in profit by changing the product lineup
- Potential for obtaining consumers beyond the genre border
- Potential for overseas markets

Threats

- A fundamental decline in sales due to the main channel, department stores, making little progress
- Decrease in sales along with shrinking formal gift market
- Decrease in market share due to heated competition against unique competitors, new brands, Western sweets
- Brand value's decline
- Accelerated vicious cycle: Decrease in sales ⇒ Deployment of new product ⇒ Increased SKU* ⇒ Diluted brand image ⇒ Decrease in sales and profit

Strengths

- Strong ties with the department store chains
- High recognition
- History and tradition
- Skilled in red-bean paste creation
- Varied products
- High repeat rate of clientele

Weaknesses

- Dependency on the department stores
- Old-fashioned brand image
- Low rate of products being considered for purchase
- Aging clientele
- Products with low appeal
- Habitual high cost
- Low productivity

The business model is collapsing. Positioning is not unique enough.

*SKU: Stock Keeping Unit. Unit used in inventory management.

First, try to stick with hypothetical thinking. Hypothetical thinking is essential in situation analysis and therefore in the strategy-building process in general. A comprehensive but vague analysis will take up a lot of your time but will not yield useful information. Before beginning each analysis separately, make sure to have a clear vision of the entire picture and come up with your own hypothesis.

Then, take those hypotheses and establish points to analyze to cement the idea. Also, identify elements and points that you are unclear about or unable to hypothesize. Only then can you begin a full-fledged situation analysis.

Second, keep mutual relationships in mind. We've introduced different ways to analyze, but instead of looking at them independently, we analyze them relative to each other. It is only natural for one issue to be related to another, and by connecting the issues and results of each analysis, you will begin to understand the mechanism.

While doing so, continue to question the true causes and issues. Don't get caught up in superficial phenomena and individual cause-and-effect relationships. You must always have micro and macro points of view to analyze the whole picture.

Third, be particular about interpretation. We've offered different frameworks and ways to analyze them. There are many more frameworks that you could use. Each framework can indeed be a useful tool in analyzing the situation. But filling out the framework doesn't lead you to 100% of the answers.

We've reiterated time and again that the key is how to interpret and understand the result of your analysis. You will have to have a reverse point of view, look at things from different angles, delve into the whys behind the result, and be suspicious. What are the true strengths? Can those actually be weaknesses? Is what you thought was an opportunity really a threat after careful examination? Don't forget to keep those points of view.

"Situation" analysis doesn't only pertain to the past or the current situation. In situation analysis, it is important to have foresight into the future. To do that, you must unravel the mechanism and dynamics behind the numerical values and facts and understand them.

Finally, don't forget to share the situation analysis. The results are meaningless if they are not shared among the parties involved. Sharing only happens by discussing extensively and coming to agreements. You can start your strategy creation process only when the situation analysis becomes the consensus. If recognition of the situation is not aligned in the first place, you will never come up with a strategy that everyone can agree on.

Forming Strategic Options

JUST GIVING OUT ORDERS SURE IS EASY...

YOU CAN'T JUST ONLY THINK ABOUT IT RATIONALLY WHEN DEALING DIRECTLY WITH CLIENTS.

...I WILL HAVE A WORD WITH THE CEO MYSELF IN REGARDS TO THIS MATTER.

BUT IT'S ALL WATER UNDER THE BRIDGE, ONCE YOU COME UP WITH A BRILLIANT STRATEGY.

THE STRATEGY WILL GIVE THE ON-SITE FRONTLINERS HOPE.

STORY 3

HOW TO SAVE A COMPANY IN TROUBLE?

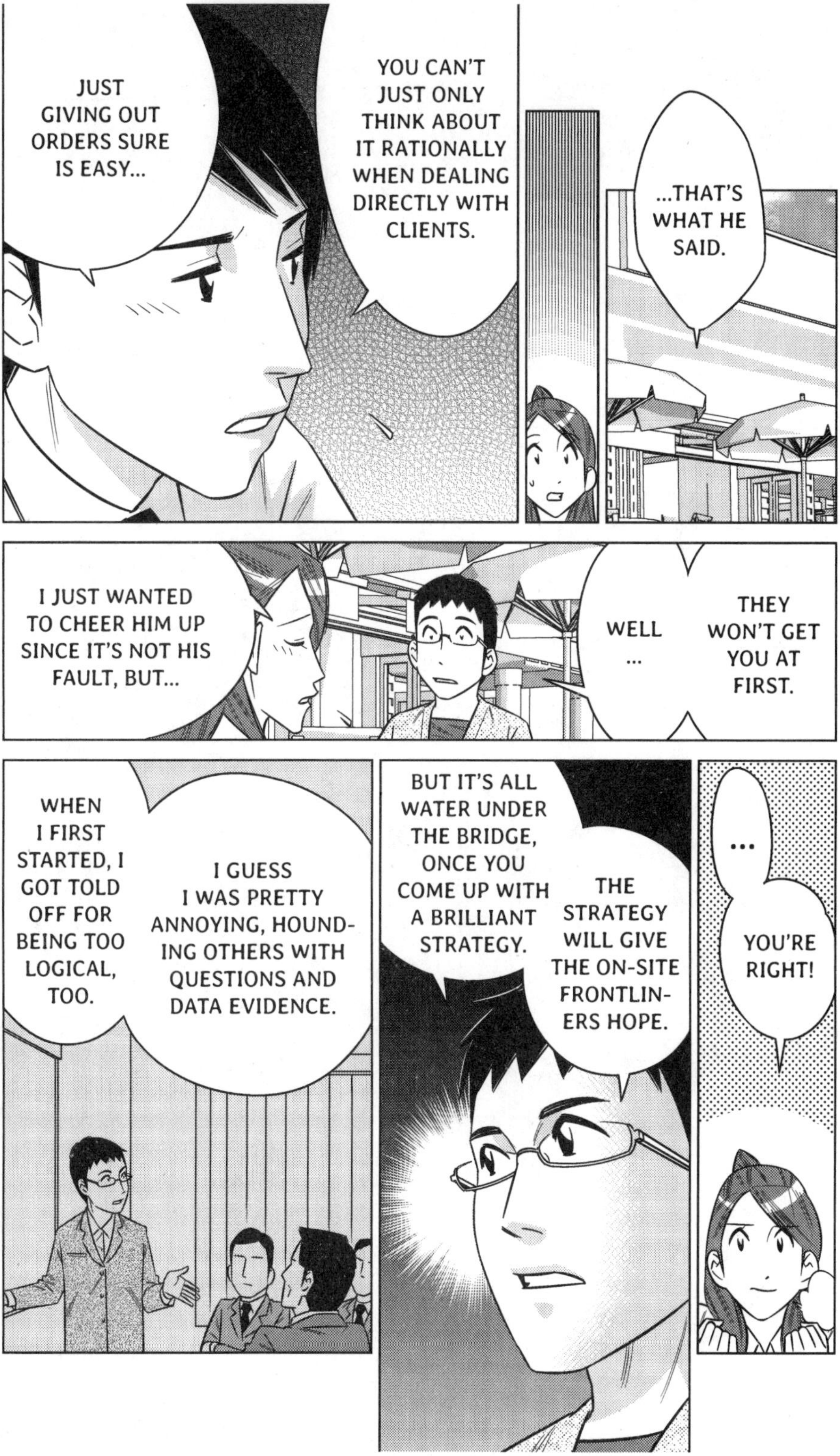
JUST GIVING OUT ORDERS SURE IS EASY...
YOU CAN'T JUST ONLY THINK ABOUT IT RATIONALLY WHEN DEALING DIRECTLY WITH CLIENTS.
...THAT'S WHAT HE SAID.
I JUST WANTED TO CHEER HIM UP SINCE IT'S NOT HIS FAULT, BUT...
WELL ...
THEY WON'T GET YOU AT FIRST.
WHEN I FIRST STARTED, I GOT TOLD OFF FOR BEING TOO LOGICAL, TOO.
I GUESS I WAS PRETTY ANNOYING, HOUND-ING OTHERS WITH QUESTIONS AND DATA EVIDENCE.
BUT IT'S ALL WATER UNDER THE BRIDGE, ONCE YOU COME UP WITH A BRILLIANT STRATEGY.
THE STRATEGY WILL GIVE THE ON-SITE FRONTLIN-ERS HOPE.
...
YOU'RE RIGHT!

NOW, LET'S GET INTO THE SPECIFICS OF STRATEGY BUILDING.

IN THIS STEP, WE WANT TO LAY OUT AS MANY OPTIONS AS POSSIBLE.

DON'T RESTRICT YOURSELF WITH SELECTIONS OR YOU MIGHT OVERLOOK A GOOD OPTION.

SO ABOUT THAT...

...I DON'T EVEN KNOW WHERE TO BEGIN.

LOOK AT THIS MESS.

A JUMBLED CHAOS

AHAHA... WELL, A SHOT IN THE DARK HAS ITS LIMIT AND CAN'T COVER EVERYTHING.

FIRST, LET'S RECONFIRM YOUR STRATEGY'S GOAL.

WHOA, YOU WROTE A LOT.

TO STOP THE DECLINING SALES, OF COURSE!

RIGHT, STOPPING THE DECLINE AND EXPANDING SALES.

SALES

IN MATSUIYA'S CASE, PROFITABILITY'S ALSO A PROBLEM.

SALES

PROFIT

IT'D BE GOOD TO STOP THE PROFIT SLUMP AND BUILD A PROFITABLE STRUCTURE.

I ALSO WANT TO MAKE SURE TO TURN THAT INTO SUSTAINABLE GROWTH!

SOUNDS GOOD.

LET'S KEEP THESE IN MIND.

★TODAY'S STRATEGY CREATION AGENDA
- STOPPING THE DECLINE AND EXPANDING THE SALES
- STOPPING THE PROFIT SLUMP AND BUILDING A PROFITABLE STRUCTURE
- IMPLEMENT SUSTAINABLE (RE)GROWTH

LET'S LOOK INTO THE MAIN ISSUES NEXT.

BASED ON THE SWOT ANALYSIS, WHAT KIND OF STRATEGIES DO YOU THINK WE NEED?

WELL WE HAVE TO RECONSTRUCT OUR EXISTING BUSINESS.

BUT I THINK WE SHOULD ALSO CONSIDER NEW VENTURES.

EITHER WAY, WE'VE GOT TO IMPROVE OUR PROFITABILITY.

YOU'RE ON THE RIGHT TRACK.

I SEE! SO THESE WILL BE THE CORES OF OUR STRATEGY BUILDING.

AND TO DELVE FURTHER INTO THESE...

★TODAY'S POINT OF ISSUES IN STRATEGY CREATION
① HOW TO RECONSTRUCT THE EXISTING BUSINESS
② POSSIBILITY OF NEW VENTURE
③ IMPROVING PROFITABILITY

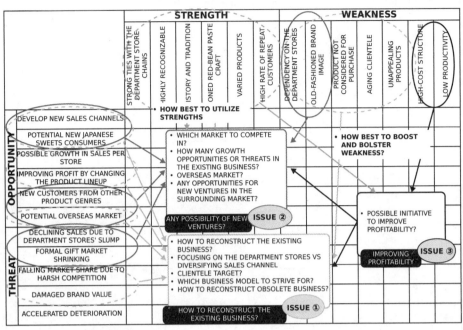

The following text is part of the image (SWOT/cross-analysis chart):

	STRENGTH						WEAKNESS						
	STRONG TIES WITH THE DEPARTMENT STORE CHAINS	HIGHLY RECOGNIZABLE	HISTORY AND TRADITION	HONED RED-BEAN PASTE CRAFT	VARIED PRODUCTS	HIGH RATE OF REPEAT CUSTOMERS	DEPENDENCY ON THE DEPARTMENT STORES	OLD-FASHIONED BRAND IMAGE	PRODUCT NOT CONSIDERED FOR PURCHASE	AGING CLIENTELE	UNAPPEALING PRODUCTS	HIGH-COST STRUCTURE	LOW PRODUCTIVITY

OPPORTUNITY
- DEVELOP NEW SALES CHANNELS
- POTENTIAL NEW JAPANESE SWEETS CONSUMERS
- POSSIBLE GROWTH IN SALES PER STORE
- IMPROVING PROFIT BY CHANGING THE PRODUCT LINEUP
- NEW CUSTOMERS FROM OTHER PRODUCT GENRES
- POTENTIAL OVERSEAS MARKET

THREAT
- DECLINING SALES DUE TO DEPARTMENT STORES' SLUMP
- FORMAL GIFT MARKET SHRINKING
- FALLING MARKET SHARE DUE TO HARSH COMPETITION
- DAMAGED BRAND VALUE
- ACCELERATED DETERIORATION

• HOW BEST TO UTILIZE STRENGTHS

- WHICH MARKET TO COMPETE IN?
- HOW MANY GROWTH OPPORTUNITIES OR THREATS IN THE EXISTING BUSINESS?
- OVERSEAS MARKET?
- ANY OPPORTUNITIES FOR NEW VENTURES IN THE SURROUNDING MARKET?

ANY POSSIBILITY OF NEW VENTURES? **ISSUE ②**

- HOW TO RECONSTRUCT THE EXISTING BUSINESS?
- FOCUSING ON THE DEPARTMENT STORES VS DIVERSIFYING SALES CHANNEL
- CLIENTELE TARGET?
- WHICH BUSINESS MODEL TO STRIVE FOR?
- HOW TO RECONSTRUCT OBSOLETE BUSINESS?

HOW TO RECONSTRUCT THE EXISTING BUSINESS? **ISSUE ①**

• HOW BEST TO BOOST AND BOLSTER WEAKNESS?

• POSSIBLE INITIATIVE TO IMPROVE PROFITABILITY?

IMPROVING PROFITABILITY **ISSUE ③**

THESE ARE SOME SPECIFIC EXAMPLES.

OOH, THIS CLARIFIES WHICH DIRECTION WE'RE GOING FOR.

START BY SORTING OUT YOUR GOALS AND ISSUES. IT'LL BE YOUR GUIDELINES.

IT ALSO EXPANDS YOUR VIEWPOINT.

NOT ENOUGH AD CAMPAIGNS!

LET'S DO AN AD.

AD...

AD...?

WHAT WAS IT AGAIN?

JUST REVERSING ISSUES NARROWS YOUR VIEWPOINTS. IT'S VERY COMMON.

OH, YEAH... I WAS LIKE THAT...

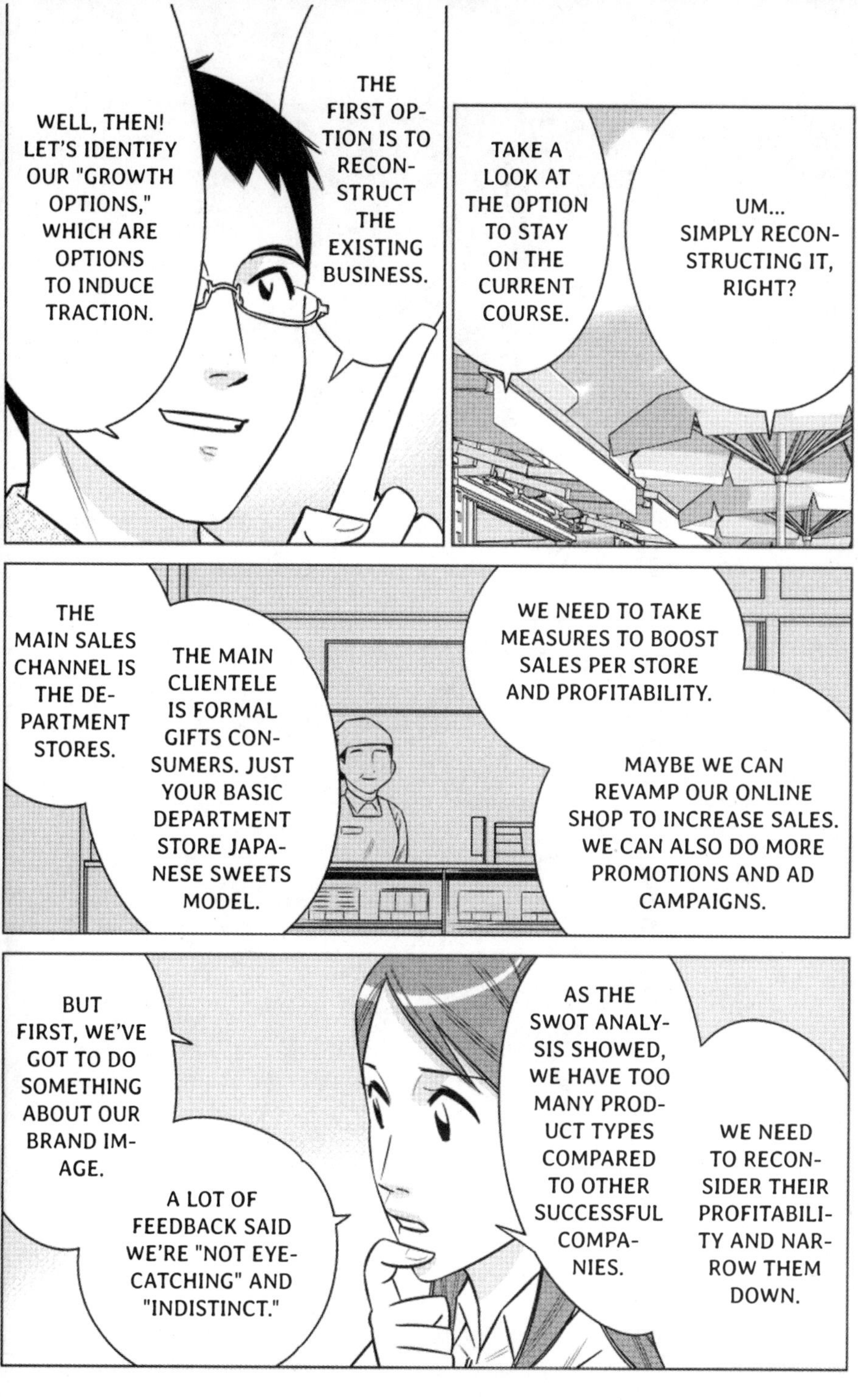
WELL, THEN! LET'S IDENTIFY OUR "GROWTH OPTIONS," WHICH ARE OPTIONS TO INDUCE TRACTION.
THE FIRST OPTION IS TO RECONSTRUCT THE EXISTING BUSINESS.
TAKE A LOOK AT THE OPTION TO STAY ON THE CURRENT COURSE.
UM... SIMPLY RECONSTRUCTING IT, RIGHT?
THE MAIN SALES CHANNEL IS THE DEPARTMENT STORES.
THE MAIN CLIENTELE IS FORMAL GIFTS CONSUMERS. JUST YOUR BASIC DEPARTMENT STORE JAPANESE SWEETS MODEL.
WE NEED TO TAKE MEASURES TO BOOST SALES PER STORE AND PROFITABILITY.
MAYBE WE CAN REVAMP OUR ONLINE SHOP TO INCREASE SALES. WE CAN ALSO DO MORE PROMOTIONS AND AD CAMPAIGNS.
BUT FIRST, WE'VE GOT TO DO SOMETHING ABOUT OUR BRAND IMAGE.
A LOT OF FEEDBACK SAID WE'RE "NOT EYE-CATCHING" AND "INDISTINCT."
AS THE SWOT ANALYSIS SHOWED, WE HAVE TOO MANY PRODUCT TYPES COMPARED TO OTHER SUCCESSFUL COMPANIES.
WE NEED TO RECONSIDER THEIR PROFITABILITY AND NARROW THEM DOWN.

SUCCESSFUL COMPETITORS HAVE ESTABLISHED A CLEAR BRAND IMAGE BY PUSHING THEIR SIGNATURE PRODUCT.

I WANNA DO THAT WITH OUR HIGHLY APPROVED RED-BEAN PASTE.

AT THE SAME TIME, WE MUST INTRODUCE FRESH NEW PRODUCTS AND SEASONAL ITEMS.

GOOD. HOW ABOUT USING THE CONNECTION WITH DEPARTMENT STORES TO OPEN A JAPANESE SWEETS CAFE?

OH! YES, SOME COMPETITORS HAVE DONE THAT!

IF IT'S IN THE DEPARTMENT STORE I THINK WE COULD PLAY TO OUR STRENGTH EVEN WITH A NEW VENTURE!

I'M JUST GETTING STARTED!

SO WE CONSIDER THE ISSUES IN RELATION TO SWOT ANALYSIS RESULTS!

OKAY, THEN. NEXT, WHAT IF WE CONSIDER DIVERSIFYING THE SALES CHANNEL WHILE STILL STAYING ON THE CURRENT COURSE...

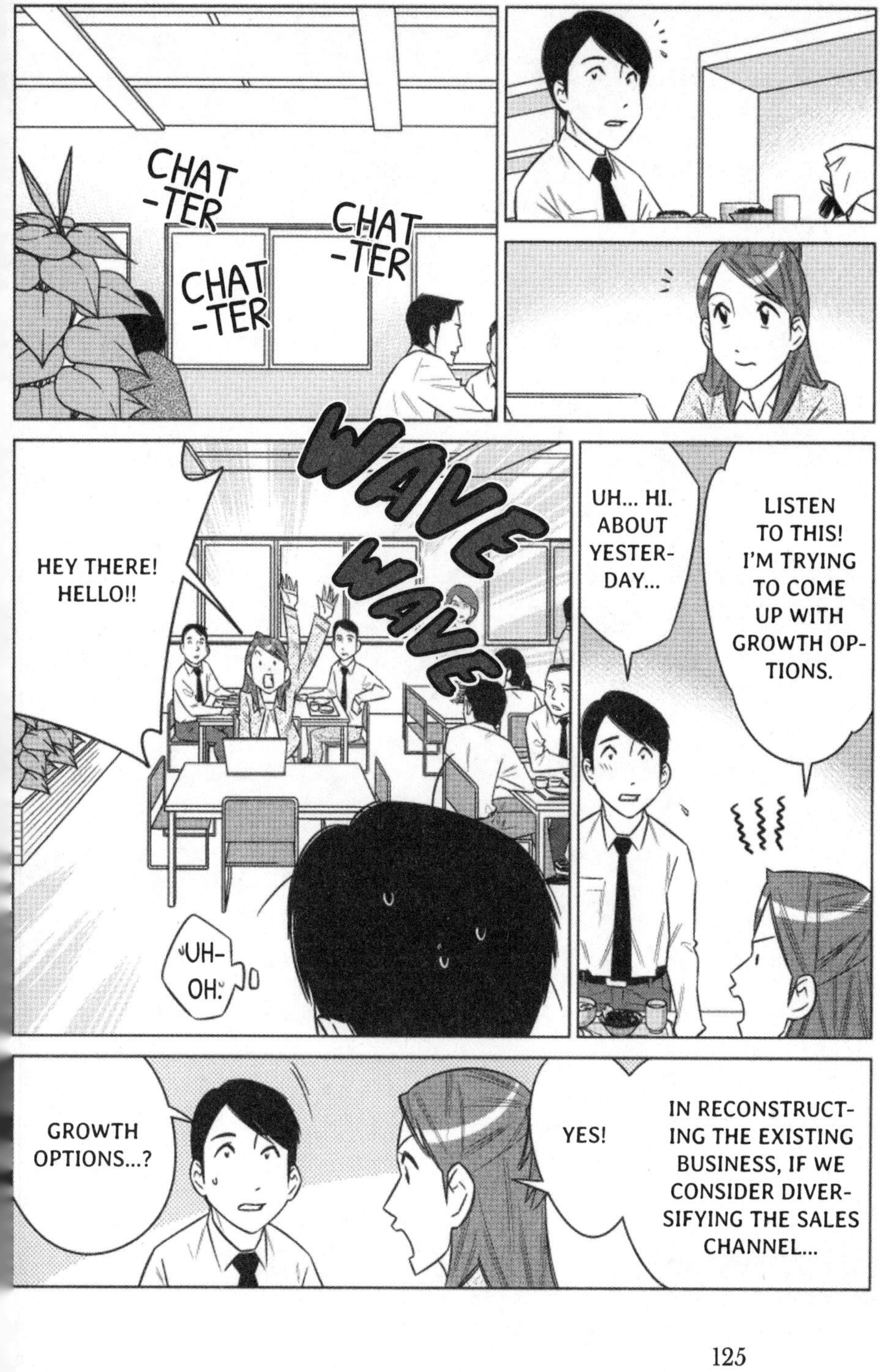
CHAT
-TER
CHAT
-TER
CHAT
-TER
HEY THERE! HELLO!!
WAVE WAVE
UH-OH.
UH... HI. ABOUT YESTER-DAY...
LISTEN TO THIS! I'M TRYING TO COME UP WITH GROWTH OP-TIONS.
GROWTH OPTIONS...?
YES!
IN RECONSTRUCT-ING THE EXISTING BUSINESS, IF WE CONSIDER DIVER-SIFYING THE SALES CHANNEL...

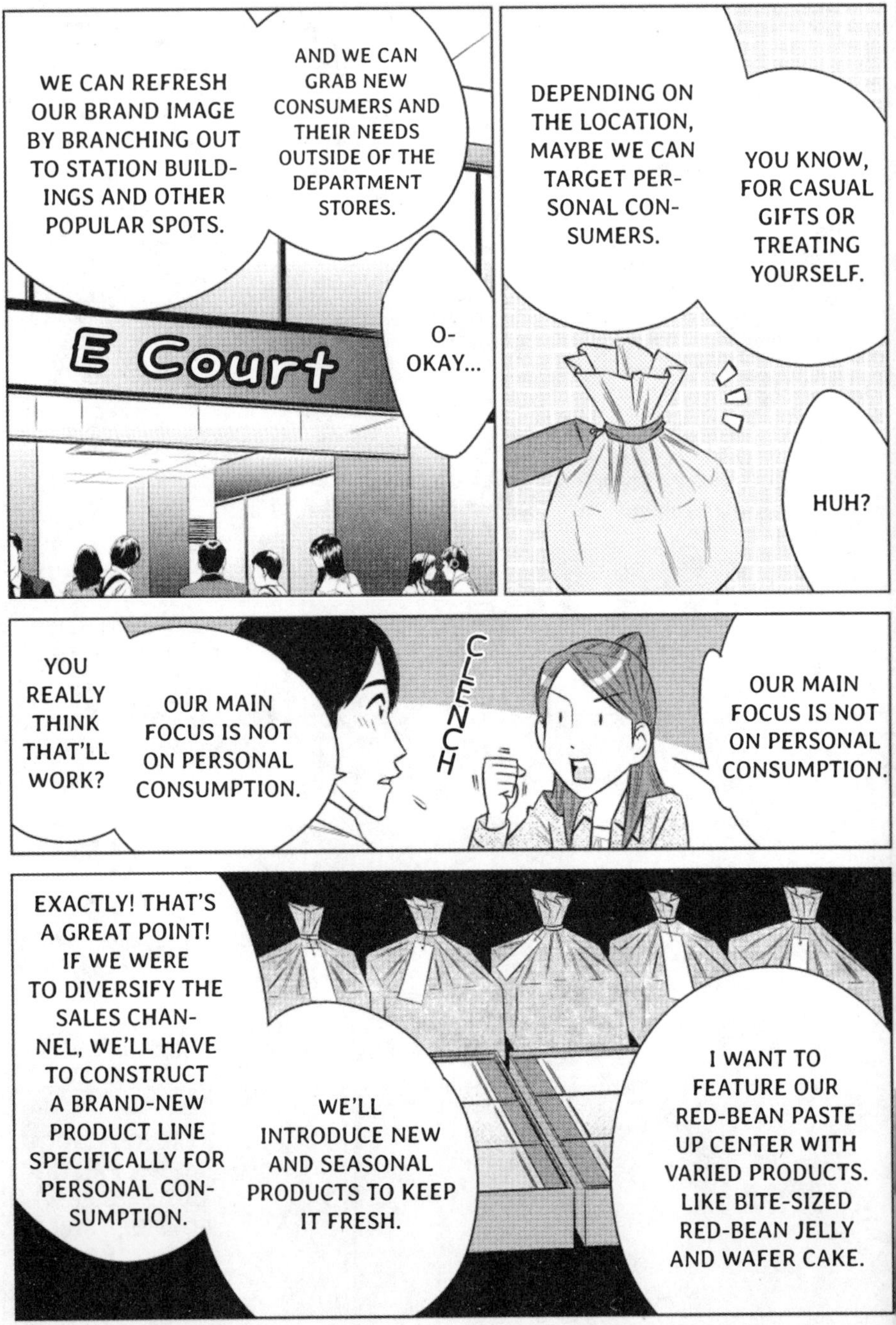
WE CAN REFRESH OUR BRAND IMAGE BY BRANCHING OUT TO STATION BUILD-INGS AND OTHER POPULAR SPOTS.
AND WE CAN GRAB NEW CONSUMERS AND THEIR NEEDS OUTSIDE OF THE DEPARTMENT STORES.
E Court
O-OKAY...
DEPENDING ON THE LOCATION, MAYBE WE CAN TARGET PER-SONAL CON-SUMERS.
YOU KNOW, FOR CASUAL GIFTS OR TREATING YOURSELF.
HUH?
YOU REALLY THINK THAT'LL WORK?
OUR MAIN FOCUS IS NOT ON PERSONAL CONSUMPTION.
CLENCH
OUR MAIN FOCUS IS NOT ON PERSONAL CONSUMPTION.
EXACTLY! THAT'S A GREAT POINT! IF WE WERE TO DIVERSIFY THE SALES CHAN-NEL, WE'LL HAVE TO CONSTRUCT A BRAND-NEW PRODUCT LINE SPECIFICALLY FOR PERSONAL CON-SUMPTION.
WE'LL INTRODUCE NEW AND SEASONAL PRODUCTS TO KEEP IT FRESH.
I WANT TO FEATURE OUR RED-BEAN PASTE UP CENTER WITH VARIED PRODUCTS. LIKE BITE-SIZED RED-BEAN JELLY AND WAFER CAKE.

OH! THAT'S A GOOD IDEA...

IT'S BEEN HARD FOR ME TO RECOMMEND PRODUCTS TO CUSTOMERS.

SO MY MOTIVATION'S LOW 'CAUSE I HAVEN'T BEEN ABLE TO WIN ANY CONTRACTS.

HMM...

RIGHT, NARROWING DOWN AND BRUSHING UP PRODUCTS IS CRUCIAL.

I DIDN'T KNOW BUSINESS PLANNING CAME UP WITH THAT STUFF.

I THOUGHT IT WAS JUST ORDERS FROM THE TOP...

NO, NO, SORRY IF I SOUNDED DISRESPECTFUL BEFORE.

I JUST WANT TO HELP EVERYONE.

THANK YOU.

YOUR IDEAS GIVE ME HOPE.

WELL, WOULD YOU LIKE TO HEAR ABOUT A NEW VENTURE, OPTION TWO?

OPTION TWO?

127

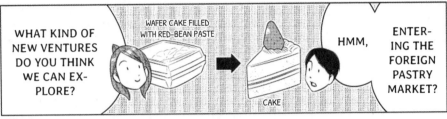

WHAT KIND OF NEW VENTURES DO YOU THINK WE CAN EXPLORE?

WAFER CAKE FILLED WITH RED-BEAN PASTE

CAKE

HMM,

ENTERING THE FOREIGN PASTRY MARKET?

WHAT ELSE?

MMM...

FREEZE

THAT'S WHERE THIS MATRIX COMES IN HANDY!

A

B

1

2

3

I'M JUST REPEATING THOUGH.

OPPORTUNITIES FOR NEW VENTURES ARE ESPECIALLY HARD TO SEE, SO LET'S PLUG IN DIFFERENT ELEMENTS AND COME UP WITH A LIST BY MAPPING THEM OUT.

FOR EXAMPLE, IF WE MATCH THE PRODUCT CATEGORY AND SALES CHANNEL...

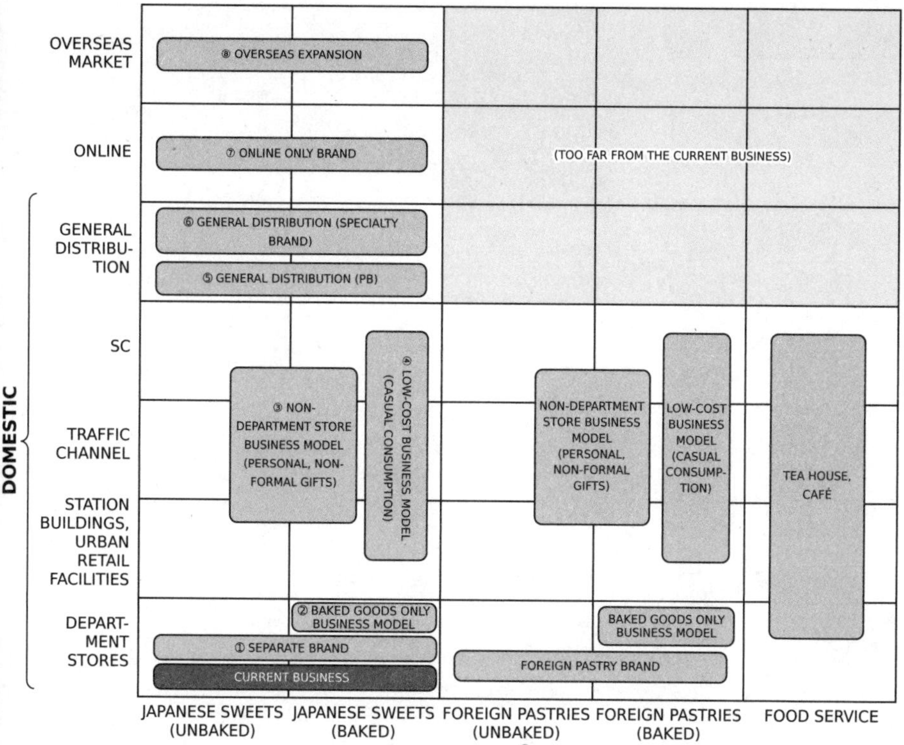
OVERSEAS MARKET
ONLINE
GENERAL DISTRIBU-TION
SC
TRAFFIC CHANNEL
STATION BUILDINGS, URBAN RETAIL FACILITIES
DEPART-MENT STORES
DOMESTIC
⑧ OVERSEAS EXPANSION
⑦ ONLINE ONLY BRAND
(TOO FAR FROM THE CURRENT BUSINESS)
⑥ GENERAL DISTRIBUTION (SPECIALTY BRAND)
⑤ GENERAL DISTRIBUTION (PB)
③ NON-DEPARTMENT STORE BUSINESS MODEL (PERSONAL, NON-FORMAL GIFTS)
④ LOW-COST BUSINESS MODEL (CASUAL CONSUMPTION)
NON-DEPARTMENT STORE BUSINESS MODEL (PERSONAL, NON-FORMAL GIFTS)
LOW-COST BUSINESS MODEL (CASUAL CONSUMP-TION)
TEA HOUSE, CAFÉ
② BAKED GOODS ONLY BUSINESS MODEL
BAKED GOODS ONLY BUSINESS MODEL
① SEPARATE BRAND
FOREIGN PASTRY BRAND
CURRENT BUSINESS
JAPANESE SWEETS (UNBAKED)
JAPANESE SWEETS (BAKED)
FOREIGN PASTRIES (UNBAKED)
FOREIGN PASTRIES (BAKED)
FOOD SERVICE

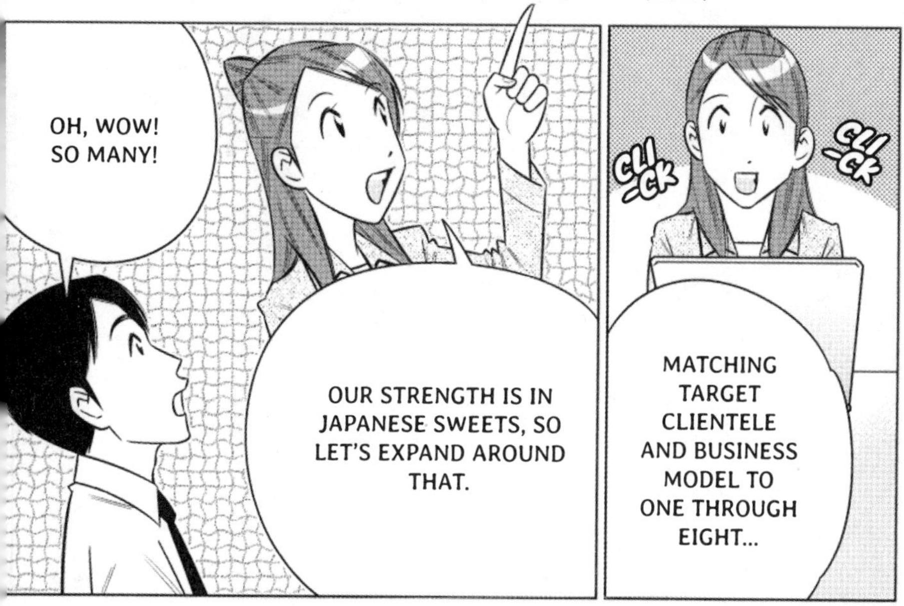
OH, WOW! SO MANY!
OUR STRENGTH IS IN JAPANESE SWEETS, SO LET'S EXPAND AROUND THAT.
CLI-CK
CLI-CK
MATCHING TARGET CLIENTELE AND BUSINESS MODEL TO ONE THROUGH EIGHT...

	TARGET CLIENTELE	BUSINESS MODEL
CURRENT BUSINESS	• FORMAL GIFT USER • (HOW FAR SHOULD WE EXPAND THE TARGET?)	• COMPREHENSIVE DEPARTMENT STORE JAPANESE SWEETS MODEL (BUT NOT FULFILLING KSFs) • BREAK AWAY FROM DEPARTMENT STORES, SHIFT TO SPECIALIZED FLAGSHIP PRODUCT?
① SEPARATE BRAND	• DIFFERENT CLIENTELE FROM THE CURRENT BUSINESS • (RECEPTIVITY, PERSONAL GIFT, PERSONAL DEMAND) • (POSSIBLE TO DIFFERENTIATE FROM THE CURRENT BUSINESS?)	• COMPREHENSIVE DEPARTMENT STORE JAPANESE SWEETS MODEL? • SPECIALIZED FLAGSHIP PRODUCT MODEL? • (IS IT EVEN POSSIBLE?)
② BAKED GOODS ONLY BUSINESS MODEL	• DIFFERENT CLIENTELE FROM THE CURRENT BUSINESS • (PERSONAL GIFT, PERSONAL DEMAND)	• LOW-COST MODEL? TOO SIMILAR TO #4? • (CAN WE PULL IT OFF?)
③ NON-DEPARTMENT STORE BUSINESS MODEL (PERSONAL, NON-FORMAL GIFTS)	• PERSONAL GIFT? • PERSONAL DEMAND? • LEVEL OF RECEPTIVITY?	• BREAK AWAY FROM THE DEPARTMENT STORE MODEL? • SPECIALIZED FLAGSHIP PRODUCT MODEL?
④ LOW-COST BUSINESS MODEL (CASUAL CONSUMPTION)	• PERSONAL CONSUMPTION • PERSONAL GIFT?	• LOW-COST MODEL? • (CAN WE PULL IT OFF?)
⑤ GENERAL DISTRIBUTION (SPECIALTY BRAND)	• PERSONAL DEMAND • PERSONAL GIFT?	• WHOLESALE BUSINESS MODEL • (CAN WE PULL IT OFF?)
⑥ GENERAL DISTRIBUTION (PB)	• PERSONAL DEMAND	• OEM (ORIGINAL EQUIPMENT MANUFACTURER) BUSINESS MODEL • (CAN WE PULL IT OFF?)
⑦ ONLINE ONLY BRAND	• FORMAL GIFT USER? • PERSONAL GIFT? • PERSONAL DEMAND?	• ONLINE SALES MODEL? • (CAN WE PULL IT OFF?)
⑧ OVERSEA EXPANSION	• OVERSEAS UPPER CLASS? OVERSEAS MASS MARKET? • GIFT DEMAND? PERSONAL DEMAND?	• MODEL FITTING FOR THE LOCAL MARKET?

YOU'LL BEGIN TO SEE SOME TRENDS.

I SEE.

LET'S EXPLORE OPTIONS FOR NEW VENTURES FROM A DIFFERENT ANGLE.

VALUE CHAIN, FOR EXAMPLE, IS A FLOW OF BUSINESS ACTIVITIES FROM US TO OUR CUSTOMERS (AND BEYOND)...

PRODUCT PLANNING → MATERIAL PROCUREMENT → MANUFACTURING → DISTRIBUTION → SALES

HERE'S A POINT OF VIEW FROM OUR VALUE CHAIN.

- UNDERTAKE OTHER COMPANIES' NEW PRODUCT PLANNING AND DEVELOPMENT
- SALE OF RAW MATERIALS (E.G., SELLING RED-BEAN PASTE TO OTHER COMPANIES)
- OEM BUSINESS (MANUFACTURE OTHER COMPANIES' BRAND PRODUCTS)
- STOCK AND SELL (PROCURE OTHER COMPANIES' PRODUCTS AND SELL THROUGH OUR SALES CHANNEL)
- ETC.

ALSO, FROM A COMPANY ASSET STANDPOINT...

- SALE OF RAW MATERIALS (UTILIZING OUR STRENGTH = "RED-BEAN PASTE")
- OEM BUSINESS (UTILIZING UNUSED MANUFACTURING LINE)
- WHOLESALE TO GENERAL DISTRIBUTION (UTILIZING OUR HIGH RECOGNITION AND BRAND POWER)
- ETC.

THERE ARE SOME OVERLAPS IN THE VALUE CHAIN AND COMPANY ASSETS.

AN ESTABLISHED VALUE CHAIN OFTEN BECOMES A COMPANY ASSET, OUR COMPANY INCLUDED.

I THINK THERE ARE MORE IDEAS WE CAN OFFER TO OUR CLIENTS.

FINALLY...

...WE CAN ALSO LOOK AT THIS FROM A BUSINESS MODEL POINT OF VIEW.

131

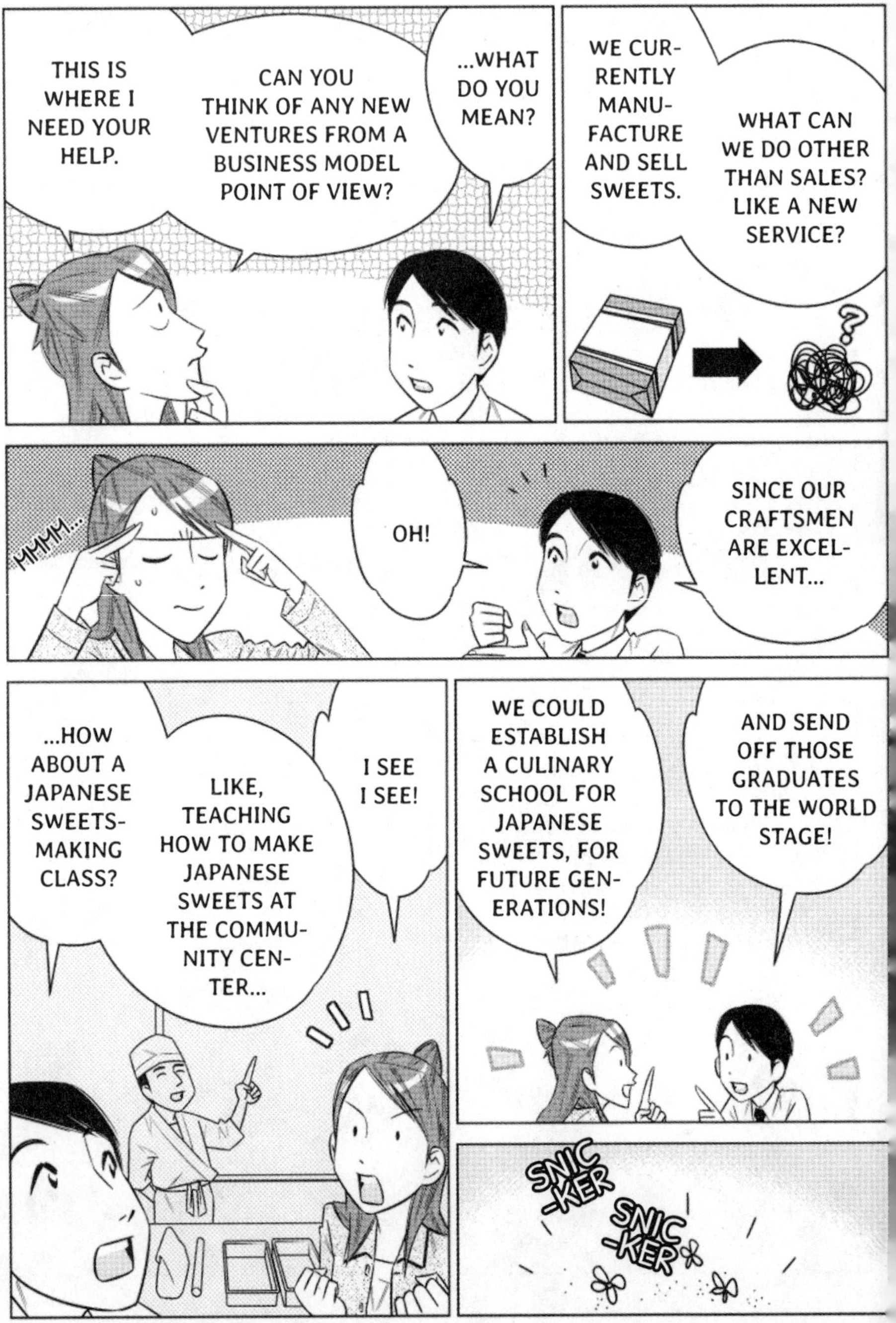
THIS IS WHERE I NEED YOUR HELP.
CAN YOU THINK OF ANY NEW VENTURES FROM A BUSINESS MODEL POINT OF VIEW?
...WHAT DO YOU MEAN?
WE CURRENTLY MANUFACTURE AND SELL SWEETS.
WHAT CAN WE DO OTHER THAN SALES? LIKE A NEW SERVICE?
?
MMMM...
OH!
SINCE OUR CRAFTSMEN ARE EXCELLENT...
...HOW ABOUT A JAPANESE SWEETS-MAKING CLASS?
LIKE, TEACHING HOW TO MAKE JAPANESE SWEETS AT THE COMMUNITY CENTER...
I SEE I SEE!
WE COULD ESTABLISH A CULINARY SCHOOL FOR JAPANESE SWEETS, FOR FUTURE GENERATIONS!
AND SEND OFF THOSE GRADUATES TO THE WORLD STAGE!
SNICKER
SNICKER

...AND WE WENT ON FOR HOURS ♪

...SOUNDS LIKE YOU HAD MORE FUN WITH HIM.

YUP!

YUP!

I'M ALWAYS IN YOUR DEBT, TAKEDA SENPAI.

OH, I SEE.

BY THE WAY...

I CAME UP WITH GROWTH OPTIONS FOR NUMBER THREE, IMPROVING PROFITABILITY.

- OVERHAUL OF THE PRODUCT LINEUP
- DECREASE PRODUCTION COST
- MINIMIZE FOOD LOSS
- LABOR COSTS AND STAFFING OPTIMIZATION
- ESTABLISH PROFIT MANAGEMENT AND MONITOR STRUCTURES
- ETC.

THESE ARE COMMON BUT IMPORTANT.

SO, HERE ARE THE POLISHED OPTIONS.

133

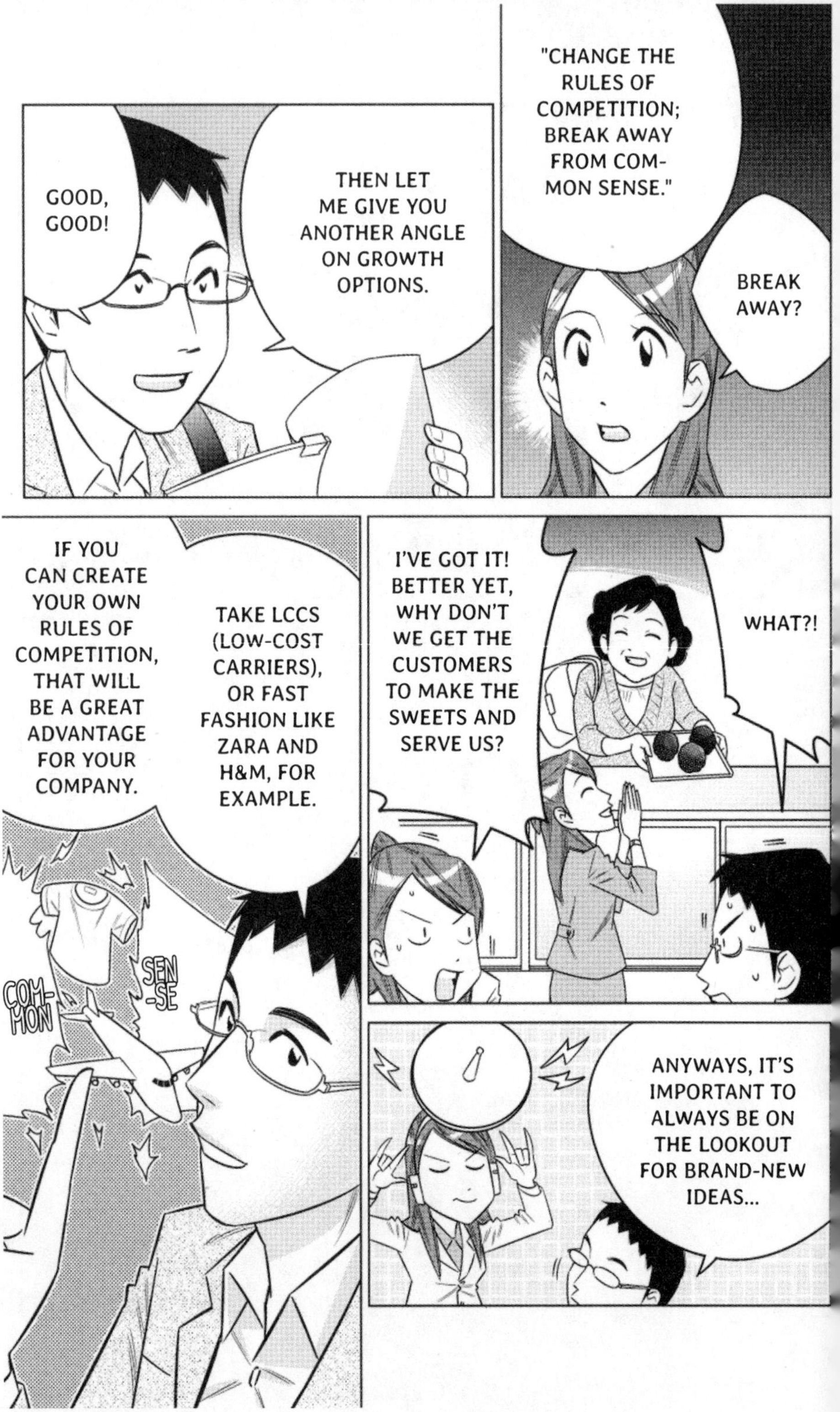
GOOD, GOOD!
THEN LET ME GIVE YOU ANOTHER ANGLE ON GROWTH OPTIONS.
"CHANGE THE RULES OF COMPETITION; BREAK AWAY FROM COM-MON SENSE."
BREAK AWAY?
IF YOU CAN CREATE YOUR OWN RULES OF COMPETITION, THAT WILL BE A GREAT ADVANTAGE FOR YOUR COMPANY.
TAKE LCCS (LOW-COST CARRIERS), OR FAST FASHION LIKE ZARA AND H&M, FOR EXAMPLE.
COM-MON
SEN-SE
I'VE GOT IT! BETTER YET, WHY DON'T WE GET THE CUSTOMERS TO MAKE THE SWEETS AND SERVE US?
WHAT?!
ANYWAYS, IT'S IMPORTANT TO ALWAYS BE ON THE LOOKOUT FOR BRAND-NEW IDEAS...

SINCE YOUR COMPANY'S SELLING POINT IS RED-BEAN PASTE, WHY NOT GROW RED BEANS?

LET'S OFFER JAPANESE SWEETS-MAKING CLASSES AND HAVE MATSUI-YA'S CRAFTSMEN TEACH THERE...

LET'S ORGANIZE.

IN MATSUI-YA'S CASE, THE BIGGEST ISSUE IS WHAT TO DO WITH THE BRAND AND THE BUSINESS MODEL.

FOR NOW, IT'S A SINGLE-BRAND, SINGLE-BUSINESS MODEL, RIGHT?

YES, WE ARE A JAPANESE SWEETS MANUFACTURER SELLING "MATSUI-YA" BRAND PRODUCTS IN DEPARTMENT STORES.

DEVELOPING A FRANCHISE CHAIN WITH THE GRADUATES ISN'T A BAD IDEA.

WE NEED TO REVIEW EVERY POSSIBLE COMBINATION OF SINGLE AND MULTIPLE OPTIONS.

	BRAND			
	SINGLE	MULTIPLE		BUSINESS MODEL
			SINGLE	
			MULTIPLE	

GO ON!

135

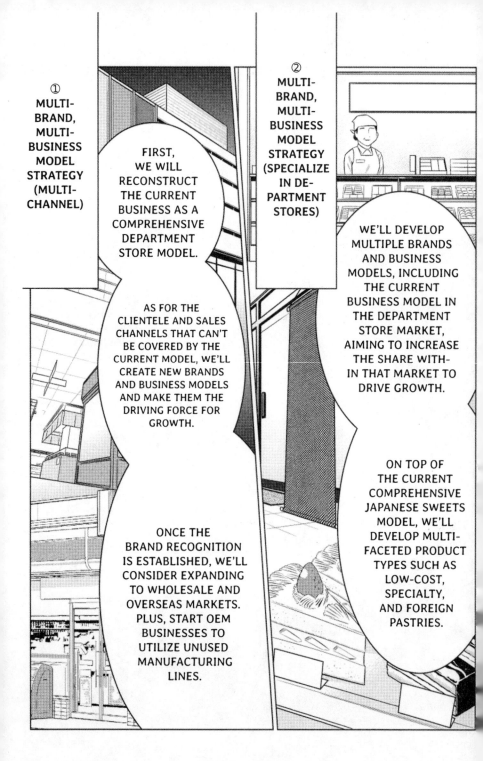

① MULTI-BRAND, MULTI-BUSINESS MODEL STRATEGY (MULTI-CHANNEL)

FIRST, WE WILL RECONSTRUCT THE CURRENT BUSINESS AS A COMPREHENSIVE DEPARTMENT STORE MODEL.

AS FOR THE CLIENTELE AND SALES CHANNELS THAT CAN'T BE COVERED BY THE CURRENT MODEL, WE'LL CREATE NEW BRANDS AND BUSINESS MODELS AND MAKE THEM THE DRIVING FORCE FOR GROWTH.

ONCE THE BRAND RECOGNITION IS ESTABLISHED, WE'LL CONSIDER EXPANDING TO WHOLESALE AND OVERSEAS MARKETS. PLUS, START OEM BUSINESSES TO UTILIZE UNUSED MANUFACTURING LINES.

② MULTI-BRAND, MULTI-BUSINESS MODEL STRATEGY (SPECIALIZE IN DEPARTMENT STORES)

WE'LL DEVELOP MULTIPLE BRANDS AND BUSINESS MODELS, INCLUDING THE CURRENT BUSINESS MODEL IN THE DEPARTMENT STORE MARKET, AIMING TO INCREASE THE SHARE WITHIN THAT MARKET TO DRIVE GROWTH.

ON TOP OF THE CURRENT COMPREHENSIVE JAPANESE SWEETS MODEL, WE'LL DEVELOP MULTI-FACETED PRODUCT TYPES SUCH AS LOW-COST, SPECIALTY, AND FOREIGN PASTRIES.

③ SINGLE-BRAND, MULTI-BUSINESS MODEL STRATEGY

THIS APPROACH WILL USE THE "MATSUI-YA" BRAND AND WILL GO AFTER VARIOUS SALES CHANNELS, NOT ONLY DEPARTMENT STORES.

WE'LL ESTABLISH A *DIFFUSION LINE ON TOP OF THE MAIN BRAND, TO MINIMIZE THE DILUTION OF THE BRAND IMAGE.

TO REVITALIZE THE BRAND, WE'LL LOOK INTO EXPANDING TO FOOD INDUSTRIES, SUCH AS CAFES, AND OVERSEA MARKETS.

④ MULTI-BRAND, SINGLE-BUSINESS MODEL STRATEGY

IN THIS, WE'LL DEVELOP MULTIPLE BRANDS FOLLOWING THE COMPREHENSIVE DEPARTMENT STORE MODEL...

WE WILL REMAIN A COMPREHENSIVE JAPANESE SWEETS MAKER, BUT ALSO DEVELOP A FOREIGN PASTRY MODEL SEPARATELY.

*DIFFUSION LINE: A SECONDARY LINE OF MERCHANDISE CREATED AT LOWER PRICES.

⑤ MULTI-BRAND, MULTI-BUSINESS MODEL STRATEGY (COMPREHENSIVE SWEETS MAKER)

⑥ JAPANESE SWEETS PLATFORM STRATEGY

THIS ONE AIMS TO ESTABLISH A "PLATFORM" WITHIN THE JAPANESE SWEETS INDUSTRY.

WE'LL AIM TO ACCOMPLISH THIS BY ESTABLISHING A CULINARY SCHOOL, HOSTING JAPANESE SWEETS-MAKING CLASSES, UNDERTAKING OEM AND PB PRODUCTS MANUFACTURING, PRODUCT DEVELOPMENT CONSULTATION, ETC.

HERE, WE DEVELOP MULTIPLE BUSINESS MODELS AND VENTURES, SUCH AS FOREIGN PASTRIES, CAFES, AND TEA HOUSES, WHICH FALL INTO THE FOOD INDUSTRY AND OEM BUSINESS.

WE'LL ALSO EXPLORE THE POSSIBILITIES OF MERGERS AND ACQUISITIONS.

WE'LL INCORPORATE PLANS TO IMPROVE PROFITABILITY IN ALL OF THE STRATEGIES.

ALSO, I'VE OMITTED THE SINGLE-BRAND/SINGLE-BUSINESS MODEL, BECAUSE STICKING WITH THE CURRENT MODEL IS MEANINGLESS.

WHAT DO YOU THINK?

I SEE... A PATH FORWARD IS STARTING TO EMERGE.

I'LL HAVE A WORD WITH THE CEO MYSELF IN REGARD TO THIS.

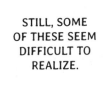

STILL, SOME OF THESE SEEM DIFFICULT TO REALIZE.

RIGHT! SO BASED ON THESE...

...WE'LL START EVALUATING AND NARROWING DOWN STRATEGIC OPTIONS.

1 What Are Strategic Options?

▶ Options Mean Choices

What are strategic options? We briefly touched on this in the prologue, but let's take a look at them further.

Options mean choices. Strategic options mean choices on which strategies to take. In building a strategy, it is vital to select your market, come up with ways to create a distinct edge from your competitors, and decide how to distribute resources. In short, strategic options means your choices for the three main strategic points (market, edge and distinction, and resource distribution). You may have more than one strategic direction you can take based on the strategic analysis results, which is common. Each of them is your strategic option.

The goal of this step is to lay out all strategic options. Afterward, we will move on to the final evaluation process and select the winning strategy.

▶ Considering a Variety of Options

Examining every available strategic option is important. If you worry too much about possibilities and risks, you'll only come up with options to play it safe and will not be able to build an effective strategy.

THE KEY TO COMING UP WITH AN EFFECTIVE STRATEGY IS TO THINK BROADLY.

In exploring options, you should not only think logically but also consider different angles and think outside the box. Otherwise, you'll end up with strategic options so ordinary, they won't be able to contribute to establishing a competitive edge. This would render the true goal of a strategy useless.

Most strategies taken by companies growing rapidly were controversial at first. Softbank is a good example. They came up with tactics such as offering free set boxes for the broadband service, innovative pricing tiers for their mobile phone service like White Plan, and proceeding with large acquisitions that turned them into a global mobile phone business giant. Their strategies were met with both praise and criticism but have certainly paid off so far.

If you think Softbank's case is a bit extreme, there are other examples of successful strategies that were out of the box. Take fast fashion brands such as ZARA and H&M. They've created a competitive edge in the fashion industry often plagued with overstock issues by limiting the production. They sold out each time and followed rapidly by releasing new products. While this is a common strategy nowadays, it was not the norm in the fashion industry up until about 10 years ago.

In short, it's crucial to come up with a variety of options in this step.

2 Make Objectives and Issues Clear

▶ What Is the Objective of Strategy Building?

Let's start coming up with strategic options. But first, don't go straight into thinking up options. There are a few things that we must keep in mind.

You must first have a clear vision of the goal and purpose of your strategy building. Now, you might think: isn't it to establish a competitive edge to come out on top? Correct. That is the ultimate objective of a strategy.

However, depending on the current situation, circumstances, as well as the company's business outlook, the specific goal might vary. For example, a strategy to double sales and a strategy focused on expanding profit are completely different. Even in the same industry, a strategy to restructure a struggling business will have a very different approach from a strategy designed to expand a steadily growing business.

SUCCESSFUL BUSINESSES TEND TO OVERLOOK THE ACTUAL GOAL, SO WATCH OUT!

Different goals will not only require different strategies, but also different choices and directions when you lay out the options. This is why it's important to make sure everyone is on the same page by sharing the result of the situation analysis, the company's vision, and the purpose of the strategy building.

Diagram 3-1 Objective of a Strategy Building

As consultants, we have run into situations where the executives are not convinced with the strategies their employees came up with. A common reason for this is due to a gap between the purpose that the employees envisioned and that of the executives. Even though the strategy is a good one, for the executives it appears as wrong because they understood the objective differently (see Diagram 3-1).

In other words, clarifying the purpose is like agreeing on a premise of the strategy building. If the existing business is already struggling, like in Matsui-ya's case, this is not a big problem. However, for a company in steady growth, opinions on where to set a goal can differ greatly depending on each party involved. A thorough discussion in advance is vital in order to set a common goal or a purpose.

In the case of Matsui-ya, their current three goals based on the situation analysis result are stopping the decrease in sales, improving profitability, and bringing about mid- to long-term sustainable growth.

▶ What Are the Issues in Building a Strategy?

Once you have a clear purpose, the next thing to flesh out is the viewpoint for the strategy evaluation. This is also a necessary step to define the strategic issues and possible problems in achieving your goal.

In the case of Matsui-ya, the three main issues are: How to reconstruct the existing business, how to utilize growth opportunities and/or threats outside the existing business (possibilities of new ventures), and how to boost the surplus structure (improving profitability).

A viewpoint is these sorts of specific questions and issues, which are the starting line of building a strategy.

It's not exaggerating to say that defining your point of view can make or break your strategy. Without recognizing the issues properly, you can't identify the correct strategy to deal with them. After all, there is no way to give a correct answer to the wrong question.

How far you delved into the core of the issues in the situation analysis is the key to defining viewpoints. We've previously touched on the plight of the Japanese home electronics industry (pages 43–44). That was all caused by not defining the viewpoint properly. They kept to strategies based on conventional market circumstances, overlooking drastic changes in market structure and rules of competition due to advances in digitalization, the expansion of emerging markets in other countries, and the rise of new competitors.

Diagram 3-2 | Setting Viewpoints

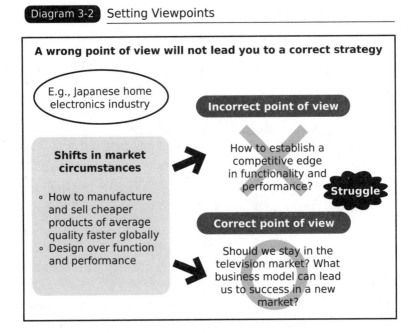

The point of view that they came up with was to establish a competitive edge in functionality and performance even within the rapidly advancing digitalization to regain their market share among emerging competitors. However, the viewpoint was incorrect. The market had already shifted to a competition of manufacturing and selling cheap products of average quality as fast as possible.

Their viewpoint was based on assumptions about the conventional market structure (or its extension). In a market structure that has dramatically changed, this is an obsolete point of view. This is

145

what led them to their decline. The viewpoints that the Japanese manufacturers should have considered are, for example, whether or not to stay in the television market, and if yes, then what business model would ensure their survival in the new market structure.

Properly defining the issues at hand will lead you to formulate an efficient strategy. If you proceed without pinning down the issues, you may end up spending fruitless hours thinking about ineffective strategies. Without clear viewpoints, you'll end up astray. You can't find an answer if there is no well-defined question.

You should have a clearer image of what to answer and what strategic options you can examine once the issues are properly specified. The scope and range of what you need to consider will be narrowed down to a certain direction. Once you've set your point of view, you won't feel like wandering in a maze with no exit.

▶ Decipher Objectives and Issues from the Result of the SWOT Analysis

Now that you have seen the importance of defining the issues before developing strategic options, how exactly do you define those purposes and issues in the first place?

First, you have to think about your objectives. As always, start with the result of your situation analysis. Consider your objectives based on the performance to date, the current market and competition, as well as future prospects. It can be increasing sales, improving profitability, restructuring an existing business, and so on. Take into account the corporate vision in setting your goal as well. If the corporate vision is to become the industry leader and the current circumstances showed that the corporate is not yet at that level, then your goal should be generating sales and profit that can contribute to that vision.

Base your issues on the result of the SWOT analysis. A good way to do it is to use a matrix to examine your company's strengths and weaknesses (SW) and opportunities and threats (OT). By doing this, you can frame your thoughts like: "What business opportunities can we realize using our strength and how to do so?" "Which weakness needs to be addressed and bolstered and for what?" and "How to utilize our strength and/or fortify our weakness to counter threats?" This will offer a crucial insight later on.

Take a look at Diagram 3-4 on page 148, which summarizes the five basic points to consider.

Diagram 3-3 Defining the Purpose

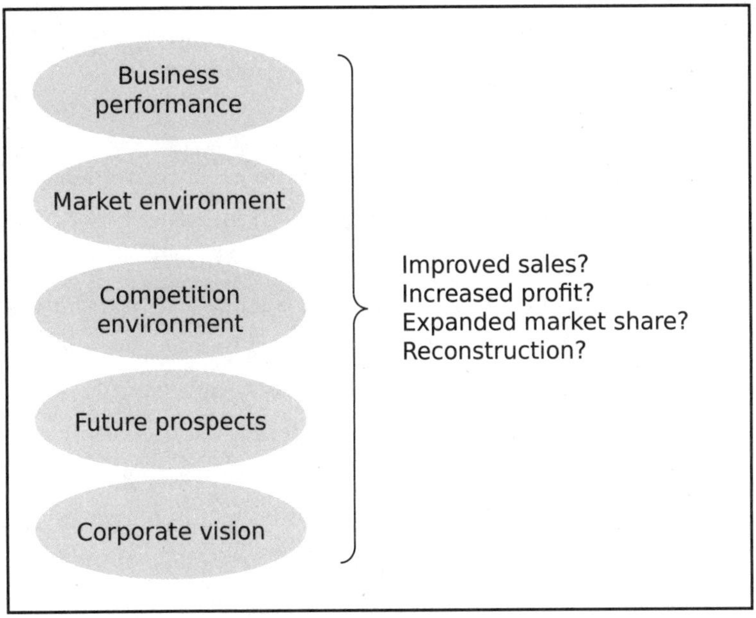
Business performance
Market environment
Competition environment
Future prospects
Corporate vision
Improved sales?
Increased profit?
Expanded market share?
Reconstruction?

① Is there any growth opportunity (improved sales) in the existing business or its extension (without drastically changing the current business model and positioning)?

② If there is but a limited growth opportunity in the existing business or its extension, where can we find the growth opportunity (if any)?

③ If there is a growth opportunity, can we capture it by changing and/or restructuring the current business model and positioning?

④ Or should we consider a new venture to gain growth opportunities?

⑤ Is there room for improving profitability?

Let's carefully examine the issues based on the above perspectives using the results of the situation review and SWOT analysis.

For Matsui-ya, Kazumi and Takeda came up with the following specific issues.

The existing business itself does have room for improvement. Not only do we have weaknesses compared to the other companies, but some industry KSFs are also not met either. If these can be improved while boosting up strengths such as the brand image and finely honed red-bean crafts, we should be able to turn things around. However, there is limited growth opportunity in the existing business and there are future potential risks. Unfortunately, that is the market-wide trend and there is little we can do about it. On the other hand, there are opportunities in other areas such as non-department stores sales channels and personal consumption consumers. It is vital to consider using these opportunities to

148

Diagram 3-5 Five Basic Points in Understanding the Issues Based on the SWOT Analysis (Matsui-ya's case)

STRENGTHS

How best to utilize strengths

- Strong ties with the department store chains
- Highly recognizable
- History and tradition
- Honed red-bean paste craft
- Varied products
- High rate of repeat customers

WEAKNESSES

How best to boost & bolster weakness

- Dependency on the department stores
- Old-fashioned brand image
- Product not considered for purchase
- Aging clientele
- Unappealing products
- High-cost structure
- Low productivity

OPPORTUNITIES

- Develop new sales channels
- Potential new Japanese sweets consumers
- Possible growth in sales per store
- Improving profit by changing the product lineup
- New customers from other product genres
- Potential overseas market

THREATS

- Declining sales due to department stores' slump
- Formal gift market shrinking
- Falling market share due to harsh competition
- Damaged brand value
- Accelerated deterioration

There are new growth opportunities

On top of the weaknesses, the KSFs in the industry are not fulfilled in the first place

Obvious room for improvement in profitability

Issue No.② How to break the limitation of the existing business and gain growth? Any new venture opportunities?

By polishing our strengths, reconstructing the existing business might be possible — Improving Profitability **Issue No. ③**

Limited room for growth in existing business

Issue No. ① How to reconstruct the existing business?

support the existing business. There is an obvious, large room for improvement in profitability.

Based on the above, Kazumi and Takeda came up with the three main issues introduced earlier.

▶ Organizing the Structure of an Issue

Once you have defined the main issues, the next thing to do is to delve into those issues and identify the secondary issues. What we came up with earlier are the primary issues. Generally, you can solve them by finding solutions to several smaller issues related to them. Thus, resolving the secondary issues should lead you to resolve the primary issues. Base your examination of secondary issues on the result of the situation analysis, especially the SWOT analysis, just as you had done with the primary issues.

Let's take a look at the primary and secondary issues Kazumi and Takeda identified.

Diagram 3-6 Issue No. ① (Matsui-ya's case)

Issue No. ①: How to reconstruct the existing business

○ Should we keep focusing on department stores, or should we diversify the sales channel?

  • Should we take the existing business away from department stores, or keep it focused on department stores and use other sales channels for the new venture?

○ Should we keep formal gift consumers as the main target, or add personal consumption and other potential clientele as well? (Targeted user)

  • Should we diversify the targeted clientele with the existing business, or let it focus only on formal gift users while targeting other types of consumers with a new venture?

○ Should we follow a comprehensive business model, specialize in a signature product, or completely break away from department stores? (Which business model to aim for?)

  • In each business model, what has the potential to be our competitive edge and/or a distinctive factor?

○ How to reconstruct an obsolete brand?

Diagram 3-7 Issue No. ② (Matsui-ya's case)

Issue No. ②: How to capture growth opportunities or handle threats the existing business couldn't face? Any possibility of a new venture?

- Which market should we compete in?
  - Identify the business areas in terms of country or region, product category, channel, price range, target clientele, business model, etc.
- How much can the existing business cover the growth opportunity and deal with threats?
- What new venture can take in high-potential channels and customers that the currently existing business can't cover?
  - Should we consider a new venture with a different positioning within the department store market?
  - A new venture targeting the non-department store market?
  - Should we try to take in personal gift users and personal consumption clientele?
  - Specialized signature product model, or low-cost operation model?
- How should we consider the overseas market?
  - Should we branch out to the overseas market or not?
  - If yes, which area should we target specifically? (Country/city, product category, channel, price range, target clientele, etc.)
  - How should we establish the business model and competitive edge?
- Is there any possible new venture within sweets manufacture and sales or its surrounding industry that could contribute to the growth?
  - From the value chain perspective (OEM business, etc.)
  - From the business model transformation perspective (from product sales to the service industry, etc.)
  - From the company assets' point of view (brand recognition, etc.)

In regards to the existing business, the issues and directions you need to examine are: what to do with the sales channel, what business model to follow, and who to target. The winning strategy patterns of the Japanese sweets industry showed that these three points are crucial. In other words, by solving these three issues, you should be able to see a possible direction to reconstruct the existing business.

In deciding how to handle opportunities and/or threats, always keep in mind what market to compete in and how much of the currently existing business can cover that market, as well as what would be the target of the new venture. Consider what new ventures apply to the target market, channel, business model, and targeted clientele.

On the other hand, there may also be possibilities for new ventures from individual perspectives like the value chain and company assets. We will go over this in more detail later.

When it comes to improving profitability, on top of the main issues such as unit cost and SG&A expenses, you'll have to consider what kind of profit management structure is needed to strengthen and sustain profitability. We'll go over these in depth later, too.

Identifying primary and secondary issues and sorting them out in relation to each other will allow you to understand the issues

Diagram 3-8 Issue No. ③ (Matsui-ya's case)

Issue No. ③: Improving Profitability
- ○ What measures should we take to improve profit?
  - Unit cost reduction
  - SG&A expenses reduction
  - Profit management
  - etc.

structurally. Identify the issue structure from the results of the situation and SWOT analysis and work in perspectives and approaches when laying out your strategic options, which we will cover in the next section.

We highly recommend you pick up other publications regarding issues and their structures, as well as how to analyze them to get a deeper understanding of this matter.

Clearing up the issue structure is a key process in building effective strategies efficiently. Skipping it risks you misjudging the direction of the strategies or overlooking important elements, which would render the strategy useless. You might also end up spending too much time discussing less essential issues.

3

Lay Out the Options 1: Growing Potentials for the Preestablished Company

▶ Aim to Grow Preestablished Business Models and Positioning

Once the issues are organized, we'll start polishing the strategic options. Let's take a look at the options in the case where there's growth potential without drastically changing the current business model and/or positioning.

A business model will give you a framework of how to earn a profit, while positioning will establish where you stand in the market relative to the competitors, defined by targeted clientele, offered value, and distinction. We'll consider growth options following these preestablished business models and positioning.

Matsui-ya's current business is a primary example of this. Poised as the "comprehensive department store Japanese sweets model," the performance has been lackluster in recent years. While they have strengths such as a rich history, acclaimed red-bean paste, and a reliable brand image, there are industry KSFs that weren't met, causing their decline. It's true the Japanese sweets market within the department store may have plateaued, but there is room for improvement.

I RECOMMEND THIS OPTION FOR COMPANIES WITH GROWTH POTEN-TIAL ON THEIR CURRENT PATH.

Therefore, without drastically changing the current business model and/or positioning,

Kazumi and Takeda believe the current business can be salvaged by improving marketing (products, price, promotion, channel) and operations (product development, procuring, production, distribution, sales, etc.).

Create a staple product using highly rated red-bean paste, offer seasonal products, clarify the brand image by narrowing down product types, and use new media and technology to change the current market environment. These measures can lead to the revitalization of the current business.

You can stay the current course if there are ways to establish a potential competitive edge, or meet the industry's KSFs sufficiently, as long as the market itself doesn't dip too low.

Diagram 3-9 Matsui-ya's Strategic Options ①

Reconstructing the current business (following current model)
- Reformation as a comprehensive department store Japanese sweets model
- The main target will be the formal gift user, pursuing a comprehensive department store Japanese sweets model as a foundation
- Pushing "red-bean paste" to the foreground as the flagship product/material
- Example: Offering "freshly cooked red-bean paste" (cooking red-bean paste at the storefront etc.)
- Coining the brand image: Gift giving means "Matsui-ya"
- Staple products + eye-catching and fresh new and seasonal products, strengthening promotion (at the storefront and the media)
- Develop a channel to broadcast the brand such as café
- Establish a flagship store
- In addition to the stores within department stores, strengthen gift centers, direct and online sales
- Aim to grow by increasing sales per store and expansion of the above channels

▶ Consider Strategic Options for the Long Run

For the established businesses, there are several ways to consider options for growth without changing the current business model and/or positioning.

First, break down the sales into individual elements: number of customers × unit price, sales per store × number of stores, sales quantity × unit price, sales per vendor × number of vendors, sales per direct sales × number of sales personnel, etc. By comparing your company's performance versus that of the competitors (or benchmark), you will identify where you can find room for improvement. For example, if your sales per store are less than the competitors', take a closer look to see if there is any room for improvement (you will have to compare with similar business models and positioning).

Also, check to see if your company is fulfilling the industry's KSFs by comparing it to similar business models and positioning. This can provide you with clues when coming up with options. If there are KSFs that are not met, you must examine the potential for gaining a competitive edge and growth by meeting those factors. This is how you can reveal ways to improve your company's marketing and operations. These will become the essentials of your strategic options.

▶ Changing the Positioning

Positioning, as we mentioned before, is where you stand in the business market, determined by clientele, offered value, and distinction. You should consider this option if your current positioning has little to no room for growth. But there is potential to grow if elements such as clientele, offered price, and distinction are changed.

156

Diagram 3-10 Example of Growth Option Evaluation by Dissecting the Sales

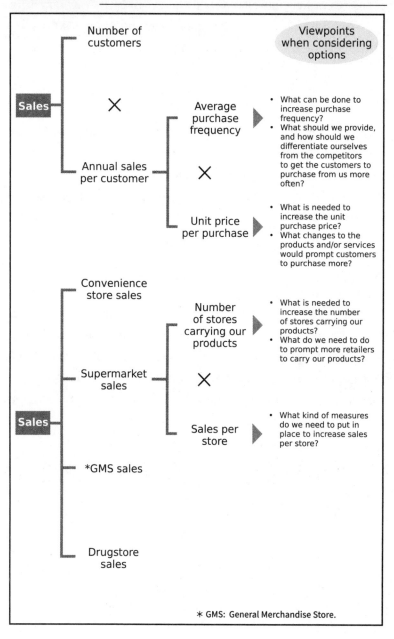

In Matsui-ya's case, its positioning within the Japanese sweets market is rather limited; it established itself by mainly targeting department store customers, especially the formal gift users, offering value such as reliability and confidence in formal gifts.

However, there are many more potential customers all across the market, and competitors are pursuing different values of their own. So Matsui-ya may benefit from changing its positioning by going after customers with personal gifts and consumption needs, exploring more casual and affordable options, and low-cost products. There are also options in how to realize those growth options, whether to pursue it by changing the current business model or establishing it as a brand-new venture.

▶ Coming Up with Growth Options by Changing the Positioning

You can examine these options and divide them into sections from the viewpoints of consumer needs and values, and purchasing action, rather than from the results of the situation and SWOT analysis. Based on each segment, identify the targeted consumer types, and offered values supported by the customers for your company and the competitors.

With those in mind, pinpoint the segments with potential growth opportunities, consumer needs that are not met or recognized by your competitors, and segments in which you can potentially win.

The key to establishing the positioning is to compartmentalize the market. It is hard to identify an effective positioning by just looking at the needs that have surfaced, and the purchasing action. In many cases, these "obvious" segments already have well-established competitors supported by consumers. It is not easy for late comers to win in such a market.

Instead, you'll have a much better chance of winning by choosing a market without competition, or identifying consumer needs that even the well-established competitors are not meeting by changing the way you look at the market segmentation.

Diagram 3-11 Example of Positioning Change

Example 1	Existing players (major electronics retailers)'s positioning	Sato Camera (page 42)'s positioning
Target clientele	• Wide consumer base within the marketing area	• Clientele includes non-camera experts such as children and the elderly • Camera beginners
Offered price	• Selling popular products at the lowest possible price	• Preserving everlasting memories

Example 2	Existing coffee chain's positioning	Starbucks Coffee's positioning
Target clientele	• Working force mainly office workers	• People looking to enjoy delicious coffee and relax
Offered price	• Affordably priced coffee • A place where you can have a quick relaxing break	• Pricy but delicious coffee • Social surroundings other than home/work where one can relax

159

Sato Camera we introduced in the prologue is a great example of this. Instead of competing with major electronics retailers by selling popular products at the lowest possible price, they realized the consumer needs were more on finding a product that best fits their needs, even at a higher price, and preserving everlasting memories. By targeting those consumers, they have successfully managed to establish a completely different positioning than that of the major electronics retailers.

Starbucks Coffee, too, followed a similar tactic. Before Starbucks, coffee shops were places where you can drink affordable but so-so coffee in sometimes not so pleasant atmosphere. Starbucks created a brand-new cafe positioning by introducing a concept of the third place, a social surrounding other than your home or work where you can relax, and offering pricier but tastier coffee with which you can have fun with flavors and customizations.

When considering strategic options from the positioning point of view, it is necessary to identify the positioning of your company and the competitors, plus the consumers' purchase actions, value, and needs based on the situation analysis. Meticulous preparation is required even from the situation analysis step.

▶ Changing the Business Model

As we mentioned before, a business model is a structure to earn profit. Based on the business situation and the market environment, you may be able to grow your business by changing the business model of your current business.

Changing a business model can be especially effective in a market that has matured with little room for growth, or an extremely competitive market that is difficult to differentiate and is becoming a losing battle.

Many companies have successfully grown by changing their business models. Uniqlo's first retailing model started as a regional fashion retailer. They accomplished this by shifting from a small retailer to a SPA (store retailer of private retail apparel) business model.

Diagram 3-12 Example of Positioning Change

Uniqlo (first retailing)	○ Improved competitive edge and transformed profit structure by integrating traditionally divided value chain (development, production, sales)
Gillette	○ Established a profit model by replacement blades (consumables) ○ Similar to the copier's sales model (profiting from the consumables such as paper and toner, not the actual machine)
Nespresso (Nestlé)	○ Selling the espresso machine at a lower price, profiting from the sale of specialized coffee pods
LCC	○ Established low-profit–high sales business model by thoroughly reducing cost and maximizing the rate of operation
Ore no French	○ Introduced standing bar style to establish a profitable business model even with high-cost price at low sale price by improving customer turnover rate

This is a bit older example, but you can take the razor manufacturer Gillette's "Gillette model" as another example of success due to a change in the business model. They have established a successful business model where they sell razor handles at a low price and profit from disposable replacement razor blades.

In recent years, Nestlé has had a similar business model. Selling their Nespresso machine at a lower price, and profiting from the sale of dedicated coffee pods. Nestlé is expanding their share in the home espresso market with this business model.

"Ore no French" gained consumer support for their extreme cost performance, which was unheard of in the Japanese restaurant industry, which is quite mature and competitive.

▶ Pairing the Positioning and the Business Model

Cases like LCC and "Ore no French" have established brand-new positioning in the conventional market for themselves. They've created new positionings while renovating their business models.

Business models and positioning quite often have a close relationship. We went over this during the positioning section (page 158 onwards), but it's hard to come up with a positioning that will create an advantage over the competition with a common overview of the market. This is where an out-of-the-box point of view is needed.

Take "Ore no French," for example. Fine French cuisine is expensive. This was the previous perception within the restaurant industry. French cuisine meant enjoying a meal that uses high-end ingredients, painstakingly crafted by an expert chef in a refined environment. No wonder it is so expensive, or so everyone thought. But what if we come up with a positioning in which contradicting elements such as low price and high quality can coexist? Customers will flock to a delicious French restaurant with a low price. But there was no business model previously that realized and profited from the low-price–high-quality French before "Ore no French." "Ore no French" hires top chefs and uses high-end ingredients, and their menu can stand its ground against their luxurious counterparts. By introducing the standing bar style and maximizing the customer turnover rate, they have established a profitable business model even with a high-cost price at a low sale price. They have developed a new way to profit from low sale prices. Without this new business model, their low-price–high-quality positioning would not work.

In many cases, it becomes necessary to evolve your business model when attempting to establish a positioning with a competitive advantage. Of course, it is possible to successfully change the positioning without changing the business model. But it is important to keep in mind how deeply connected they are.

An industry's winning pattern, too, is often defined by the positioning and the business model. This was true in the Japanese sweets market. One of the winning patterns was a low-cost model. This low-price–high-quality model targeted the casual and personal consumption clientele and earned profit by rigorously sticking to the low-cost operation.

To successfully establish this positioning, in other words, target clientele looking for affordable products that can be personally

Diagram 3-13 Matsui-ya's Strategic Options ②

Reconstruction of the current business (by changing positioning and business model)

○ Developing specialized flagship product model, breaking away from department stores (multi-channel) model

- Evaluate the product lineup and narrow it down centered on flagship products
- Develop a lineup to meet personal gift and consumption needs, separate from the formal gift sector
- Develop sales channels other than the department stores (mainly for personal consumption clientele)
- Expand to popular commercial facilities and locations to refresh the brand image
- Continue sales within the department store market
- Strengthen promoting and marketing
- Expand to opportunities such as café to broadcast brand image
- Aim mainly to grow through increased numbers of stores and sales channels

○ Develop a low-cost model, breaking away from the department stores (multi-channel) model

- Target clientele looking for casual and personal consumption with a focus on low-unit price products. Expand to different sales channels with large potential clientele such as station buildings and shopping centers.
- A structure is needed to profit from low-unit price products, by concentrating on products with low-cost rates, operating the stores at a minimal cost, and narrowing down and cutting unnecessary costs meticulously.

and casually consumed, they will need a business model that would allow them to sell low-unit price products and still profit from them, by narrowing down and cutting unnecessary costs meticulously.

From this standpoint, Kazumi and Takeda are discussing Matsui-ya's strategic options with the positioning and the business model as a pair.

▶ Coming Up with Growth Options by Changing the Business Options

To be honest, it's not easy to come up with options for growth by changing the business model. In most cases, there is little to no precedent, and it'll require highly creative and flexible ideas.

First, it is a given that you must review and organize the current business models used by your company and its competitors. Understanding the current situation and how each company is competing with what kind of business model and positioning will become your springboard.

Next, see if there are any clientele, consumer needs, and values that are not covered by your company or the competitors. For "Ore no French," this was "quality French cuisine at a low price."

In many cases, untapped sectors usually mean a market is too small to profit from, or too difficult to profit from with a conventional business model. It's not beneficial to consider the former, but the latter has a growth potential by changing the business model. What needs to be changed from the previous business model to establish a profitable positioning? Put your imagination and creativity to good use.

Of course, you won't come up with good ideas and great business models just by thinking. Let's look for more clues that can help you. One of them is examining examples of business model change within and outside of the industry you are in. As you can see from many examples we've provided previously, many companies worldwide are always evolving and changing their business models to grow their business. Learn from the predecessors. Study them regardless of the industries and business types. Examples from different industries can often provide valuable insight. It is often true that common sense in one industry may not be so in another.

For an average manufacturer, it is common to produce just enough to sell and procure just enough to produce. This is considered "JIT (just-in-time)" manufacturing. But in the fashion industry, this way of thinking was unheard of until recently. JIT manufacturing is becoming more and more commonplace, resulting in the evolution of the business model centered on fast fashion.

Lay Out the Strategic Options 2: Options for the Newly Established Businesses

4

▶ Analyze from the Market Point of View

Aiming to grow through a new venture can be one of the main pillars of your strategic options. This option becomes especially important if some opportunities or threats cannot be dealt with by the current business or its extension, or by changing the business model.

A great example of a successful growth strategy by a new venture is Fujifilm. Fujifilm, as the name suggests, was originally in the photography industry manufacturing photographic films and cameras. They knew the market for photographic film would shrink drastically due to the advance of the digital camera. That is why they sought out strategic options based on new business opportunities that can sustain growth in the future. They targeted the field where they could utilize their skills and technology, and reviewed their options carefully for almost two years. In the end, they came up with growth strategies in completely different fields such as cosmetics and medical equipment. Fujifilm is continuing to grow to this day, while its American competitor, Kodak, filed for bankruptcy in 2012.

THIS IS THE OPTION FOR WHEN THE CURRENT BUSINESS IS IN A TOUGH SITUATION!

As you can see from this example, the business field is one of the key standpoints when considering a new venture. Many different aspects define the market, such as product category, channel, clientele, region, and so on.

167

Take these aspects in many different combinations and look for a business field with great potential that is not covered currently by your company.

When you are polishing strategic options, don't get too caught up in the strength and resources of your company. That can narrow your viewpoints. However, in cases like Fujifilm, if the entire premise hinges on your company's strengths such as skills and resources, it is okay to select a new market based on those strengths.

Also, you will have to consider what kinds of positionings and business models can be applied in this market while coming up with options for expanding to a new field. Positionings and business models or the winning patterns of the major players already in that potential market can give you clues. You'll have to consider what kind of winning patterns your company can establish upon entering that market.

Kazumi flushed out options for a new venture based on viewpoints such as product category, channel, and region with Takeda's help (Diagram 3-14). Mapping essential aspects in a matrix form like that diagram can give you a better understanding.

LET'S BEGIN BY IDENTIFYING WHAT KIND OF BUSINESSES ARE IN THAT MARKET.

They delved further into the new venture options that were starting to emerge from targeted clientele and business model standpoints and began examining what kind of business opportunities can be found with each new venture option.

Diagram 3-14 Matsui-ya's Strategic Options ③ - 1

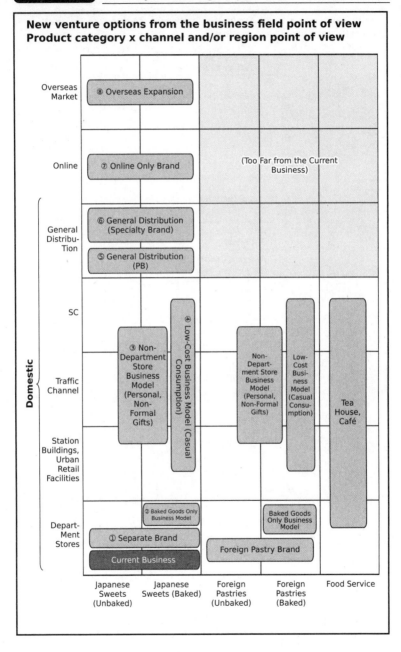

New venture options from the business field point of view
Product category x channel and/or region point of view

	Japanese Sweets (Unbaked)	Japanese Sweets (Baked)	Foreign Pastries (Unbaked)	Foreign Pastries (Baked)	Food Service
Overseas Market	⑧ Overseas Expansion				
Online	⑦ Online Only Brand		(Too Far from the Current Business)		
General Distribution	⑥ General Distribution (Specialty Brand) ⑤ General Distribution (PB)				
SC / Traffic Channel / Station Buildings, Urban Retail Facilities	③ Non-Department Store Business Model (Personal, Non-Formal Gifts)	④ Low-Cost Business Model (Casual Consumption)	Non-Department Store Business Model (Personal, Non-Formal Gifts)	Low-Cost Business Model (Casual Consumption)	Tea House, Café
Department Stores	① Separate Brand / Current Business	② Baked Goods Only Business Model	Foreign Pastry Brand	Baked Goods Only Business Model	

(Domestic)

Diagram 3-15 | Matsui-ya's Strategic Options ③ - 2

New venture options from the business field point of view
Matsui-ya's strategic option 3-1 x positioning x business
model

	Target Clientele	Business Model
Current Business	• Formal Gift User (How Far Should We Expand the Target?)	• Comprehensive Department Store Japanese Sweets Model (But Not Fulfilling KSFs) • Break away from Department Stores, Shift to Specialized Flagship Product?
① Separate Brand	• Different Clientele from the Current Business (Receptivity, Personal Gift, Personal Demand) (Possible to Differentiate from the Current Business?)	• Comprehensive Department Store Japanese Sweets Model? • Specialized Flagship Product Model? (Is It Even Possible?)
② Baked Goods Only Business Model	• Different Clientele From the Current Business (Personal Gift, Personal Demand)	• Low-Cost Model? Too Similar to #4? (Can We Pull It Off?)
③ Non-Department Store Business Model (Personal, Non-Formal Gifts)	• Personal Gift? • Personal Demand? • Level of Receptivity?	• Break away from The Department Store Model? • Specialized Flagship Product Model?
④ Low-Cost Business Model (Casual Consumption)	• Personal Consumption • Personal Gift?	• Low-Cost Model? (Can We Pull It Off?)
⑤ General Distribution (Specialty Brand)	• Personal Demand • Personal Gift?	• Wholesale Business Model (Can We Pull It Off?)
⑥ General Distribution (Pb)	• Personal Demand	• OEM (Original Equipment Manufacturer) Business Model (Can We Pull It Off?)
⑦ Online Only Brand	• Formal Gift User? • Personal Gift? • Personal Demand?	• Online Sales Model? (Can We Pull It Off?)
⑧ Oversea Expansion	• Overseas Upper Class? Overseas Mass Market? • Gift Demand? Personal Demand?	• Model Fitting for the Local Market?

170

▶ Analyze from the Value Chain Point of View

You can also examine options for a new venture from the value chain point of view. Utilizing a specific function on the company's value chain flow, focusing on a specific function, and expanding upstream or downstream of the value chain can all lead to a new venture.

In many cases, the IT industry, which deals with personal computers, mobile phones, and semiconductors, handles product development, planning, and manufacturing separately by different companies that specialize in each field. You can develop a business specializing in a specific function upon the industry-wide value chain.

Major food manufacturers are starting to take on consignment businesses producing a private brand (PB) for major retailers such as convenience stores in recent years. This, too, can be considered a new venture utilizing the company's specific function.

On the other hand, Uniqlo, which started out as a apparel retailer, shifted into the SPA business model by streamlining from product development straight through production (the actual manufacturing is done by outsourcing, but they do have a control over it) by expanding the upstream of their value chain. This is not exactly a brand-new venture, but is a good example of growth due to the value chain expansion.

Automobile manufactures, such as Toyota, expanding in markets such as used cars, leasing, rental cars, and financial business is another example of successful new ventures by expanding the value chain (in this case the downstream), or by utilizing specific functions upon the value chain.

▶ Analyze from the Asset Point of View

You can come up with a new venture from the asset point of view, by utilizing your company's strengths and resources. The premise in Fujifilm's case was first and foremost to take advantage of the skills the company possessed. This is a prime example of coming up with a new venture by utilizing the skills you already have.

What about another aspect of a company's strengths, its resources? First, there are tangible and intangible assets. Tangible assets can be funds, real estate, factories and equipment, products, and stores. They are something that can be given a monetary value, or something that can be seen. On the other hand, intangible assets can be brand recognition, skills, function, organizational

Diagram 3-16 Matsui-ya's Strategic Options ④

Options for new ventures from the value chain point of view
- Undertaking other companies' new product planning and development
- Sale of raw materials (e.g. selling red-bean paste to other companies)
- OEM business (manufacture other company's products)
- Stock and sell (procure other companies' products and sell through our sales channel)
- etc.

Research and development → Product planning → Procurement → Production → Distribution → Sales

Product development business

Raw material (e.g., red-bean paste) sales business

OEM business

Stock and Sell business (a one-stop shop for sweets and snacks)

abilities (marketing, product development, etc.), and so on. It is something that is not easily given monetary value, or something that cannot be seen. Business partners and networks, client base, and personnel can be considered tangible assets, but intangible assets are more fitting for them.

In general, intangible assets have a greater importance when it comes to the company assets. Intangible assets are often utilized in developing a new venture.

Diagram 3-17 From the Company Assets' Point of View

	Examples of assets	Examples of new business developments by assets
Tangible Asset	○ Funds, real estate, factories, equipment, etc.	○ Developing new ventures by using the company's real estate and facilities • Example: Station buildings owned by the railroad company
Intangible Asset	○ Brand power, business partners, client base, technologies, etc.	○ Expanding the business by utilizing the brand recognition ○ Providing new products and services to business partners and client base • Example: Retailers, credit card business, popular brands branching out to the hospitality industry, such as restaurants and hotels
	○ Anything relating to organization, such as organizational structure, HR system, personnel, climate, and culture, etc.	○ Developing new ventures reflecting personnel, climate, and culture • Example: Virgin Group (British multinational venture capital conglomerate)
	○ Functions and performance relating to value chain, such as research and development, marketing skills, procurement/ production/distribution, sales, and sales force	○ Expansion to new markets utilizing company's skills and functions • Example: Food and drink manufacturers expanding to medical and health food industries

There are many examples of new ventures taking advantage of brand recognition. Sony has used the brand recognition they have established in the electronics business and branched out into the financial and gaming fields. AEON, Seven & Seven Bank, and i Holdings, too, have successfully expanded into the financial sector by taking advantage of their impressive ability to attract customers. We've already mentioned Fujifilm, which succeeded in new sectors like cosmetics with their skills and technologies. Xerox has used relationships with their business partners and the network they have built to start a solution service business.

There are instances in which tangible assets came into play. Seven Bank, the financial sector of the Seven & i Holdings mentioned before, centers on a business model that profits from the service fees of their ATM machines. This model is possible due to 7-Eleven's ability to attract customers, as well as its over 16K stores countrywide. Therefore, this is an example of utilizing a tangible asset, their store network. There are more extreme cases of new ventures by tapping into abundant funds.

When thinking about options for new ventures from the asset point of view, you might come up with similar ideas from that of the value chain point of view. Kazumi also points this out, but this is often because the established value chain itself and its function can be considered an asset.

▶ Analyze from the Business Model Point of View
Another way to consider new venture options is from the business model point of view. Here are some examples: Is it possible to shift or expand from the manufacturing sector to the servicing sector? How about a shift from direct sales to a franchising model? Can

we shift from the manufacturing and sales model to specializing only in manufacturing, or only in sales?

It's not easy to consider options for a new venture from the value chain, company asset, or business model point of view. To broaden your view, it's important to learn from various examples, including ones from other industries and business types.

Take a look at various examples and see if you can apply them in your own business. Identify the key essence from these examples and adopt them for your company. These trials and errors will help broaden the options for a new venture.

▶ Change the Rules of Competition, Think Outside of the Box

Finally, let us add one more thing. We've mentioned this before, but when it comes to thinking up a new venture it is vital to think outside of the box. If you can come up with a new venture with a business model that can rewrite the rules of the competition, that will be a great advantage. Of course, the very viewpoint (change the rules of competition, think outside of the box) is extremely important not only to a new venture, but also when considering a change in the positioning and/or the business model of the current business.

We've looked at LCCs (low-cost carriers) before, but they changed the rules of competition within the aviation industry. Previously, what determined the advantage were the service quality and benefits and how to improve them. The rise of LCCs has created a brand-new way to compete, low cost. Conventional carriers (FSCs, or full-service carriers) can't ignore this change. They may not be able to

175

compete with the same low price range, but a price war is certainly under way, and even FSCs have to look into ways to cut spending and strengthen their profitability.

The introduction of iPhones and other smartphones has significantly changed the rules of competition in the mobile phone industry. In Japan, the mobile phone carrier integrated everything from the network to the device. But in the age of iPhones and smartphones, consumers can choose what service to use by downloading an app, without being tied to the carrier. A mobile phone carrier is becoming a "pipeline" providing the network. Because the difference in devices is shrinking, major mobile phone carriers are now competing with elements such as call quality, pricing structures (though they are still neck to neck), and the superiority of the network itself.

Diagram 3-18 Matsui-ya's Strategic Options ⑤

Options for new ventures from the company asset point of view
- Sale of raw materials (utilizing our strength = "red-bean paste")
- OEM business (utilizing unused manufacturing line)
- Wholesale to general distribution (utilizing our high recognition and brand power)
- etc.

Diagram 3-19 Matsui-ya's Strategic Options ⑥

Options for new ventures from the business model point of view
- Establishing a culinary school specializing in Japanese sweets-making (shift from sales to service)
- Dispatching Japanese sweets craftsmen (shift from sales to service)
- Organizing Japanese sweets-making classes (shift from sales to service)
- Franchising
- etc.

Diagram 3-20 Matsui-ya's Strategic Options ⑦

Options from the standpoint of changing the rules and breaking the norm
- Develop full vertical integration of red-bean production and sales by starting from the red-bean cultivation, strengthen the commitment to the red-bean paste
- Made-to-order model

Lay Out the Strategic Options 3: Improve Profit

5

▶ Options to Lower Cost and Improve Gross Profit Margin

For options from the profitability point of view, the first ones to come into mind are decreasing the cost rate and improving the gross profit margin. These options are important if competitive edge can be gained from the change in the profit structure by cutting down the cost rate.

There are several ways to bring down the cost. One way is to lower the production cost. Lowering the raw material cost, improving production rate, cutting down on personnel involved in production or improving productivity, and outsourcing are some examples.

Cutting down the raw material cost can be done either by lowering the price by lowering the spec, or lowering the material cost by consolidating suppliers to save on the raw material cost. In some cases, you can lower the cost by simply changing the suppliers.

Decreasing unnecessary production steps and increasing productivity can result in cost cutting. You can also reevaluate the price setting itself to bring down the cost rate.

THIS IS IMPORTANT IF YOU THINK YOU CAN INCREASE THE COMPETITIVE ADVANTAGE BY CHANGING THE PROFIT STRUCTURE!

Overhauling the product lineup and portfolio is another effective way if you have several product types. By decreasing the number of products with relatively high cost rate, or altogether stopping production and sales of those products, you can bring down the cost rate as a whole. In some cases, inefficient procurement and production due to excessive product types can increase the cost rate. If that is the case, narrowing down the product lineup can also be effective.

As you can see, there are many different ways to bring down cost and cost rate, but what's important here is clarifying how lowering the cost rate can contribute to the improvement of competitive edge, and to not let the cost rate decrease result in the loss of that advantage. There's no point if you lose customers due to the decrease of the product quality as a result of the reduced cost.

In order to avoid such a case and aim to grow by improving competitive advantage, it's important to clarify where in profit structure the issues and room for improvement lie by analyzing the situation accurately. The same goes for the management cost, which we'll go over next. It's useful to compare with the benchmark set by the competitors. However, it is not as simple as aiming to reach the same level as the competitors. Some cases are incomparable due to differences in bookkeeping. The profit and cost structures can differ if the business models are different. You have to spend money where needed. You must analyze carefully so as not to lose the competitive edge by eliminating necessary costs.

If you think issues can be overcome and there is room for improvements, it'll become vital to analyze the cause structurally: Is the issue high cost price, or the high managing cost, or both? We mentioned this in the prologue, but without identifying the true cause, you won't be able to counter effectively. In the worst-case scenario, you can make a bad situation worse.

▶ Options to Lower Managing Cost

When it comes to managing cost, we'll discuss the room for reduction by cost category. As we mentioned in the cost section, we'll come up with improvements and solutions by referring to the competitors' benchmark, identifying where to improve in order to gain competitive edge, or which profit structure to aim for, in addition to the current cost structure.

Specifically, look into volume reduction (quantity and/or frequency) and the ways to lower unit price. As for the unit price, some effective ways are: Exploring the possibility of saving by narrowing down the suppliers, consider changing the suppliers by obtaining comparable estimates, and downgrading the specs of the product.

For managing cost reduction, visualize each and every spending category and meticulously pinpoint unnecessary and/or inefficient spending. When doing so, be sure to carefully examine each cost to avoid eliminating necessary cost, especially related to competitive edge.

▶ Options to Improve Efficiency

There are some overlaps with material cost and managing cost reduction, but you can also look at options from the efficiency and productivity point of view and strengthen the profit structure. Examples are: Shortening the lead time from production to sales, increasing the amount of product produced per person, or the amount of sales per person, and increasing stock turnover rate. Improving the effectiveness and productivity of these and other business activities can lead to strengthening the profitability.

It's not easy to judge if the current level of production or efficiency is reasonable or not. You can compare it with the other companies' levels, or to your company's past record. You can also compare among different departments within your company or between different industries. Evaluate possibilities by the information obtained.

▶ Improve Ways to Manage and Improve Profit Structures

The situation can worsen if the improvement of the profit structure is only temporary. Only continuous improvement to the profit structure will yield results. Constant and accurate monitoring of the profit and measures to quickly respond to the signs of inflation are needed. These systems for profit management and monitoring are indispensable in profit structure improvement.

Diagram 3-21 Matsui-ya's Strategic Options ⑧

Options to improve profit structure (example)

- ○ Options to increase gross profit margin
  - • Overhaul of product lineup (eliminating products with a low profit margin)
  - • Decreasing production cost (reevaluating raw materials, production process, outsourcing rate, etc.)
  - • Minimize food loss
  - • Overhaul of price setting
  - • etc.
- ○ Options to decrease management cost
  - • Labor cost and staffing optimization
  - • Overhaul (negotiate) handling fees and rent
  - • Overhaul of promotional cost
  - • etc.
- ○ Others
  - • Establish profit management and monitoring structures
  - • etc.

Summarizing Strategic Options

6

▶ Organizing All Available Options

We're now in the final step of strategic option polishing. We've gone over various viewpoints in order to handpick strategic options. In fact, we have too many options, making it difficult to narrow them down. So let's first organize the polished options.

There are several ways to organize them. The first way is to organize options by similarities. We've come up with options from different points of view, but there are bound to be similar or overlapping options. Go ahead and combine similar options.

Next, list the organized options and separate them by whether they can be applied simultaneously or not. If they can be used concurrently, you can adopt them and turn them into a growth strategy. If not, you will have to pick and choose.

Also list potential advantages, opportunities, threats, weaknesses, and KSFs needed when utilizing each option. You'll get a better picture of your options as a whole.

TRY TO PREPARE SEVERAL OPTIONS FOR THE MOST IMPORTANT ISSUE.

▶ Coming Up with Growth Options and Scenarios by Organizing Strategic Options

Once options are organized to some degree, we'll review them objectively to select the growth scenario options. The growth scenario is a road map to success by combining multiple

strategic options. This also has many options, thus we are defining it as growth scenario options.

A trick to putting together a scenario is to prepare various options for the essential aspect of strategy building.

In Matsui-ya's case, the bottom lines were how to reconstruct the current business, how to deal with growth opportunities and threats that are not covered by the current business (possibility of a new venture), and how to strengthen the profit structure (improving profitability). The final point of contention began to emerge after considering different strategic options from various angles: Whether to proceed with a single- or multi-brand, and with a single- or multi-business model.

Focusing on these as the core of the issue, organize various growth options and combine them with the options we have identified. The result is the six growth scenario options seen in Diagram 3-22.

*All strategies will incorporate plans to improve profitability
*Single-brand/single-business model is logically possible but has low appeal and probability as an option (due to growth limit) and has been omitted

Diagram 3-22 Matsui-ya's Growth Scenario Option

① Multi-brand, multi-business model strategy (multi-channel)	◦ Reconstruct the current business according to the comprehensive department store model, establishing it as the Matsui-ya's flagship brand, steady operation contributing to the profit ◦ Develop and deploy a new business model to cover the clientele and sales channels that aren't covered by the current model, making it a driving force for growth • Clear differentiation from the current model, such as a specialized flagship product model and low-cost model ◦ Consider expanding to the wholesale and overseas markets once the brand recognition is reestablished and the business is stabilized ◦ Develop the OEM business to utilize the unused manufacturing lines • No plans for shrinking the manufacturing capacity at this time, taking future prospects into consideration.
② Multi-brand, multi-business model strategy (specialize in department stores)	◦ Develop multiple brands and business models in addition to the current business model, aiming to increase the share within the department store market to drive the growth ◦ Develop multifaceted product types such as low-cost, specialty, and foreign pastries on top of the current comprehensive Japanese sweets model
③ Single-brand, multi-business model strategy	◦ Shift from the current business model, going after clientele other than the formal gift users both in and out of the department store markets ◦ Develop multiple brands and business models tailored to fit each (non-department store) sales channel, and establish brands separate from the main brand for the department store market, such as a diffusion brand targeting non-department store customers, to minimize the dilution of the brand image ◦ Expand into the food industry such as cafés to revitalize the brand ◦ Look into the prospect of overseas markets for the future ◦ A strategy to utilize the strength such as brand recognition, tradition, and history to the fullest
④ Multi-brand, single-business model strategy	◦ Develop multiple brands following the comprehensive department store model ◦ Keep current business as comprehensive Japanese sweets, developing a new comprehensive foreign pastry model separately
⑤ Multi-brand, multi-business model strategy	◦ Pursue multiple business models and ventures, such as foreign pastries, food industries such as cafes and tea houses, and OEM business ◦ Consider mergers and acquisitions as options
⑥ Japanese sweets platform strategy	◦ Aim to become a "platform" within the Japanese sweets industry • Train and dispatch craftsmen (culinary school) • Take on production consignments (OEM and PB businesses) • Supply "red-bean paste" • Provide product planning and development service • Provide new business model development and consulting service • Become a purveyor of Japanese sweets (culinary school for Japanese sweets, revitalization of current brand, food industry, overseas expansion)

STEP
3

Review and Select Options

BUT... TIME HAS CHANGED.

BUT THEY'RE TOO PRETTY TO EAT...

THEY'RE GOOD BE-CAUSE YOU CAN EAT THEM.

IF EVERYONE AGREES, THEN I'D LIKE TO ASK FOR YOUR COOP-ERATION!

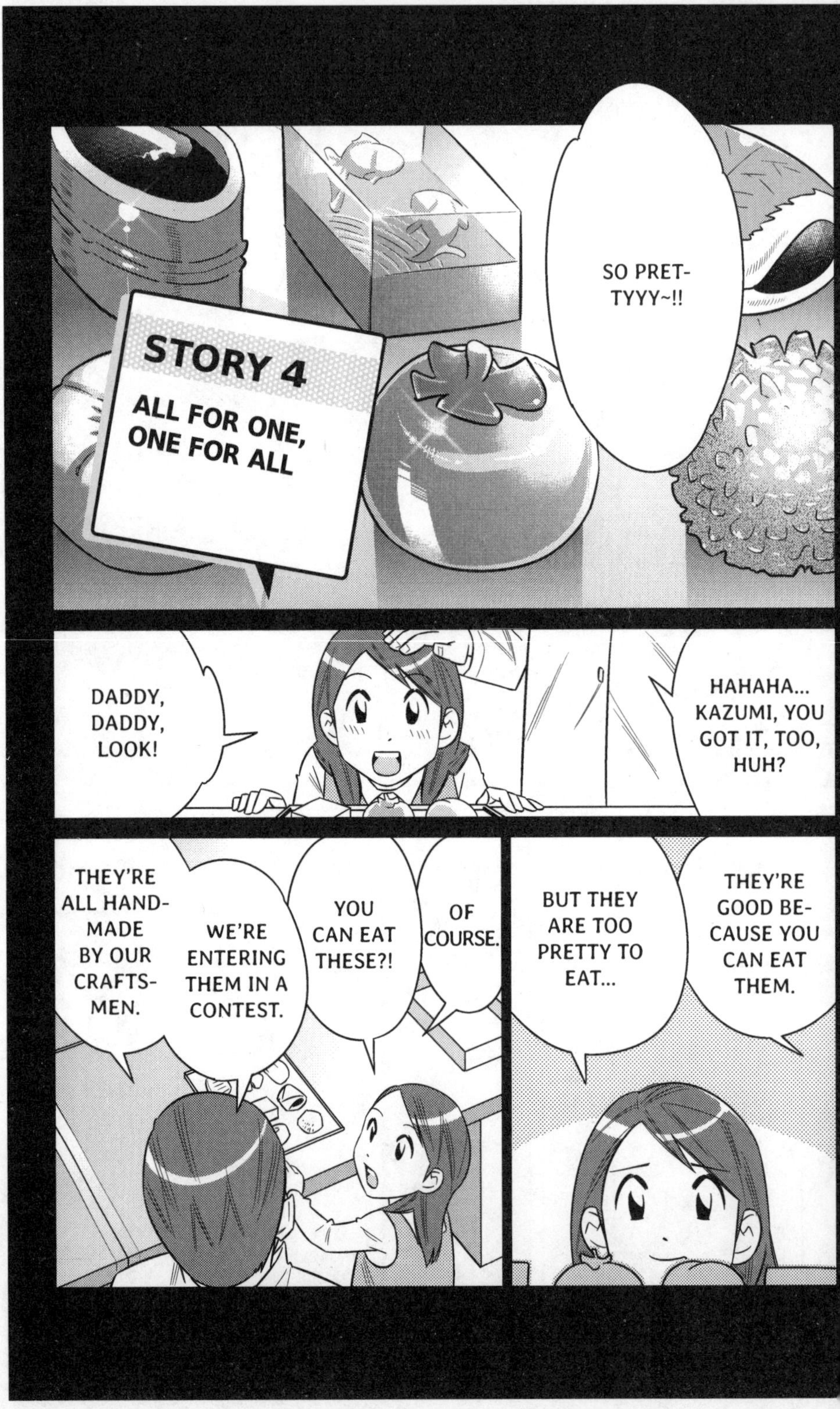
SO PRET-
TYYY~!!
STORY 4
ALL FOR ONE,
ONE FOR ALL
HAHAHA... KAZUMI, YOU GOT IT, TOO, HUH?
DADDY, DADDY, LOOK!
OF COURSE.
YOU CAN EAT THESE?!
WE'RE ENTERING THEM IN A CONTEST.
THEY'RE ALL HAND-MADE BY OUR CRAFTS-MEN.
THEY'RE GOOD BE-CAUSE YOU CAN EAT THEM.
BUT THEY ARE TOO PRETTY TO EAT...

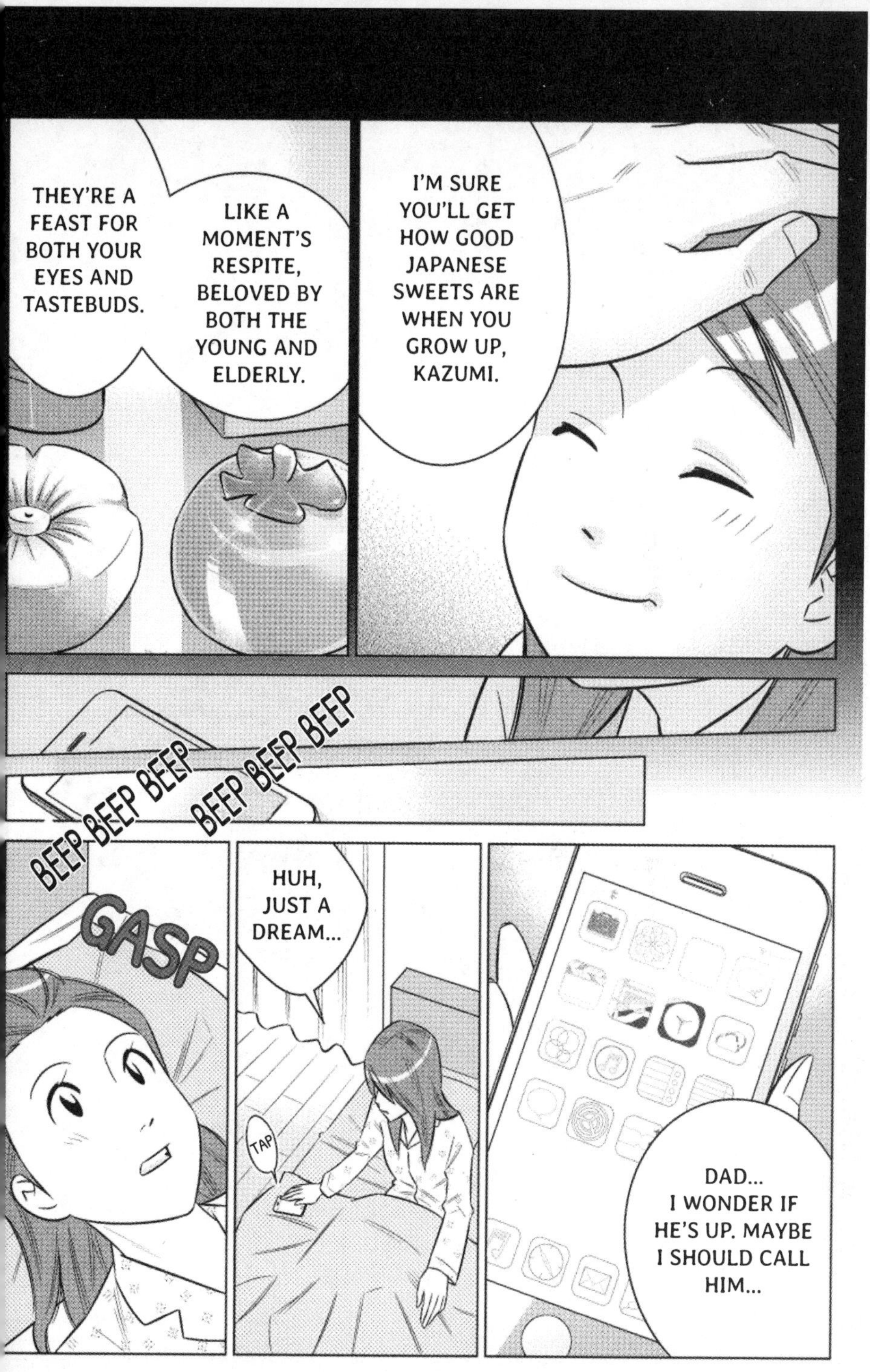
THEY'RE A FEAST FOR BOTH YOUR EYES AND TASTEBUDS.
LIKE A MOMENT'S RESPITE, BELOVED BY BOTH THE YOUNG AND ELDERLY.
I'M SURE YOU'LL GET HOW GOOD JAPANESE SWEETS ARE WHEN YOU GROW UP, KAZUMI.
BEEP BEEP BEEP
BEEP BEEP BEEP
GASP
HUH, JUST A DREAM...
TAP
DAD... I WONDER IF HE'S UP. MAYBE I SHOULD CALL HIM...

...

NO, NOT TILL I FINISH THE STRATEGY. I DON'T WANT TO WORRY HIM.

NOW, TO SELECT STRATEGIC OPTIONS...

WE'LL FOCUS ON REVIEWING "RATIONALITY" AND "FEASIBILITY".

CLI-CK

CLI-CK

"RATIONALITY" IS THE EXECS' VIEWPOINT.

IT'S BASED ON THE COMPANY'S WHOLE VISION AND MAINLY SEES POTENTIAL GROWTH AND PROFITABILITY.

EXECUTION

GROWTH

ON THE OTHER HAND, "FEASIBILITY" IS THE VIEWPOINT OF THE FRONTLINERS ON-SITE.

IS IT FEASIBLE WITH THE ORGANIZATIONAL CAPABILITY? WHAT ARE THE RISKS AND SHORTCOMINGS? IT'S A MORE PRACTICAL VIEWPOINT.

LET'S REVIEW THEM ONE BY ONE SO THAT WE DON'T OVERLOOK ANYTHING.

FIRST, EVALUATING RATIONALITY.

THE POINTS TO EVALUATE INCLUDE: THE POTENTIAL SALES GROWTH, POTENTIAL PROFIT IMPROVEMENT, RETURN ON INVESTMENT (ROI), STRENGTHS AND WEAKNESSES, OPPORTUNITIES AND THREATS, AND SO ON.

RATIONALITY EVALUATION

*SEE NEXT PAGE FOR DETAILS

	POTENTIAL SALES GROWTH	POTENTIAL PROFIT IMPROVEMENT	ROI	PROSPECT TO APPLY STRENGTHS	PROSPECT TO FORTIFY WEAKNESSES	POSSIBLE OPPORTUNITIES TO SEIZE	ABILITY TO HANDLE THREATS	ODDS OF WINNING
RATIONALITY EVALUATION	◎=HIGH X=LOW	◎=HIGH X=LOW	◎=HIGH X=LOW	◎=HIGH X=LOW	◎=HIGH X=LOW	◎=HIGH X=LOW	◎=HIGH X=LOW	◎=HIGH X=LOW
① MULTI-BRAND, MULTI-BUSINESS MODEL STRATEGY (MULTI-CHANNEL)	◎	○	○	○	◎	◎	◎	○
② MULTI-BRAND, MULTI-BUSINESS MODEL STRATEGY (SPECIALIZE IN DEPARTMENT STORES)	△	○	◎	○	△	△	△	△
③ SINGLE-BRAND, MULTI-BUSINESS MODEL STRATEGY	○	○	◎	◎	○	○	○	◎
④ MULTI-BRAND, SINGLE-BUSINESS MODEL STRATEGY	△	△	△	△	△	△	△	△
⑤ MULTI-BRAND, MULTI-BUSINESS MODEL STRATEGY	◎	△	○	○	○	◎	◎	△
⑥ JAPANESE SWEETS PLATFORM STRATEGY	◎	◎	△	◎	◎	○	◎	◎

RATIONALITY EVALUATION DETAILS

	POTENTIAL SALES GROWTH	POTENTIAL PROFIT IMPROVEMENT	ROI
RATIONALITY EVALUATION	◎=HIGH X=LOW	◎=HIGH X=LOW	◎=HIGH X=LOW
① MULTI-BRAND, MULTI-BUSINESS MODEL STRATEGY (MULTI-CHANNEL)	◎ (Potential needs and clientele currently unreached in non-department store sales channel.)	○ (Profit management will be more difficult due to the multiple businesses model, but may improve profitability if a profitable structure can be established in each business.)	○ (A considerable amount of investment is needed to develop and establish the new venture, but we may expect a high return if successful.)
② MULTI-BRAND, MULTI-BUSINESS MODEL STRATEGY (SPECIALIZE IN DEPARTMENT STORES)	△ (Better odds than now, but specializing in the department store will limit the growth. May cause market cannibalization between the current business and the new venture.)	○ (Harder profit management. The profitability of the existing business may decrease due to market cannibalism. Improvement is possible if we can establish a suitable profit structure in each business.)	◎ (Targeting the department store market for the new venture keeps investment amount low.)
③ SINGLE-BRAND, MULTI-BUSINESS MODEL STRATEGY	○ (Potential needs and clientele currently unreached in non-department store sales channel, but in a smaller scope due to the single-brand model.)	○ (Developing profit structures suited for each channel/business model may improve profitability.)	◎ (Due to utilizing an existing brand, if successful, we may expect a relatively high return. Only needs a short start-up period.)
④ MULTI-BRAND, SINGLE-BUSINESS MODEL STRATEGY	△ (Better odds than now, but specializing in the department store will limit the growth.)	△ (Extremely difficult to establish a profitable structure as we are inexperienced in the Western sweets field.)	△ (Limited expected return even if the new brand is successful due to using the comprehensive department store model.)
⑤ MULTI-BRAND, MULTI-BUSINESS MODEL STRATEGY	◎ (Large room for sales growth once the new venture is up and running.)	△ (Integration may limit improvements in profitability.)	○ (We may expect a relatively high return for some of the businesses.)
⑥ JAPANESE SWEETS PLATFORM STRATEGY	◎ (If successfully established, this can turn into a wide range of revenue streams.)	◎ (Possibility of establishing a highly profitable model by expanding into fields other than product sales.)	△ (A considerable amount of investment is needed to develop and establish a new venture.)

PROSPECT TO APPLY STRENGTHS	PROSPECT TO FORTIFY WEAKNESSES	POSSIBLE OPPORTUNITIES TO SEIZE	ABILITY TO HANDLE THREATS	ODDS OF WINNING
◎=HIGH X=LOW	◎=HIGH X=LOW	◎=HIGH X=LOW	◎=HIGH X=LOW	◎=HIGH X=LOW
○ (Using our strength in history and tradition to offer a wide range of product variety.)	◎ (Prospect to break away from the department store market, possible brand image renewal.)	◎ (Potential needs and clientele currently unreached in non-department store sales channel.)	◎ (Reducing dependency on department stores, expanding out of the shrinking formal gift market, escaping the vicious cycle.)	○ (Due to the highly competitive market, it's not easy to win with a new brand and business model. However, we may have some winning odds in the expanding non-department store market.)
○ (Strengths such as the relationship with the department stores, history, tradition, and product variety can all be utilized. However, they may not be as useful if we were to expand into the Western sweets market.)	△ (Cannot cut ties with the department stores. Running the existing business while separately managing a new venture may enable us to take in new clientele.)	△ (Limited room in taking new, unreached clientele in the department store market.)	△ (Cannot tackle diversifying sales channel. Meeting needs outside of gift-giving might be possible, but...)	△ (Due to the highly competitive and oversaturated market, even with a strong relationship with department stores, establishing new brands and business will be challenging.)
◎ (We will be able to utilize our strengths such as high recognition, history, tradition, and honed red-bean paste craft to the fullest.)	○ (If we succeed in developing a new sales channel, it will help refresh the brand image and take in new clientele.)	○ (Potential needs and clientele currently unreached in non-department store sales channel, but in a smaller scope due to the single-brand model.)	○ (Limited opportunity to reduce dependency to department stores, expand out of the shrinking formal gift market, and escape the vicious cycle.)	◎ (By utilizing our already highly recognized brand, as long as the new business model works out, the odds of winning are fairly good.)
△ (We can utilize our strong relationship with the department stores, but not our strengths as a Japanese sweets manufacturer.)	△ (Cannot cut ties with the department stores.)	△ (Limited room in taking new, unreached clientele in the department store market.)	△ (Cannot tackle diversifying sales channel.)	△ (Very low winning odds due to inexperience in the Western sweets market. If we can create a new fusion genre with our "red-bean paste," we might have a chance...)
○ (We can utilize our strong relationship with the department stores, but not our strengths as a Japanese sweets manufacturer. However, current assets may be utilized for OEM business and such.)	◎ (If the new venture is a success, we can refresh the brand image and stop our dependency on the department stores.)	◎ (Potential needs and clientele currently unreached non-department store sales channel.)	◎ (Reducing dependency on department stores, expanding out of the shrinking formal gift market, escaping the vicious cycle.)	△ (Low odds of winning with the comprehensive model, considering our assets, strengths, and history.)
◎ (We will be able to utilize our strengths such as high recognition, history, tradition, and honed red-bean paste craft to the fullest.)	◎ (Prospect to break away from the department store market, possible brand image renewal.)	○ (Potential expansion into the market unreached by the current business.)	◎ (Reducing dependency on department stores, expanding out of the shrinking formal gift market, escaping the vicious cycle.)	◎ (Little to no competition with a similar business model, high chance of winning if we can establish ourselves.)

NEXT UP, WE HAVE "FEASIBILITY".

AMONG THE POINTS TO EVALUATE ARE ORGANIZATIONAL CAPABILITY, INVESTMENT SCALE AND RESERVE, DIFFICULTY OF EXECUTION, RISKS AND SHORTCOMINGS, AND SO ON.

RATIONALITY EVALUATION

*SEE NEXT PAGE FOR DETAILS

FEASIBILITY EVALUATION	ORGANIZATIONAL CAPABILITY ◎=HIGH X=LOW	INVESTMENT SCALE AND RESERVE ◎=SMALL X=LARGE	DIFFICULTY OF EXECUTION ◎=HIGH X=LOW	RISKS AND SHORTCOMINGS ◎=HIGH X=LOW
① MULTI-BRAND, MULTI-BUSINESS MODEL STRATEGY (MULTI-CHANNEL)	△	△	△	○
② MULTI-BRAND, MULTI-BUSINESS MODEL STRATEGY (SPECIALIZE IN DEPARTMENT STORES)	○	◎	△	△
③ SINGLE-BRAND, MULTI-BUSINESS MODEL STRATEGY	△	○	○	○
④ MULTI-BRAND, SINGLE-BUSINESS MODEL STRATEGY	△	△	△	X
⑤ MULTI-BRAND, MULTI-BUSINESS MODEL STRATEGY	X	X	△	△
⑥ JAPANESE SWEETS PLATFORM STRATEGY	△	△	X	△

LASTLY, WE COMBINE BOTH RATIONALITY AND FEASIBILITY AND SEE THE OVERALL REVIEW.

THE RESULTS WILL CHANGE DEPENDING ON WHAT YOU FOCUS ON.

ANY STRATEGY HAS ITS PROS AND CONS, SO LET'S LAY OUT A FEW PATTERNS FOR THE COMBINED EVALUATION.

RATIONALITY EVALUATION

FEASIBILITY EVALUATION	ORGANIZATIONAL CAPABILITY ◎=HIGH X=LOW	INVESTMENT SCALE AND RESERVE ◎=SMALL X=LARGE	DIFFICULTY OF EXECUTION ◎=HIGH X=LOW	RISKS AND SHORTCOMINGS ◎=HIGH X=LOW
① MULTI-BRAND, MULTI-BUSINESS MODEL STRATEGY (MULTI-CHANNEL)	△ (Capability to run multi-brand or business models, and to develop and run non-department store model, are not adequate)	△ (A considerable amount of investment is needed to develop and establish the new venture)	△ (A rather difficult challenge to develop multi-brand and non-department store businesses)	○ (Developing a new business will not be easy, but controlling investment will limit the risk)
② MULTI-BRAND, MULTI-BUSINESS MODEL STRATEGY (SPECIALIZE IN DEPARTMENT STORES)	○ (Capability to run multi-brand or business models is not high, but we have experience in the department store market)	◎ (Targeting the department store market to develop new brands/business keeps investment amount low)	△ (A highly difficult challenge to establish a new brand/business while avoiding market cannibalism)	△ (Developing a new venture for the department store market with our experience is not difficult, but there is a high risk of market cannibalism)
③ SINGLE-BRAND, MULTI-BUSINESS MODEL STRATEGY	△ (Inadequate capability to run multiple businesses. Our ability to develop and run the non-department store sales channel is still unknown)	○ (Utilizing an existing brand will keep the investment amount fairly low compared to a new brand)	○ (Shifting to a multi-business model is rather difficult, but using an existing brand will give some familiar grounds)	○ (Relatively low risk, but can we establish a profit structure in other sales channels? There are also risks of brand damage and dilution)
④ MULTI-BRAND, SINGLE-BUSINESS MODEL STRATEGY	△ (Lacking experience in the Western sweets field)	△ (Requires investment in personnel and manufacturing equipment to expand to the Western sweets field)	△ (Extremely difficult to successfully develop a comprehensive brand in the Western sweets market)	X (Establishing a comprehensive brand outside of our expertise [Western sweets] is extremely risky)
⑤ MULTI-BRAND, MULTI-BUSINESS MODEL STRATEGY	X (Not only do we lack experience in the Western sweets field, but we also have no expertise in the non-department store and wholesale markets)	X (Requires investment to expand into a new market/business such as Western sweets and cafés)	△ (Shifting into being both Japanese and Western sweets manufacturer by running multiple businesses will not be easy)	△ (Risk of failure due to targeting multiple fields/industries which affects resource distribution)
⑥ JAPANESE SWEETS PLATFORM STRATEGY	△ (Capability to run business models other than Japanese sweets manufacturing and sales is unknown)	△ (Requires investment to expand into businesses we have not touched previously, such as the service industry)	X (Entering a completely different field such as the service industry will be highly difficult)	△ (A highly ambitious plan with equally high risk)

COMBINED EVALUATION

*SEE NEXT PAGE FOR DETAILS

COMBINED EVALUATION	RATIONALITY (GROWTH AND PROFIT IMPROVEMENT) FOCUSED ◎=HIGH X=LOW	RATIONALITY (INVESTMENT RETURN) FOCUSED ◎=SMALL X=LARGE	FEASIBILITY FOCUSED ◎=HIGH X=LOW
① MULTI-BRAND, MULTI-BUSINESS MODEL STRATEGY (MULTI-CHANNEL)	◯	◯	◯
② MULTI-BRAND, MULTI-BUSINESS MODEL STRATEGY (SPECIALIZE IN DEPARTMENT STORES)	△	◎	◯
③ SINGLE-BRAND, MULTI-BUSINESS MODEL STRATEGY	◯	◯	◎
④ MULTI-BRAND, SINGLE-BUSINESS MODEL STRATEGY	✕	✕	✕
⑤ MULTI-BRAND, MULTI-BUSINESS MODEL STRATEGY	△	△	✕
⑥ JAPANESE SWEETS PLATFORM STRATEGY	◎	△	△

BUT THESE ARE ONLY THEORETICAL.

YOU ALSO NEED TO CONSIDER THE INTENT OF ALL PARTIES INVOLVED.

MAKE SURE TO HAVE A THOROUGH DISCUSSION WITH EVERYONE INVOLVED.

EVERY-ONE'S INTENT ...?

PEOPLE WOULDN'T WANT TO DO WHAT THEY DON'T AGREE ON.

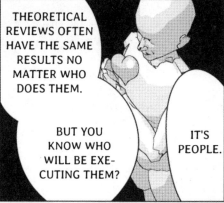

THEORETICAL REVIEWS OFTEN HAVE THE SAME RESULTS NO MATTER WHO DOES THEM.

BUT YOU KNOW WHO WILL BE EXE-CUTING THEM?

IT'S PEOPLE.

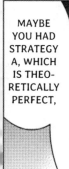

MAYBE YOU HAD STRATEGY A, WHICH IS THEO-RETICALLY PERFECT,

BUT STRATEGY B, WHICH IS A LITTLE UNREA-SONABLE, IS MORE EXCITING.

TALK TO EVERYONE AND DECIDE ON THE OPTION THAT EVERYONE CAN AGREE ON, REGARDLESS OF WHICH STRATEGY IS RIGHT.

BUT DON'T GET CAUGHT UP IN THE HEAT OF THE MOMENT. BALANCE YOUR-SELF WITH OBJECTIVITY.

IGNORING OTHERS' OPINIONS MIGHT LEAD YOU TO A STRATEGY THAT ISN'T UNIQUE OR DISTINCT WITHOUT ANY WINNING ODDS.

LACKING THE FINISH-ING TOUCH, SO TO SPEAK.

195

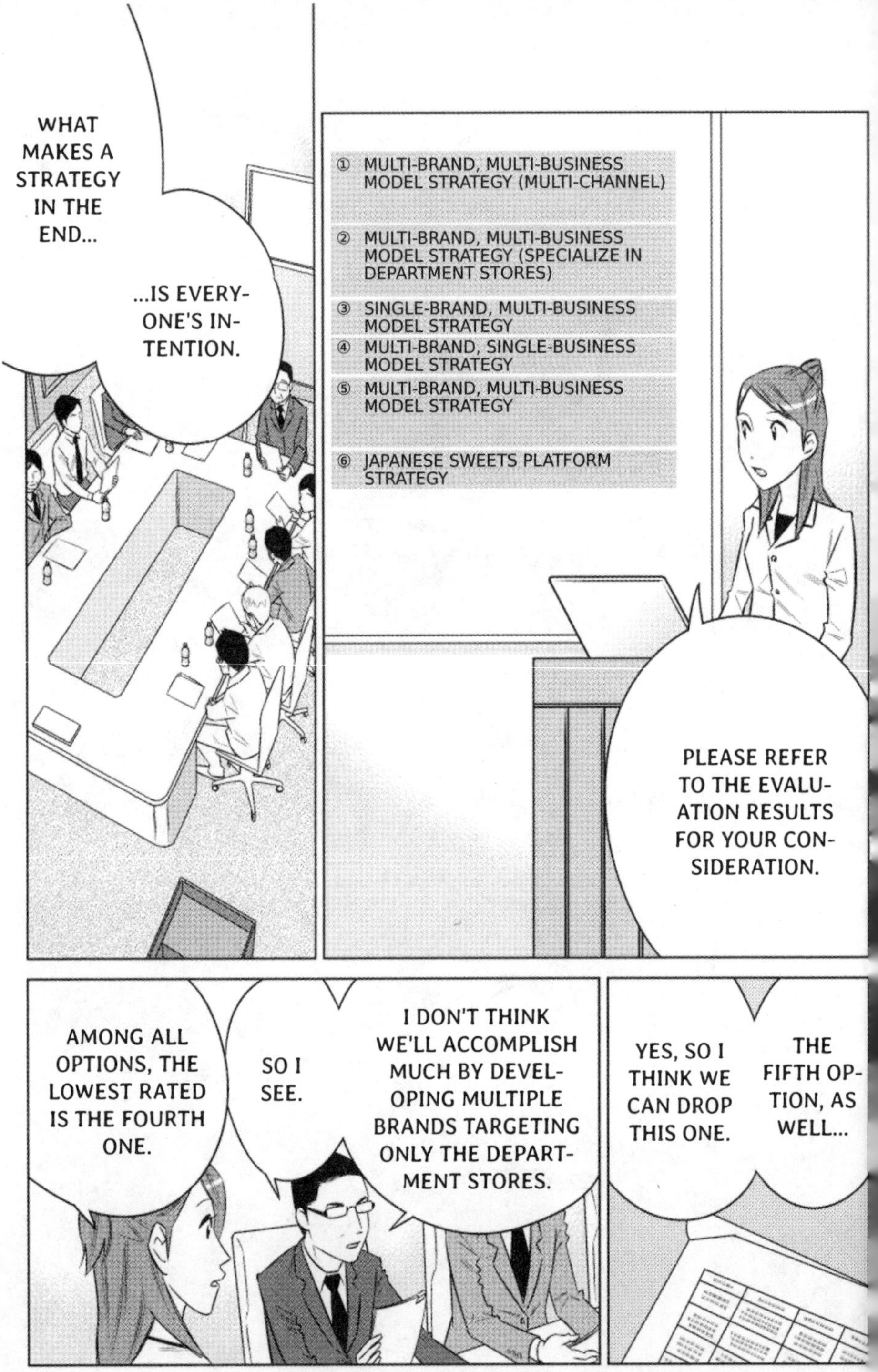
WHAT MAKES A STRATEGY IN THE END...
...IS EVERYONE'S INTENTION.
① MULTI-BRAND, MULTI-BUSINESS MODEL STRATEGY (MULTI-CHANNEL)
② MULTI-BRAND, MULTI-BUSINESS MODEL STRATEGY (SPECIALIZE IN DEPARTMENT STORES)
③ SINGLE-BRAND, MULTI-BUSINESS MODEL STRATEGY
④ MULTI-BRAND, SINGLE-BUSINESS MODEL STRATEGY
⑤ MULTI-BRAND, MULTI-BUSINESS MODEL STRATEGY
⑥ JAPANESE SWEETS PLATFORM STRATEGY
PLEASE REFER TO THE EVALUATION RESULTS FOR YOUR CONSIDERATION.
AMONG ALL OPTIONS, THE LOWEST RATED IS THE FOURTH ONE.
SO I SEE.
I DON'T THINK WE'LL ACCOMPLISH MUCH BY DEVELOPING MULTIPLE BRANDS TARGETING ONLY THE DEPARTMENT STORES.
YES, SO I THINK WE CAN DROP THIS ONE.
THE FIFTH OPTION, AS WELL...

TAKING MATSUI-YA'S BUSINESS SIZE, ASSETS, AND HISTORY INTO CONSIDERATION...

I DON'T THINK IT'S A GOOD IDEA TO SHIFT THE BUSINESS ITSELF DRASTICALLY.

THE SIXTH ONE IS VERY BOLD...

I GET THAT THE POTENTIAL IS HUGE. PROVIDING GROUNDWORK FOR CRAFTS TRAINING, DEVELOPMENT, AND MANUFACTURING FOR OTHER COMPANIES...

MAYBE IF WE CAN COMBINE THIS WITH OTHER STRATEGIES?

MATSUI-YA GENERAL MANAGER OF PRODUCTION

I AGREE. LET'S PUT THIS ASIDE FOR NOW.

...D, MULTI-BUSINESS ...TEGY

...ETS PLATFORM

I JUST DON'T THINK WE CAN WIN WITH THE SIXTH STRATEGY ALONE.

SO WE'RE LEFT WITH THE FIRST THREE OPTIONS.

① MULTI-BRAND, MULTI-BUSINESS MODEL STRATEGY (MULTI-CHANNEL)

② MULTI-BRAND, MULTI-BUSINESS MODEL STRATEGY (SPECIALIZE IN DEPARTMENT STORES)

③ SINGLE-BRAND, MULTI-BUSINESS MODEL STRATEGY

CONSIDERING THE DECLINE IN THE DEPARTMENT STORE MARKET ITSELF, I DON'T THINK IT'S WISE TO SPECIALIZE THERE.

HOLD ON!

I KNOW WHAT YOU'RE SAYING, BUT SALES DOESN'T HAVE ANY EXPERTISE IN OTHER MARKETS.

MATSUI-YA GENERAL MANAGER OF SALES

197

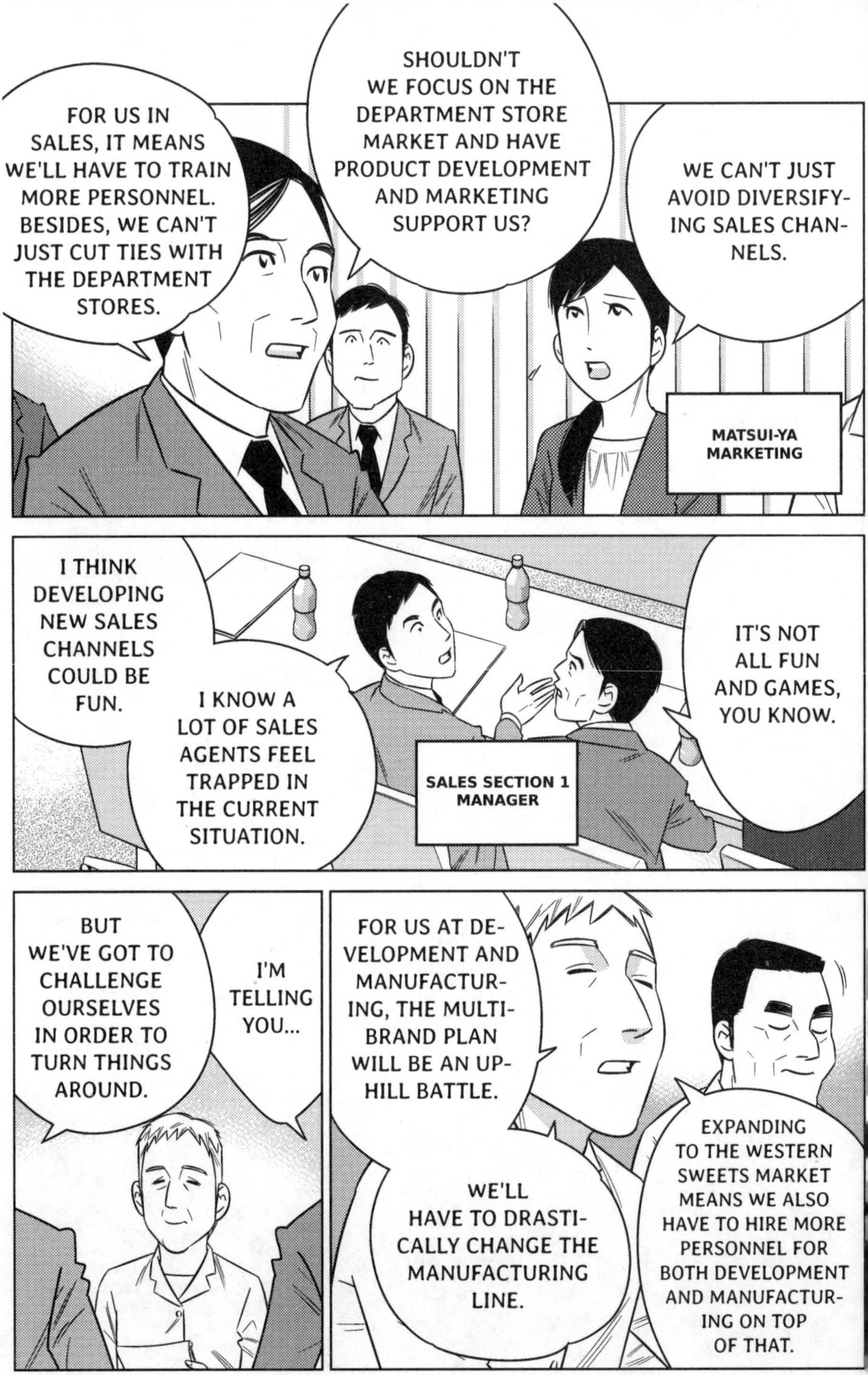
FOR US IN SALES, IT MEANS WE'LL HAVE TO TRAIN MORE PERSONNEL. BESIDES, WE CAN'T JUST CUT TIES WITH THE DEPARTMENT STORES.
SHOULDN'T WE FOCUS ON THE DEPARTMENT STORE MARKET AND HAVE PRODUCT DEVELOPMENT AND MARKETING SUPPORT US?
WE CAN'T JUST AVOID DIVERSIFY-ING SALES CHAN-NELS.
MATSUI-YA MARKETING
I THINK DEVELOPING NEW SALES CHANNELS COULD BE FUN.
I KNOW A LOT OF SALES AGENTS FEEL TRAPPED IN THE CURRENT SITUATION.
SALES SECTION 1 MANAGER
IT'S NOT ALL FUN AND GAMES, YOU KNOW.
BUT WE'VE GOT TO CHALLENGE OURSELVES IN ORDER TO TURN THINGS AROUND.
I'M TELLING YOU...
FOR US AT DE-VELOPMENT AND MANUFACTUR-ING, THE MULTI-BRAND PLAN WILL BE AN UP-HILL BATTLE.
WE'LL HAVE TO DRASTI-CALLY CHANGE THE MANUFACTURING LINE.
EXPANDING TO THE WESTERN SWEETS MARKET MEANS WE ALSO HAVE TO HIRE MORE PERSONNEL FOR BOTH DEVELOPMENT AND MANUFACTUR-ING ON TOP OF THAT.

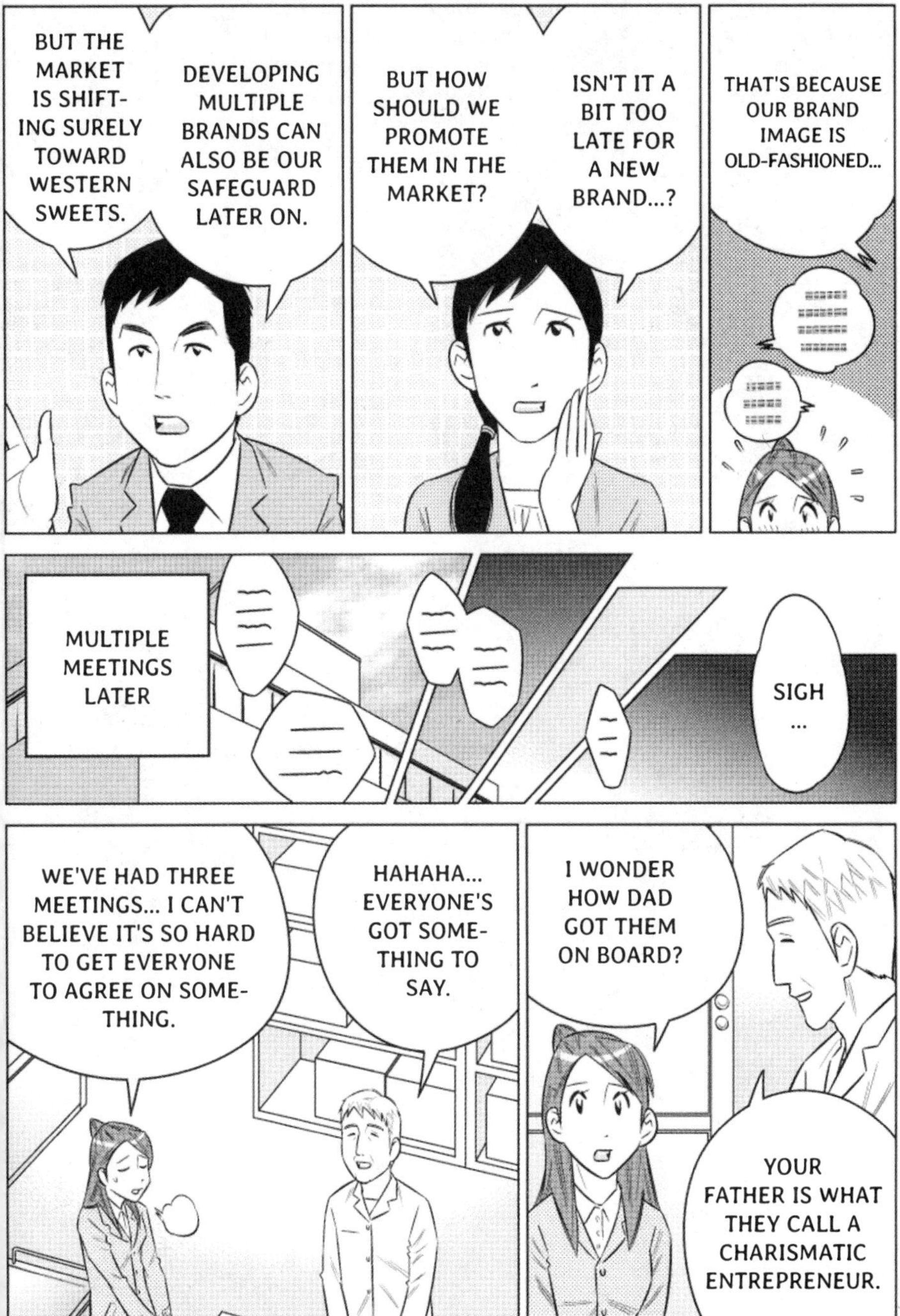
BUT THE MARKET IS SHIFT-ING SURELY TOWARD WESTERN SWEETS.
DEVELOPING MULTIPLE BRANDS CAN ALSO BE OUR SAFEGUARD LATER ON.
BUT HOW SHOULD WE PROMOTE THEM IN THE MARKET?
ISN'T IT A BIT TOO LATE FOR A NEW BRAND...?
THAT'S BECAUSE OUR BRAND IMAGE IS OLD-FASHIONED...
MULTIPLE MEETINGS LATER
SIGH ...
WE'VE HAD THREE MEETINGS... I CAN'T BELIEVE IT'S SO HARD TO GET EVERYONE TO AGREE ON SOME-THING.
HAHAHA... EVERYONE'S GOT SOME-THING TO SAY.
I WONDER HOW DAD GOT THEM ON BOARD?
YOUR FATHER IS WHAT THEY CALL A CHARISMATIC ENTREPRENEUR.

HE WAS A JAPANESE SWEETS CRAFTSMAN HIMSELF, SO HE WAS ACTIVELY INVOLVED WITH PRODUCT DEVELOPMENT.

HIS INTUITION IN READING THE MARKET WAS GREAT.

EVEN IF THE ECONOMY GENERALLY WAS BETTER THEN,

I THINK YOUR FATHER'S IDEAS CONTRIBUTED A LOT TO THE COMPANY'S GROWTH.

BUT... TIME HAS CHANGED.

SURE, A COMPANY CAN DEPEND ON A SINGLE PERSON'S TALENT TO GROW, FOR A TIME.

BUT I WONDER IF THAT'LL BE ENOUGH.

A SYSTEMATIC ANALYSIS... WHAT I BELIEVE YOU'RE DOING RIGHT NOW, IS VERY IMPORTANT, MISS KAZUMI.

...

I THINK YOU'RE CARRYING ON YOUR FATHER'S AGENDA.

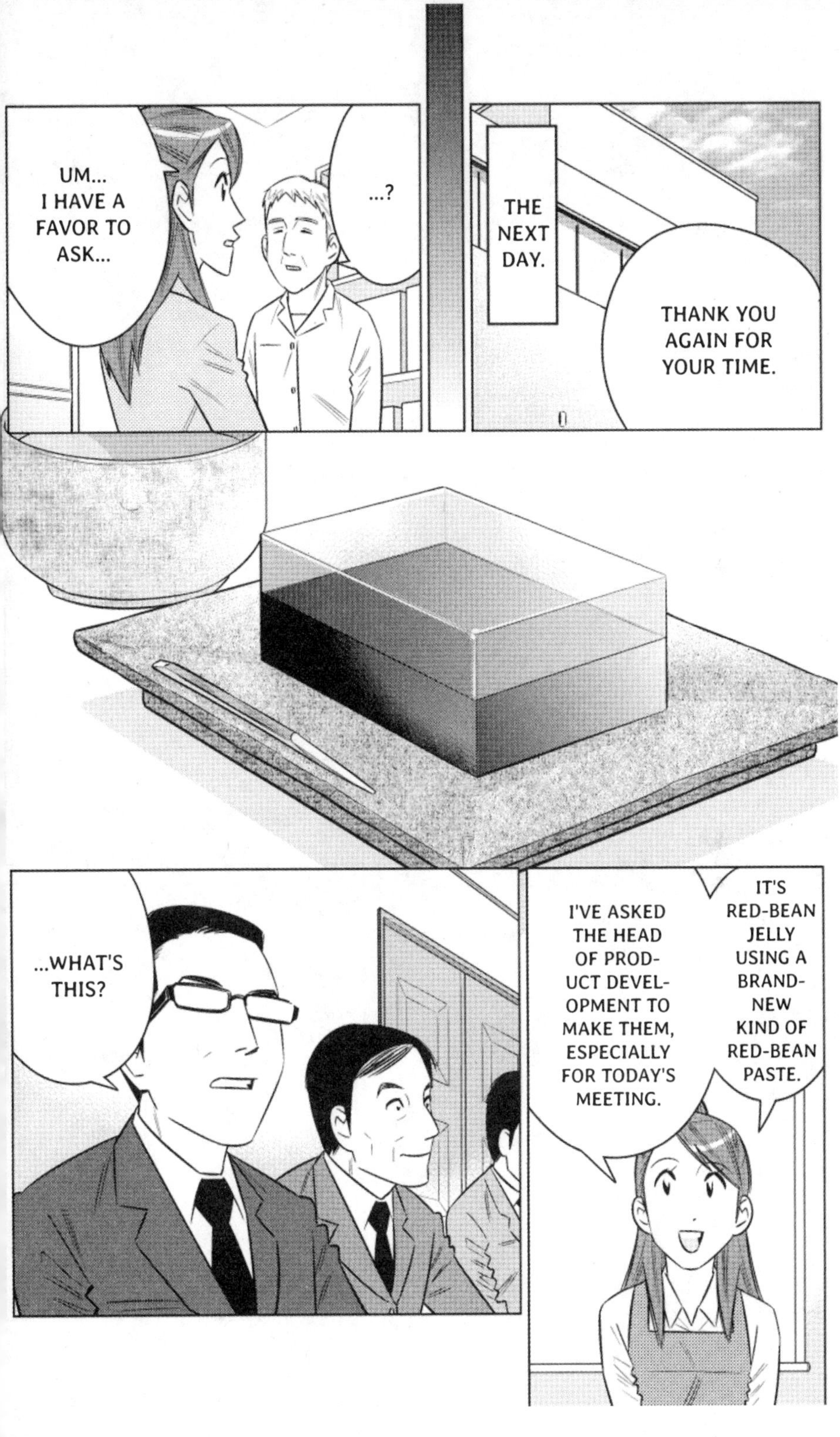
THE NEXT DAY.
THANK YOU AGAIN FOR YOUR TIME.
UM... I HAVE A FAVOR TO ASK...
...?
IT'S RED-BEAN JELLY USING A BRAND-NEW KIND OF RED-BEAN PASTE.
I'VE ASKED THE HEAD OF PROD-UCT DEVEL-OPMENT TO MAKE THEM, ESPECIALLY FOR TODAY'S MEETING.
...WHAT'S THIS?

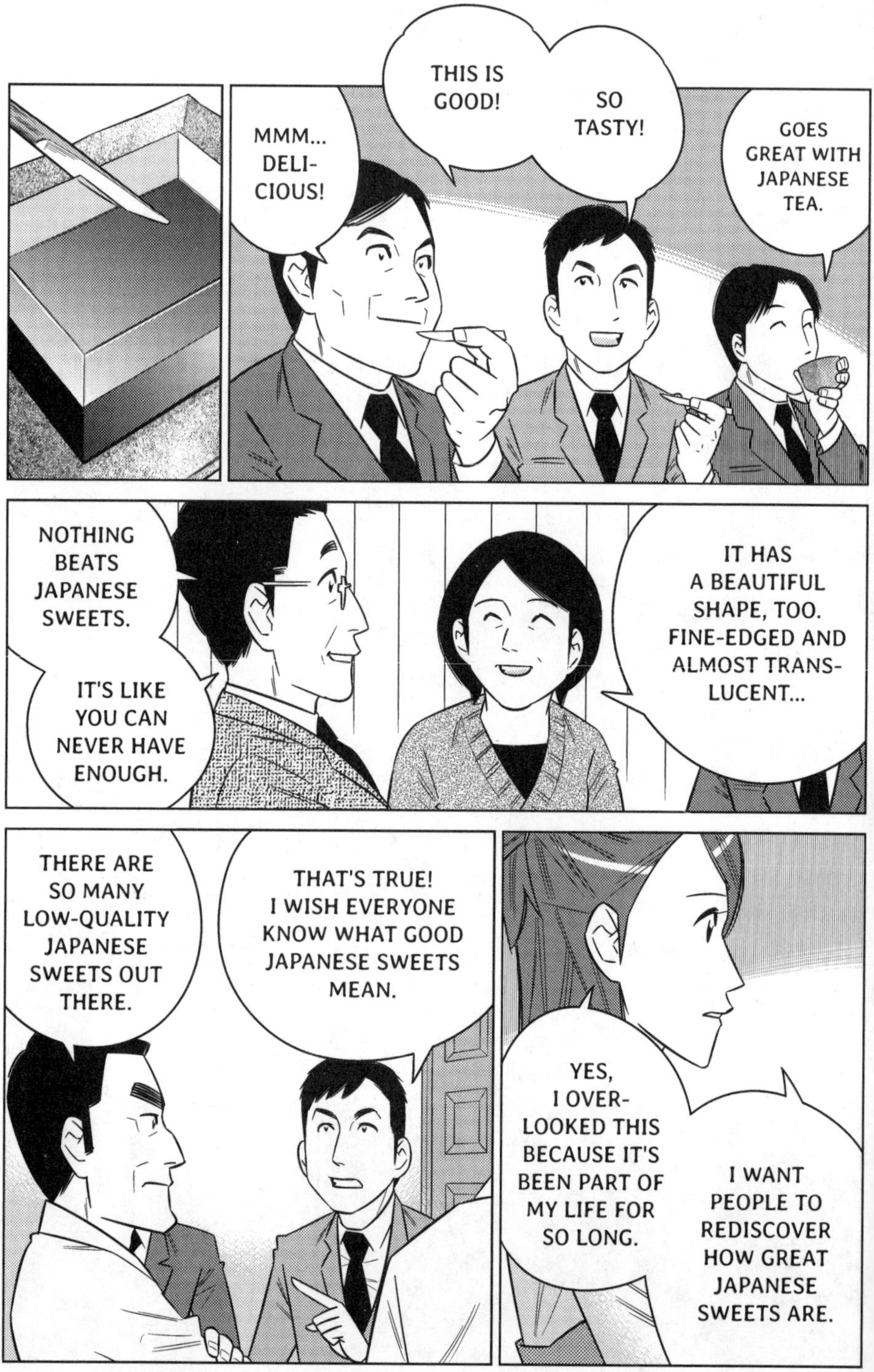
MMM... DELI-CIOUS!
THIS IS GOOD!
SO TASTY!
GOES GREAT WITH JAPANESE TEA.
NOTHING BEATS JAPANESE SWEETS.
IT'S LIKE YOU CAN NEVER HAVE ENOUGH.
IT HAS A BEAUTIFUL SHAPE, TOO. FINE-EDGED AND ALMOST TRANS-LUCENT...
THERE ARE SO MANY LOW-QUALITY JAPANESE SWEETS OUT THERE.
THAT'S TRUE! I WISH EVERYONE KNOW WHAT GOOD JAPANESE SWEETS MEAN.
YES, I OVER-LOOKED THIS BECAUSE IT'S BEEN PART OF MY LIFE FOR SO LONG.
I WANT PEOPLE TO REDISCOVER HOW GREAT JAPANESE SWEETS ARE.

HEARING YOUR FEEDBACK JUST NOW CONVINCED ME.

OUR COMPANY HAS A PASSION FOR JAPANESE SWEETS.

USING OUR HIGHLY RECOGNIZED "MATSUI-YA" BRAND, I'D LIKE TO SPREAD THE APPEAL OF JAPANESE SWEETS ALL OVER THE WORLD.

PERSONALLY, MY TOP PICK WOULD BE THE THIRD OPTION OF THE SINGLE-BRAND, MULTI-BUSINESS MODEL.

THE REASON BEING THE LACK OF RESOURCES TO ESTABLISH A NEW BRAND AT THE MOMENT.

BUT WE CAN'T SURVIVE WITHOUT DEVELOPING NON-DEPARTMENT STORE CHANNELS.

WE CAN'T AVOID THE MULTI-BUSINESS MODEL IF WE WANT TO ATTRACT NEW CLIENTELE.

203

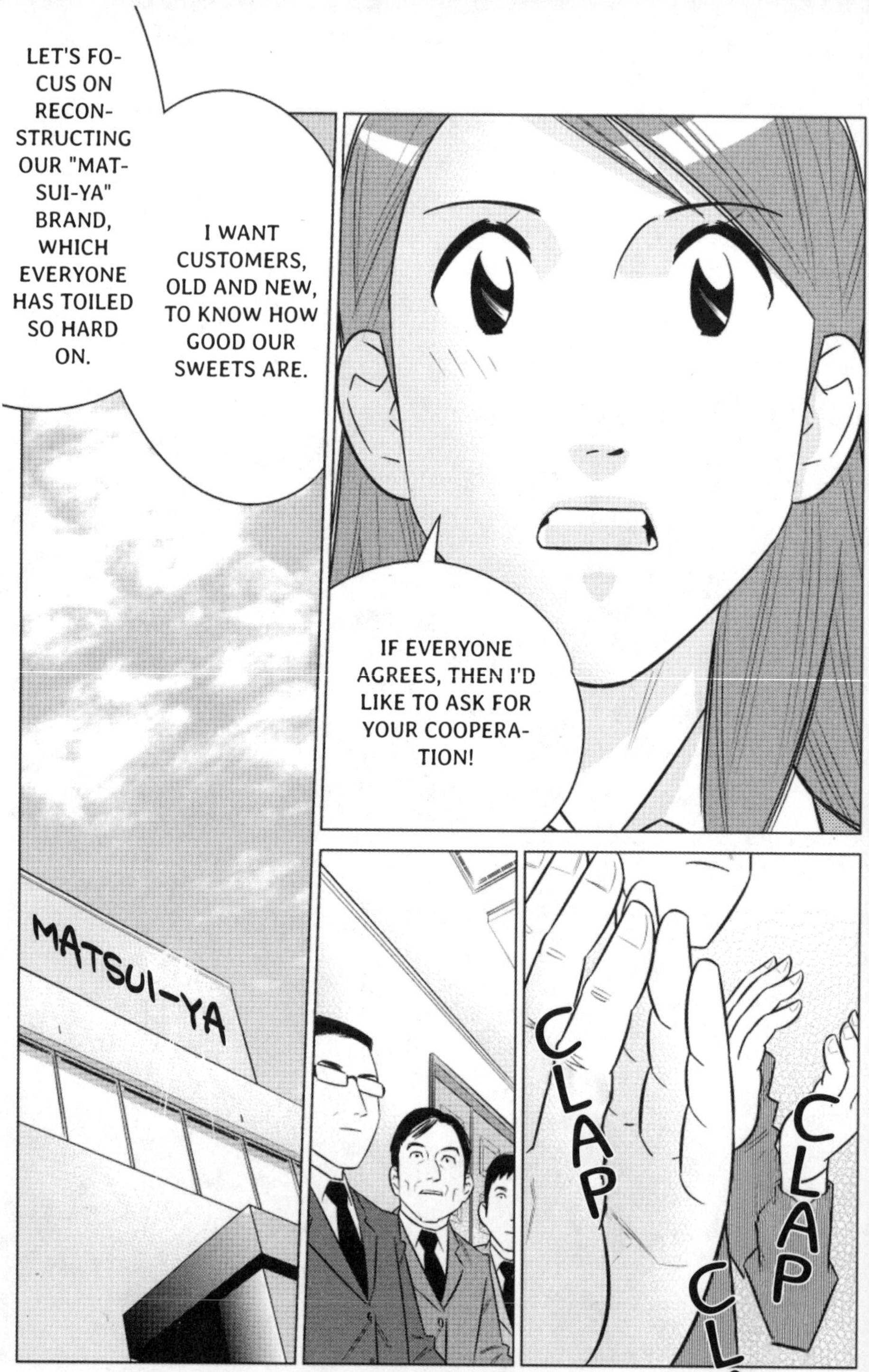
LET'S FO-CUS ON RECON-STRUCTING OUR "MAT-SUI-YA" BRAND, WHICH EVERYONE HAS TOILED SO HARD ON.
I WANT CUSTOMERS, OLD AND NEW, TO KNOW HOW GOOD OUR SWEETS ARE.
IF EVERYONE AGREES, THEN I'D LIKE TO ASK FOR YOUR COOPERA-TION!
MATSUI-YA
CLAP
CLAP
CLAP

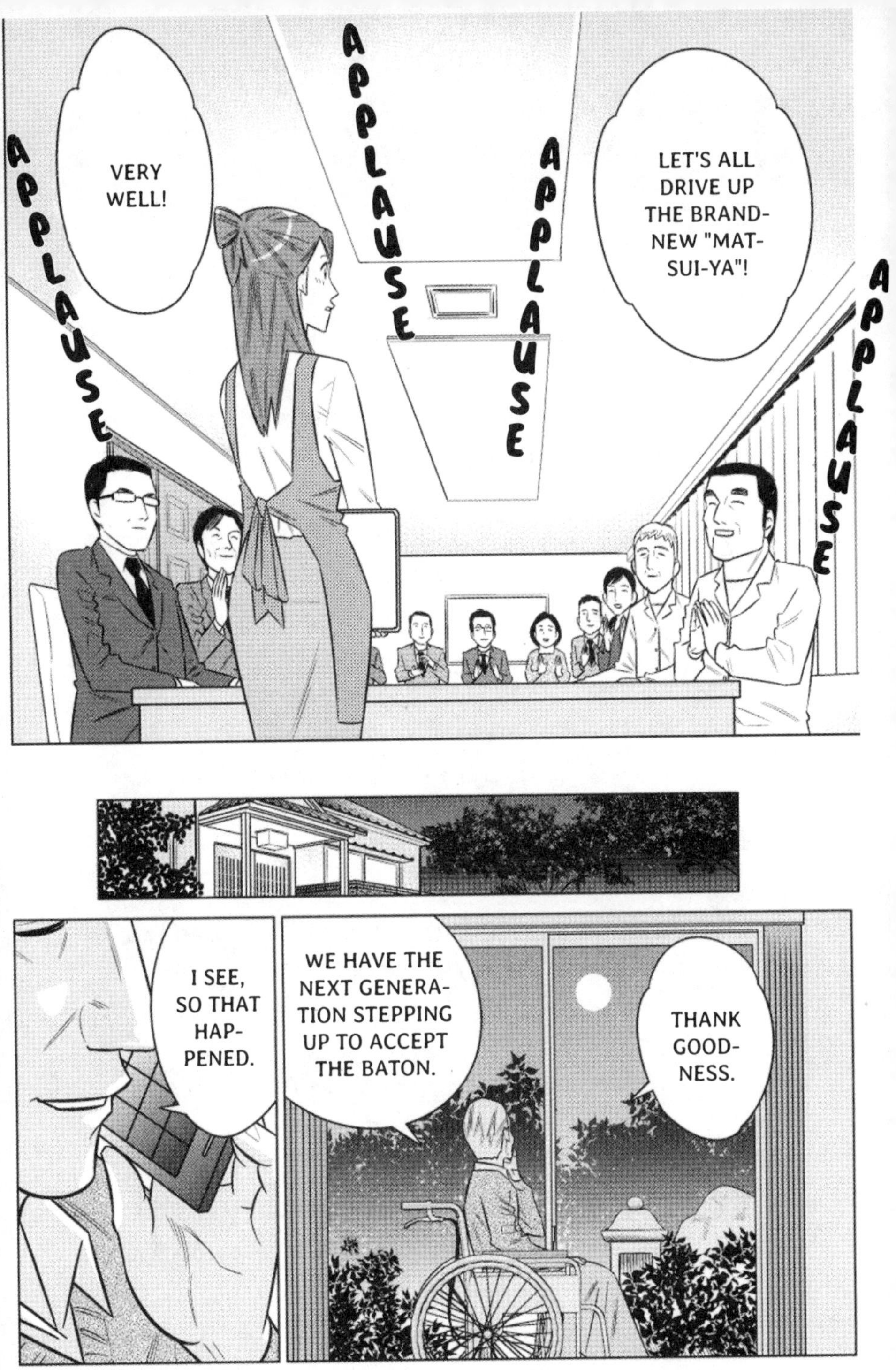
LET'S ALL DRIVE UP THE BRAND-NEW "MAT-SUI-YA"!
APPLAUSE
APPLAUSE
APPLAUSE
VERY WELL!
APPLAUSE
WE HAVE THE NEXT GENERA-TION STEPPING UP TO ACCEPT THE BATON.
THANK GOOD-NESS.
I SEE, SO THAT HAP-PENED.

1

Reviewing Options

▶ How to Review Options

You can't execute every strategic option you come up with. Only a few strategies can be implemented, and you can't have it all. This is why we need to narrow down strategies that are executable from the many options you have.

To do so, first, we need to evaluate the merits and shortcomings of each strategic option. This is what it means to review options. It is a vital process as the outcome of the review will decide which strategies to execute.

What you need to review is not every possible strategic option, but only the options of growth scenarios compiled at the end of step 2.

▶ Three Perspectives in Reviewing Options

You will be focusing on the following three perspectives to review and narrow down your options: Rationality, Feasibility, and Intent of all parties involved (see Diagram 4-1).

LET'S LOOK AT THE PERSPECTIVES USED TO REVIEW THE OPTIONS.

Rationality means evaluating the options' merits and shortcomings based on objective and rational viewpoints. This includes the potential sales growth, potential profit improvement, return on investment (ROI), the possibility of utilizing strengths and bolstering weaknesses,

and the ability to seize opportunities and handle threats. To put it simply, whether you can win or not.

Feasibility, on the other hand, means whether that option is executable based on the organizational capability, investment scale and reserve, difficulty of execution, risks and shortcomings, etc.

Thirdly, the intent of all parties involved refers to what the company and/or everyone involved wants. Things boil down to whether they want to do it or not.

When Fujifilm was trying to come up with new ventures to replace their photography business, they narrowed down their options using three perspectives: "Can we do it?" "Do we want to do it?" and "Should we do it?" While slightly different from "Can we win?," "Can we do it?" and "Do we want to do it?" introduced

Diagram 4-1 Perspectives to Review Options

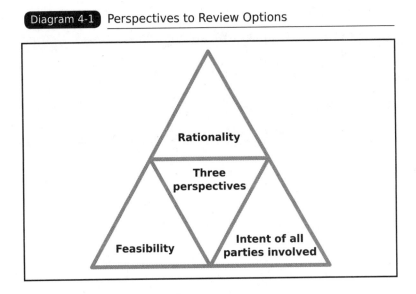

above, the "Should we do it?" perspective includes the question if the company can win in that field, so they are still quite similar.

▶ Reviewing with Both a Cool Head and a Burning Passion

If you are too caught up in objective rationality and feasibility, the result most likely will be the same regardless of who had done them. However, focusing too much on intent, enthusiasm, and intuition might also mislead you.

In order words, you'll need to balance a cool head for objectivity with a burning passion when reviewing your options.

To maintain a calm head, set a clear list of criteria and basis to evaluate objectively without emotional investment.

At the same time, reflect intent and enthusiasm into the strategy in deciding on the evaluation result to come up with a strategy that resounds with your passion and soul.

These two contradicting elements are necessary for reviewing your options.

▶ The Main Points in Reviewing Rationally

Let's take a look at the points used to evaluate rationality. In each category, assess the result of each option if they are selected.

◦ Potential sales growth

Let's look at the potential sales growth first. Here we gauge the prospect of improvement in sales in the future if this option is chosen. Base your evaluation on statistical viewpoints, such as expected market growth, and how much market share can be gained in the competitive environment.

If it is difficult to estimate the market scale and the potential market share gained, or if the estimate itself is not very useful because the market is highly dispersed, break down the sales components (parameters) and try to estimate the potential sales based on the outlook of each parameter. For example, you can estimate the sales and how each parameter will change in the future by using formulas like store × sales per store, and the number of customers × revenue per customer.

TRY TO STICK WITH QUANTITA-TIVE EVAL-UATION!

◦ Potential profit improvement

For profitability, we'll evaluate based on the estimated profit margin and the expected amount of profit if we were to select that option. If the option includes measures to improve profitability, include their effects. Take into consideration

Diagram 4-2 Points in Evaluating Rationality

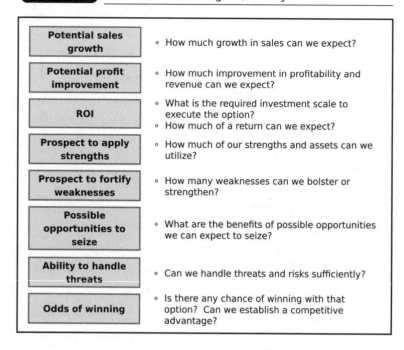

Potential sales growth	◦ How much growth in sales can we expect?
Potential profit improvement	◦ How much improvement in profitability and revenue can we expect?
ROI	◦ What is the required investment scale to execute the option? ◦ How much of a return can we expect?
Prospect to apply strengths	◦ How much of our strengths and assets can we utilize?
Prospect to fortify weaknesses	◦ How many weaknesses can we bolster or strengthen?
Possible opportunities to seize	◦ What are the benefits of possible opportunities we can expect to seize?
Ability to handle threats	◦ Can we handle threats and risks sufficiently?
Odds of winning	◦ Is there any chance of winning with that option? Can we establish a competitive advantage?

the potential changes in the competitive environment and the market structure. Add in your company's prospect of improved competitive edge if this option is implemented. Quantify the potential profit improvement for each option when executed.

◦ **Return on Investment (ROI)**

Estimate the required amount of investment for each option to be executed. To do this, assume the necessary implemented measures for each option and calculate the funds needed for them. The extent of the required investment depends on the situation, but you should include all necessary expenses based on the current situation such as the required facilities and personnel, R&D, marketing, sales promotion, and so on.

Once you have estimated the required amount of investment, compare it to the estimated sales and/or profitability, and determine the investment return. Sometimes, you may have to evaluate the investment return based on the duration viewpoint. For example, if the option takes a long time to implement, but the ROI stays small. Of course, this is harder to quantify, but you can compare options relatively to decide which option has more merits to it.

In some cases, executing certain options may be difficult without skilled personnel or new equipment for an already existing factory. Consider these the human resources and facility investment. They also count in addition to the financial investment.

○ **Prospect to apply strengths**
This evaluates how much of the company's strength can be utilized. Go over the strengths of your company that you identified in the situation analysis, and determine how much can be applied to each option.

○ **Prospect to fortify weaknesses**
We assess the possibility of supporting or strengthening your company's weaknesses if an option is executed. Look at your situation analysis again and determine the potential to fortify any weaknesses.

How to strengthen the weakness upon executing an option (if fortifying the weakness is required to implement an option) will be evaluated separately under feasibility evaluation.

◦ **Possible opportunities to seize**

We'll evaluate how much of the currently unreached business opportunities can be seized by executing an option. This is closely related to the sales and profitability estimations that decided the target market. Evaluate the opportunities in conjunction with the estimated results.

◦ **Ability to handle threats**

This evaluates how many threats and risks the selected option can handle. If the company is facing a threat to the current market itself, expected results can be gauged from the sales estimation. On the other hand, any threat of declining profitability due to increasing competition can be evaluated through profitability estimation.

◦ **Odds of winning**

Ask yourself: if a particular option is chosen, what are the odds of winning? Can we win? In other words, can you establish a competitive advantage with that option?

It's not easy to evaluate, but we can gauge from how much of the business' winning patterns and the KSFs the company can fulfill once a certain option is implemented.

Another evaluation point you can use is to see how much your company can surpass or catch up to the level of products and/ or services the major players in that field are at if the option is implemented.

Options that will change the rules or norms of the industry are hard to gauge. However, you'll have more chances in establishing a competitive edge with them. In such cases, feasibility might weigh more in the overall review.

▶ How to Review Each Point

Now that we've gone over each evaluation point, how do we actually evaluate them? First of all, stick with quantitative evaluation as much as possible. Sales, profitability, and investment returns are relatively easy to appraise by numbers.

Points like the prospects to apply strengths and fortify weaknesses, and odds of winning are harder to quantify. These you will have to evaluate qualitatively. In order to remain objective, you need to first break down the evaluation points into sub-categories and analyze them in detail. For example, the prospect to apply strengths is just one single point, which may result in a very generic evaluation. But you can list the strengths into sub-points and review the potential of each option according to it in order to come to the generalized overall evaluation result.

Also, others' opinions can be used as valid evaluation tools. You can have the relevant personnel score each evaluation point, and make a decision based on them. It'll be helpful to break down everything into sub-categories, have them scored, and see the total score to determine the overall evaluation.

Either way, you'll have to decide whether you want to weigh each point equally, or if you want to focus on certain points more. It goes for the overall evaluation as well (e.g., do you consider potential sales growth evaluation more or equally important to the potential profit improvement), but we'll talk about it later. For this, the deciding factors should be the intent of all parties involved, as well as the relationship between the strategy's goal and the issues at hand. For instance, if there is a particular fatal threat, then give more weight to the threats in the evaluation.

It's also important to clarify the grounds for evaluation. Evaluation is mostly based on hypotheses and conditions. Take the estimates for sales and profit for example. To estimate them, you need to first assume the conditions. Identify and clear up these conditions so that you may discuss if the conditions are properly set, or if it needs to be slightly changed. While you're at it, try clarifying the perspective used for evaluation as well.

Matsui-ya' was using a pretty simple review system. Foregoing the quantitative evaluation completely, they chose to review with a two-step qualitative evaluation of "likely" and "unlikely." Having more details is better, but in reality, you will have time and workload constraints. A consultant specializing in these processes may be able to devote 100% of their time to these analyses, but that's often not the case in a normal company. In most cases, you will have to work on building the strategy while also doing your regular duties.

A review process can be simplified, like in Matsui-ya's case, if time constraints prevent you from doing a more in-depth analysis. You run the risk of being arbitrary, but it is a valid way.

▶ The Main Points in Reviewing the Feasibility

Let's look at the main points to review feasibility next. As with reviewing rationality, we'll review the possible outcome of each option.

As mentioned before, feasibility is asking whether or not it "can be done" and if it is suitable with the current capability of your company.

Sometimes, a drastic decision is needed for a company to grow. However, you need a "suitable" strategy to support it. Of course, some strategies exceed the company's capability, such as Softbank's case when they acquired Sprint Nextel. Bold decisions might yield significant opportunities. Softbank is certainly a company that grew into what it is today by taking seemingly reckless strategies at the time.

But not all companies can take extreme measures like that. Playing it too safe might not be good, but it's necessary to know your limit. Even when you decide on a reckless option, you must be aware of the fact that it exceeds your capabilities, and that this is a deliberate choice made for potentially drastic growth. This is why feasibility evaluation is essential.

EVALUATE THE FEASIBILITY FROM VARIOUS ANGLES.

Feasibility evaluation not only lets you assess whether or not you "can do it," but also gives you an idea of what "conviction" you'll need to push through with the plan.

- **Organizational capability**

This point evaluates whether the organization's capability can execute the selected option.

You must first clarify what kind of organizational capability is required when executing that option. Or to establish a competitive advantage. Identify the abilities needed based on your understanding of the result of the situation analysis, the winning patterns, and the KSFs in that industry.

Diagram 4-3 Organizational Capability

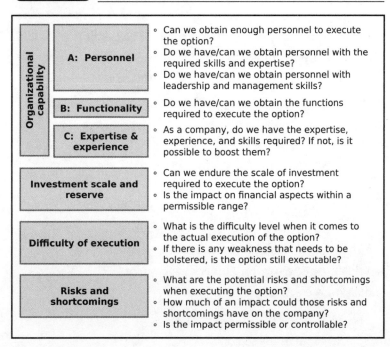

Organizational capability	A: Personnel	◦ Can we obtain enough personnel to execute the option? ◦ Do we have/can we obtain personnel with the required skills and expertise? ◦ Do we have/can we obtain personnel with leadership and management skills?
	B: Functionality	◦ Do we have/can we obtain the functions required to execute the option?
	C: Expertise & experience	◦ As a company, do we have the expertise, experience, and skills required? If not, is it possible to boost them?
Investment scale and reserve		◦ Can we endure the scale of investment required to execute the option? ◦ Is the impact on financial aspects within a permissible range?
Difficulty of execution		◦ What is the difficulty level when it comes to the actual execution of the option? ◦ If there is any weakness that needs to be bolstered, is the option still executable?
Risks and shortcomings		◦ What are the potential risks and shortcomings when executing the option? ◦ How much of an impact could those risks and shortcomings have on the company? ◦ Is the impact permissible or controllable?

Organizational capability is composed of various elements, but the three main ones are personnel, capability, and expertise and experience. There might be other elements, of course. Depending on the industry, you might want to break down those elements further for more in-depth analysis. For instance, if a specific technology is crucial to execute the strategy, you should separate technical capability from the expertise and experience element and evaluate it on its own.

a. Personnel

There are three main points to evaluating personnel.

First of all, question whether or not the company is capable of allocating and organizing the number of people required for the option. This includes reviewing the possibility of personnel transfer from the existing business, hiring new ones, acquiring external ones, and so on. After all, one of the essential keys to a strategy is resource distribution.

The second one is the personnel's skills and expertise. Do you have the personnel with the required skills and expertise to execute the option? If not, acquiring such personnel from external sources is a possibility, so you need to consider it in the review as well.

Thirdly, you must determine whether you have the personnel with leadership skills to manage the entire process if you execute the option. This is crucial especially if the option requires shifting the positioning and/or business model of the current business, or tackling a new venture. Again, see if you have a suitable candidate internally, and if not, include the possibility of bringing in an external source in the evaluation.

b. Functionality
This aspect evaluates whether the company has the required in-house capabilities to execute the option and if not, the chances of obtaining it externally.

For functionality, you can evaluate from the value chain perspective. What function is needed on the value chain flow if that option is executed? Can the existing internal organizational structure cover it? If not, is there a plan to compensate for it? These are the points you might want to evaluate.

c. Expertise and experience (intangible)
While we had discussed expertise and skills under personnel, here we'll talk about expertise and experience as an organization, including information databases and such. Not only on an individual level, but does the company have sufficient expertise and knowledge to execute the option on the organizational level?

This includes, but is not limited to, a lot of soft skills such as technical capabilities, product development, in-depth knowledge of the consumers, market observation skill, customer service expertise, and client information. If it's clear a certain functionality is required to execute the option chosen, you'll be smart to identify and evaluate it separately.

Just like the personnel and functionality aspects, if you are lacking the expertise and experience required, you will have to evaluate the possibility of obtaining them externally as well.

○ **Investment scale and reserve**

We've estimated and evaluated how much investment is required, or what kind of resource is needed, for each option under the rationality review. While the estimation in the rationality review was numerically based, in the feasibility review, we take a look at whether the required investment is within the acceptable limit of the company's resources (funds, personnel, etc.), or whether it's within the investment reserve.

We can evaluate based on several points. Whether a company has the capacity to invest in the first place is one. If it's short of funds and personnel, has difficulties in raising funds, or has limited possibility to obtain personnel from external sources, unfortunately, that means the investment scale for this particular option is unaffordable.

Even with a good investment capacity, you need to consider what kind of impact it will have on the financial aspects. You don't want to end up with a daily precarious cash flow as a result of an investment.

Of course, you can cover the resources needed for investment by obtaining funds and personnel externally. If that's the case, you'll have to examine the financial impact, as well as the actual possibility of securing resources.

○ **Difficulty of execution**

Now let's take a look at the difficulty level to execute the option. It's not easy to evaluate difficulty evenly, but you can assess it by breaking them down into several factors.

For instance, will the option be executed within the already existing business field, or is it in a new business field? The former most likely has a lower difficulty level.

Similarly, you can evaluate by determining if the option is focused on improving or reforming an already existing business. If you are aiming to grow by improvement on the current business trajectory, the difficulty level will be relatively low. On the other hand, you can say the difficulty level is quite high if the option hinges on reforming the positioning and business model.

The difficulty level is also affected by how easily you can read the market and how many unknown factors are in it. With a strategic

Diagram 4-4 Difficulty of Strategy Execution

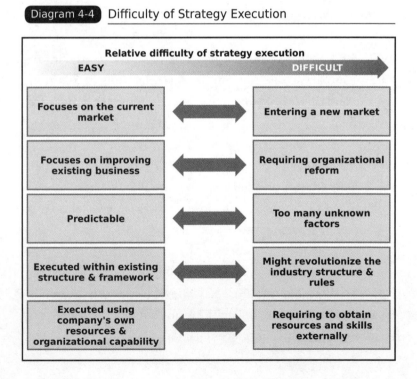

option that is highly predictable in the relatively easy-to-read market and very few unknown factors, the difficulty level will be considerably low. However, if the market itself is hard to read or contains too many unknown factors, and the strategic option itself is unpredictable, the difficulty level will be extremely high.

Options that will change the existing rules and the norms of the market will also be highly difficult to execute.

If the company's organizational capabilities and resources are insufficient and obtaining external resources is the prerequisite for executing a certain option, you can mark that as highly difficult as well. The same goes for an option that requires reinforcing the company's weakness. Those will increase unknown factors, and you will find it hard to predict if the acquired capabilities and resources can be aptly controlled and utilized.

- ○ **Risks and shortcomings**

The last point in the feasibility evaluation focuses on risks and shortcomings. Are there any, and how big are they? Generally, some risks and shortcomings exist regardless of the option, but their sizes and the possible impacts vary. In fact, an option without risks and shortcomings is not an effective strategic option.

A strategy directs focus and deployment of resources, or as some would say, all about choices and focus. Which, in turn, means you will have to compromise on some points. Some sort of trade-off is always required. By compromising, you may increase the possibility of creating risks and shortcomings. Therefore, the better the strategic option is, the more risks and shortcomings it contains. So how should we evaluate risks and shortcomings?

First, consider the impact and its size if the chosen strategy did not work out or was ineffective. Not only are you losing anticipated sales and profit, but the investment will also be wasted. Evaluate its ramification.

You'll also have to consider the lost opportunities upon executing the option. For instance, options for a new venture often involve diverting resources from the existing business, which means it will, in turn, lose opportunities.

Ideally, the new venture would yield a greater result (sales, profit, etc.) than if an equal amount of resources are applied toward the current business. However, if the new venture fails, or does not yield as much as expected, you'll be losing what you would have achieved from the existing business originally on top of the expected result from the new venture.

Other negative impacts on the already existing business include market cannibalism. It is a possible risk if you were to establish a new brand in the same market as the existing business.

Sometimes, there are indirect impacts that should be considered if the option fails. This can include a negative impact on brand image, losing trust from the business partners, and a declining customer base.

Depending on the option chosen, there may be opportunities and threats that cannot be handled. These should also count as risks and/or shortcomings.

The key is to proceed with the evaluation while keeping in mind points such as the executed option's impact on the company and the current business, expected risks, and what opportunities and threats are not fully addressed.

After that, evaluate how they might impact the company. Consider if these risks and shortcomings are controllable, and if not, tolerable. If yes, then you don't have to put too much weight on them. However, if they cannot be controlled or tolerated, then you should regard them as extremely important factors in the review.

▶ How to Review Each Point

Compared to reviewing rationality, it's even harder to objectively evaluate feasibility with a quantitative approach. While investment and anything relating to money can be easily translated into numerical values and reviewed objectively, other points need to be evaluated qualitatively in most cases.

Therefore, we'll be using the qualitative approach for this. As the options are evaluated by the company insiders, however, we can't eliminate subjectivity. This is why it is important to involve as many opinions as possible and review each option based on that. Just like in the rationality evaluation, you need to break down the points into sub-categories, have everyone score them one by one, and then get an overall score for each point.

Again, clarifying the grounds for evaluation such as the hypothesis, conditions, and viewpoints beforehand will be vital in the discussions to come. Have them organized in an easy-to-understand form.

Kazumi's done a preliminary evaluation for Matsui-ya with Takeda's help. Just like the rationality evaluation, they also evaluated the feasibility with a simplified two-step method, which is useful when faced with time and workload constraints. Also, it is important to note that Kazumi is maintaining a relatively objective point of view. When reviewed by the parties involved, there's a risk of losing objectivity as the result will inevitably be affected by personal opinions and intents (the feasibility evaluation has a higher risk of this compared to the rationality evaluation).

Preferably, this process should include not only the parties involved but those who are not directly involved as well. If that's too difficult, then the parties involved should be aware that they need to maintain objectivity as best as they can.

▶ Fostering Agreement and Understanding with "Face-to-face Discussions"

In this part, we have to narrow down the options. This is actually the most crucial step in building an effective and applicable strategy.

Systematically selecting options based on both rationality and feasibility evaluations alone will not result in an effective strategy. To build an effective and practical strategy, you need all parties involved to agree on one option that they can believe that they can and want to do.

The ones who will execute a strategy will be the people. As Takeda said, "People wouldn't want to do what they don't agree on." A strategy that people involved can't agree on and commit to its execution is nothing more than a pie in the sky, even if the strategy itself is brilliant.

So it's not always about choosing the logically correct option. Not that it means you should select an option that's obviously wrong, but it is vital to settle on one that everyone will commit to, regardless of the shortcomings.

ON TOP OF THE REVIEW RESULTS, EVERYONE HAS TO AGREE ON IT!

To do this, thorough discussions among parties involved, including executives, must be done to review options and evaluation results. We call

this a face-to-face discussion, which is a direct meeting where everyone is gathered to hold open dialogues to foster agreement and understanding.

▶ The Groundwork for Discussions: Situation Analysis and Strategic Options

In Matsui-ya's case, Kazumi went over the evaluation results with the executives, but the meeting erupted in various thoughts and opinions, and couldn't get to a consensus (see page 199). That is okay. You can't expect everyone to be on the same page from the start. Everyone comes from a different background, with different opinions, experiences, values, and perceptions of the issues. Some may even have a different goal in mind.

What's important is for everyone to understand that there are differences in their perceptions. It is not about who's right and

| Diagram 4-5 | Fostering Conviction and Agreement through Face-to-Face Discussion |

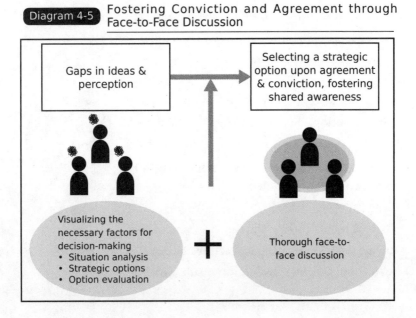

who's wrong. Simply recognizing that there is a gap in their understanding is enough.

With that in mind, proceed with thorough discussions to fill the gap and get everyone on the same page. The situation analysis, strategic options, and evaluations are all for aligning everyone's opinions. Without discussion items, you can't have an effective and fruitful argument. You must first lay the groundwork for discussion. And what we've done thus far, the situation analysis, strategic options, and their evaluation results, is the very groundwork for discussions.

In other words, visualizing the issues is the purpose of the situation analysis, option formulation, and evaluation. It is pointless to have an aimless discussion. With the visualized issues and items to discuss, you can go over everything until everyone is on the same page and committed, no matter how many meetings it takes.

▶ Which Reviewed Points to Prioritize

A thorough discussion is needed, but you can't spend all your time on it. A swift decision is required, especially in today's market, which changes rapidly. So effectiveness and efficiency are needed as the layer above thoroughness in a discussion.

One of the issues when narrowing down the strategic options is how to understand the evaluation results and lead them to the final decision. In most cases, the key element is deciding which items of evaluation, out of many, to focus on.

Of course, there may be a difference in opinions, or the evaluation result itself may be questioned. In such instances, you must go back to the viewpoints, hypotheses, and conditions and see if those are set appropriately. An evaluation, by nature, needs a hypothesis and conditions to some extent, so the degree of accuracy is limited, no matter how many times you argue over them. It is important to set a standard or a condition, but it's pointless to discuss its accuracy beyond its limit.

Instead, place importance on which evaluation results to focus and base the final decision on. The intentions of the parties involved are reflected here. An evaluation tends to end up similar and ordinary the more objectively it is done, just as the overall evaluation ends up unremarkable and not so useful when done without focusing on the evaluation items. Such evaluation doesn't help create individuality and character, which means it'll be harder to differentiate your company from your competitors and establish a competitive advantage over them.

For a company to highlight its competitive edge, you have to not only capture the evaluation results objectively but also put heart and soul into them. That is the passion we mentioned at the beginning of this chapter. The rationality and feasibility evaluations should be done calmly, but in the final step where the evaluation results are analyzed and decided upon, what becomes essential is the passion of everyone involved.

Should you choose a difficult option, but aim to grow dramatically, or a safe one to go after steady growth? Should you focus on using your company's strengths or focus on the market opportunities and go after the one with the most potential? They are neither right nor wrong. In the end, it all comes down to how everyone involved feels about it. Make sure to have exhaustive discussions until everyone is on board with the same goal.

Here's one example. Suntory, for years, had been in the red in the beer business. Common sense would have told you to get out of the market a long time ago. However, Suntory stuck with the beer business, staying the course tenaciously. As a result, they succeeded in developing a hit product, their Premium Malts, in 2008. They turned the beer business into a profit for the first time in 46 years. That was the result of the passion and commitment of everyone, from top to bottom. It is a great example of passion as the driving force.

▶ How to Understand and Decide on the Results

Understanding the evaluation results can also reflect everyone's intentions and enthusiasm. The same evaluation result can be interpreted differently by each person. What if the fact presented was "the market share is low"? Some people may think it's over, but others may see the possibility of finding a niche market.

There's always room for interpretation, even for the same fact or evaluation result. Go over these differences in depth and guide them toward one direction in the end.

▶ How to Expand Options

It is possible to evolve an option itself during the face-to-face discussion phase. You may end up combining several options into one and turn them into a brand-new option or change the details of a specific option.

Tackle these changes proactively as long as everyone can agree on them. You may very well be able to improve the effectiveness and feasibility of an option by taking in the experience and knowledge of predecessors and evolving your options accordingly.

▶ Making Decisions Based on What You Want to Do

You can only come to a consensus on which evaluation item to focus on or interpretation of the results to decide on, by vigorously discussing among the involved parties. Logical or mechanical results won't lead to results.

Based on the results of the analysis and discussions, the final decision is up to management. The decisive factor is if you want to or not. Discuss as many times as needed, and select an option that everyone wants to do.

As for the option you choose, use it in these ways. Organize and share the vision, use it as the basis for strategy (purpose, aim, etc.), use it as a pillar for strategy (core measures), direct the resource distribution, and so on.

▶ Always Have a Plan B Ready

Don't just stick with one option. Always have a plan B. It's always possible for changes in the environment, in and out of the company, to interfere with the execution of the option chosen. This could result in weaker results compared to expectations. Have options ready for those situations.

STEP 4

How to Translate Options into Plans and Actions

STORY 5 **What Becomes of a Strategy**

MATSUI-KUN, YOU MEAN...?

NOD

MATSUI-KUN, YOU MEAN... IN REGARDS TO THE FUTURE LOAN, INAHO BANK IS DEMANDING YOU RESIGN FROM YOUR POSITION...?

WE ARE ON THE HOME-STRETCH NOW.

LET'S COME UP WITH SPECIFIC EXECUTIONS AND ACTIONS BASED ON THESE.

THE STRATEGY FRAMEWORK TO REVITALIZE "MATSUI-YA" HAS BEEN DECIDED.

STORY 5
WHAT BECOMES OF A STRATEGY

BUSINESS STRATEGY FRAMEWORK FOR MATSUI-YA REVITALIZATION

NEW MATSUI-YA VISION	"BRINGING JOY TO THE LIVES OF PEOPLE AROUND THE WORLD THROUGH JAPANESE SWEETS" "PROVIDING A RESPITE TO PEOPLE AROUND THE WORLD WITH JAPANESE SWEETS"
BASIC CONCEPTS FOR THE STRATEGY	• REVITALIZE "MATSUI-YA" BRAND, UTILIZING THE BRAND ASSETS TO THE FULLEST TO PURSUE THE POTENTIAL OF JAPANESE SWEETS, PROVIDING JOY AND RESPITE TO PEOPLE AROUND THE WORLD WITH MATSUI-YA'S JAPANESE SWEETS • CLARIFY THE BRAND IDENTITY BY COINING "MATSUI-YA" = "RED-BEAN PASTE" BRAND IMAGE, AND ESTABLISH SIGNATURE PRODUCTS. • MAINTAIN THE FOCUS AROUND THE COMPREHENSIVE DEPARTMENT STORE JAPANESE SWEETS BUSINESS MODEL, BUT ALSO DEVELOP MULTIPLE BUSINESS MODELS SUITED FOR EACH SALES CHANNEL • REFRESH THE BRAND IMAGE THROUGH AGGRESSIVE PROMOTIONS, RELEASING SEASONAL PRODUCTS, DIVERSIFYING THE RED-BEAN PASTE FLAVORS, AND NEW BUSINESS MODELS • CHALLENGES FOR THE FUTURE: STREAMLINE PRODUCTION FROM RED-BEAN CULTIVATION TO RED-BEAN PASTE PRODUCTION, TRAINING JAPANESE SWEETS CRAFTSMEN, AND HOSTING JAPANESE SWEETS-MAKING CLASSES, ALL AIMING TO REVITALIZE THE JAPANESE SWEETS INDUSTRY ITSELF • REFORM THE PROFIT STRUCTURE DRASTICALLY TO STRENGTHEN IT, GUARANTEEING REINVESTMENT FOR THE FUTURE GROWTH

THREE MAIN PILLARS OF THE STRATEGY	**1** REVITALIZING THE "MATSUI-YA" BRAND	**2** SHIFT TO A MULTI-BUSINESS MODEL	**3** DRASTIC REFORM OF THE PROFIT STRUCTURE

WE ARE ON THE HOME-STRETCH NOW.

LET'S COME UP WITH SPECIFIC EXECUTIONS AND ACTIONS BASED ON THESE.

THE KEY IS IN THE DETAILS AND PRECISION!

DECIDE ON EVERYTHING, INCLUDING SCHEDULING AND WHO'S IN CHARGE.

ALSO, MAKE SURE TO BUILD A STRUCTURE TO MONITOR THE PROGRESS.

IN CHARGE

THIS IS VITAL SO THAT IT WON'T TURN INTO A PIE IN THE SKY.

ONCE AGAIN, A BUSINESS STRATEGY IS MEANINGLESS UNLESS IT IS EXECUTED!

YOU CAN ONLY SAY YOU'RE DONE WITH THE STRATEGY BUILDING AFTER FINISHING ALL THESE STEPS.

OH BOY... IT REALLY IS A MAJOR TASK...

"MEASURES" ARE REQUIREMENTS FOR THE EXECUTION OF THE STRATEGY.

"ACTIONS" ARE WHAT'S BEING DONE AT THE ON-SITE LEVEL.

"ACTIONS" COME AFTER "MEASURES."

ACTION

ACTION

ACTION

ACTION

MEASURES

1

REVITALIZING THE "MATSUI-YA" BRAND

FOR EXAMPLE... HERE'S ONE OF THE MAIN PILLARS: REVITALIZING THE "MATSUI-YA" BRAND.

WHAT DO YOU THINK IS NEEDED TO REALIZE THIS?

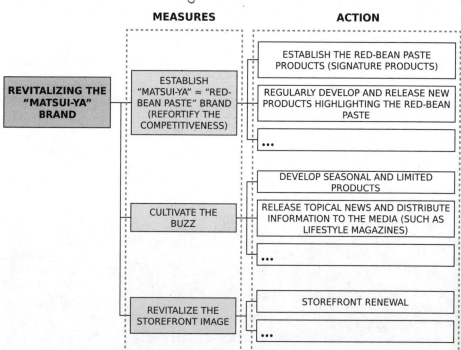

	MEASURES	ACTION
REVITALIZING THE "MATSUI-YA" BRAND	ESTABLISH "MATSUI-YA" = "RED-BEAN PASTE" BRAND (REFORTIFY THE COMPETITIVENESS)	ESTABLISH THE RED-BEAN PASTE PRODUCTS (SIGNATURE PRODUCTS)
		REGULARLY DEVELOP AND RELEASE NEW PRODUCTS HIGHLIGHTING THE RED-BEAN PASTE
		...
	CULTIVATE THE BUZZ	DEVELOP SEASONAL AND LIMITED PRODUCTS
		RELEASE TOPICAL NEWS AND DISTRIBUTE INFORMATION TO THE MEDIA (SUCH AS LIFESTYLE MAGAZINES)
		...
	REVITALIZE THE STOREFRONT IMAGE	STOREFRONT RENEWAL
		...

234

I THINK I GET IT.

WE SHOULD PROCEED BY DISCUSSING THESE WITH EACH DEPARTMENT.

DON'T FORGET TO PRIORITIZE BOTH MEASURES AND ACTIONS.

DON'T FORGET TO ASSIGN PRIORITY TO EACH MEASURE AND ACTION.

LASTLY, TURN EVERYTHING INTO A SCHEDULE.

AS I SAID BEFORE, DON'T FORGET TO SET WHO'S IN CHARGE TO EXECUTE EACH ONE.

YOU'VE GOT TO MOTIVATE EVERYONE SO THAT THEY'RE PUMPED TO EXECUTE IT!

STRATEGY

TO DO SO, EVERYONE IN THE COMPANY NEEDS TO BE ON THE SAME PAGE.

AND YOU NEED TO GET THE EXEC'S SUPPORT IN SHOULDERING THE RESPONSIBILITY.

ALL RIGHT. I'M ON FIRE AGAIN!

THANK YOU SO MUCH!

SLAM

235

SO WITH CO-OPERATION FROM EACH DEPARTMENT...

...MEASURES AND ACTIONS FOR THE THREE MAIN PILLARS OF THE STRATEGY BEGAN TO TAKE SHAPE.

BREAKDOWN OF SPECIFIC MEASURES AND ACTIONS

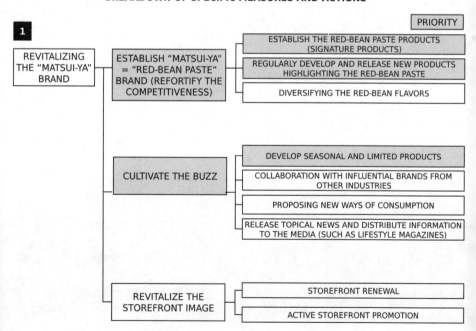

1

REVITALIZING THE "MATSUI-YA" BRAND

PRIORITY

ESTABLISH "MATSUI-YA" = "RED-BEAN PASTE" BRAND (REFORTIFY THE COMPETITIVENESS)
- ESTABLISH THE RED-BEAN PASTE PRODUCTS (SIGNATURE PRODUCTS)
- REGULARLY DEVELOP AND RELEASE NEW PRODUCTS HIGHLIGHTING THE RED-BEAN PASTE
- DIVERSIFYING THE RED-BEAN FLAVORS

CULTIVATE THE BUZZ
- DEVELOP SEASONAL AND LIMITED PRODUCTS
- COLLABORATION WITH INFLUENTIAL BRANDS FROM OTHER INDUSTRIES
- PROPOSING NEW WAYS OF CONSUMPTION
- RELEASE TOPICAL NEWS AND DISTRIBUTE INFORMATION TO THE MEDIA (SUCH AS LIFESTYLE MAGAZINES)

REVITALIZE THE STOREFRONT IMAGE
- STOREFRONT RENEWAL
- ACTIVE STOREFRONT PROMOTION

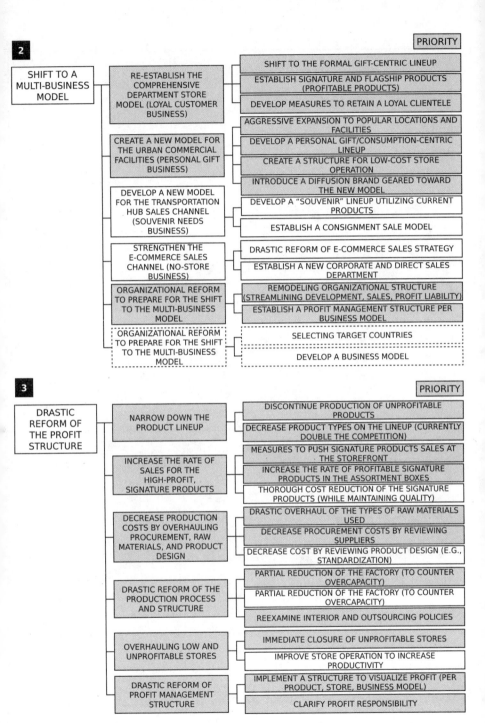

2

PRIORITY

SHIFT TO A MULTI-BUSINESS MODEL

- **RE-ESTABLISH THE COMPREHENSIVE DEPARTMENT STORE MODEL (LOYAL CUSTOMER BUSINESS)**
  - SHIFT TO THE FORMAL GIFT-CENTRIC LINEUP
  - ESTABLISH SIGNATURE AND FLAGSHIP PRODUCTS (PROFITABLE PRODUCTS)
  - DEVELOP MEASURES TO RETAIN A LOYAL CLIENTELE

- **CREATE A NEW MODEL FOR THE URBAN COMMERCIAL FACILITIES (PERSONAL GIFT BUSINESS)**
  - AGGRESSIVE EXPANSION TO POPULAR LOCATIONS AND FACILITIES
  - DEVELOP A PERSONAL GIFT/CONSUMPTION-CENTRIC LINEUP
  - CREATE A STRUCTURE FOR LOW-COST STORE OPERATION

- **DEVELOP A NEW MODEL FOR THE TRANSPORTATION HUB SALES CHANNEL (SOUVENIR NEEDS BUSINESS)**
  - INTRODUCE A DIFFUSION BRAND GEARED TOWARD THE NEW MODEL
  - DEVELOP A "SOUVENIR" LINEUP UTILIZING CURRENT PRODUCTS
  - ESTABLISH A CONSIGNMENT SALE MODEL

- **STRENGTHEN THE E-COMMERCE SALES CHANNEL (NO-STORE BUSINESS)**
  - DRASTIC REFORM OF E-COMMERCE SALES STRATEGY
  - ESTABLISH A NEW CORPORATE AND DIRECT SALES DEPARTMENT

- **ORGANIZATIONAL REFORM TO PREPARE FOR THE SHIFT TO THE MULTI-BUSINESS MODEL**
  - REMODELING ORGANIZATIONAL STRUCTURE (STREAMLINING DEVELOPMENT, SALES, PROFIT LIABILITY)
  - ESTABLISH A PROFIT MANAGEMENT STRUCTURE PER BUSINESS MODEL

- **ORGANIZATIONAL REFORM TO PREPARE FOR THE SHIFT TO THE MULTI-BUSINESS MODEL**
  - SELECTING TARGET COUNTRIES
  - DEVELOP A BUSINESS MODEL

3

PRIORITY

DRASTIC REFORM OF THE PROFIT STRUCTURE

- **NARROW DOWN THE PRODUCT LINEUP**
  - DISCONTINUE PRODUCTION OF UNPROFITABLE PRODUCTS
  - DECREASE PRODUCT TYPES ON THE LINEUP (CURRENTLY DOUBLE THE COMPETITION)

- **INCREASE THE RATE OF SALES FOR THE HIGH-PROFIT, SIGNATURE PRODUCTS**
  - MEASURES TO PUSH SIGNATURE PRODUCTS SALES AT THE STOREFRONT
  - INCREASE THE RATE OF PROFITABLE SIGNATURE PRODUCTS IN THE ASSORTMENT BOXES
  - THOROUGH COST REDUCTION OF THE SIGNATURE PRODUCTS (WHILE MAINTAINING QUALITY)

- **DECREASE PRODUCTION COSTS BY OVERHAULING PROCUREMENT, RAW MATERIALS, AND PRODUCT DESIGN**
  - DRASTIC OVERHAUL OF THE TYPES OF RAW MATERIALS USED
  - DECREASE PROCUREMENT COSTS BY REVIEWING SUPPLIERS
  - DECREASE COST BY REVIEWING PRODUCT DESIGN (E.G., STANDARDIZATION)

- **DRASTIC REFORM OF THE PRODUCTION PROCESS AND STRUCTURE**
  - PARTIAL REDUCTION OF THE FACTORY (TO COUNTER OVERCAPACITY)
  - PARTIAL REDUCTION OF THE FACTORY (TO COUNTER OVERCAPACITY)
  - REEXAMINE INTERIOR AND OUTSOURCING POLICIES

- **OVERHAULING LOW AND UNPROFITABLE STORES**
  - IMMEDIATE CLOSURE OF UNPROFITABLE STORES
  - IMPROVE STORE OPERATION TO INCREASE PRODUCTIVITY

- **DRASTIC REFORM OF PROFIT MANAGEMENT STRUCTURE**
  - IMPLEMENT A STRUCTURE TO VISUALIZE PROFIT (PER PRODUCT, STORE, BUSINESS MODEL)
  - CLARIFY PROFIT RESPONSIBILITY

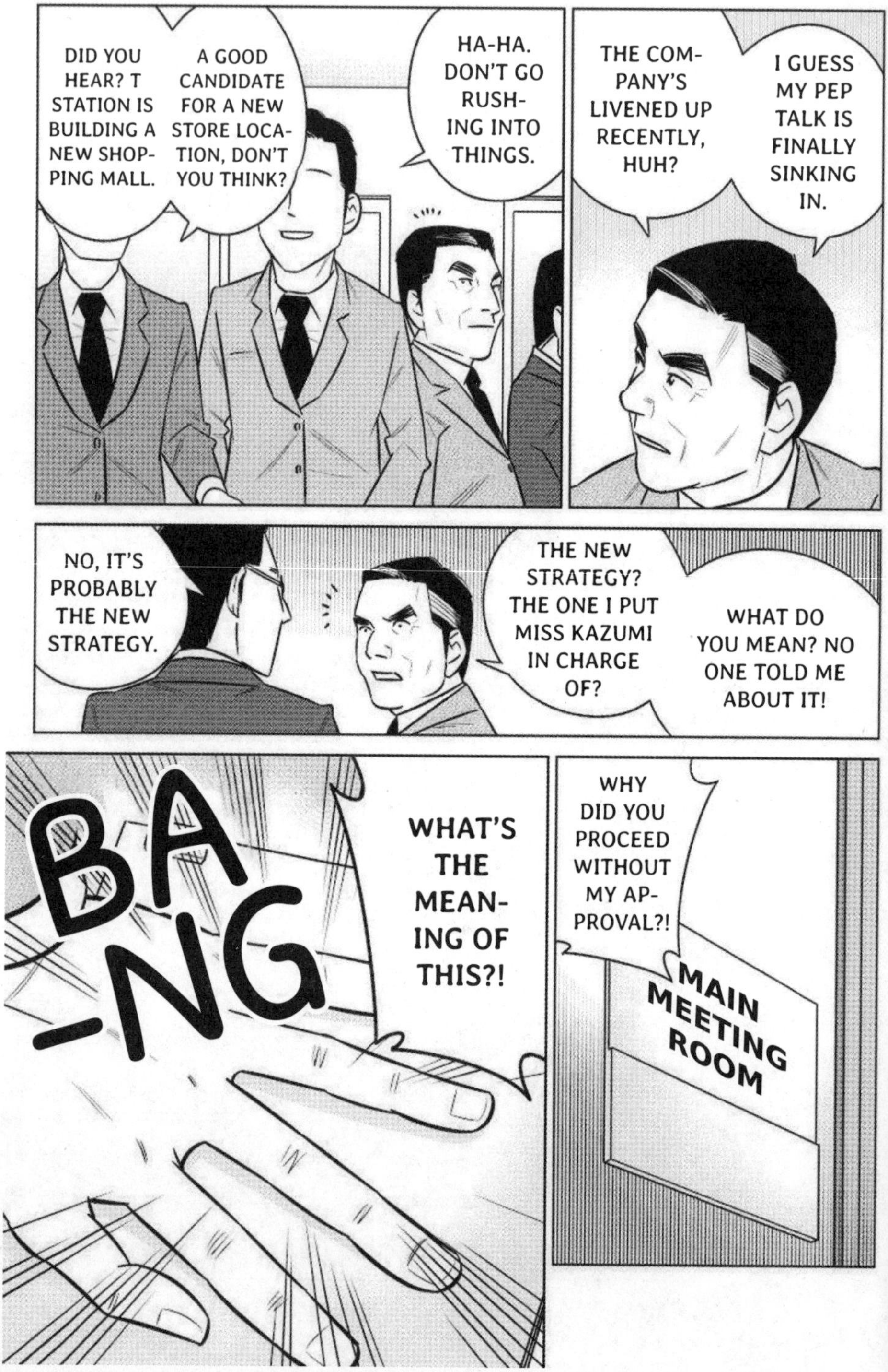
DID YOU HEAR? T STATION IS BUILDING A NEW SHOPPING MALL.
A GOOD CANDIDATE FOR A NEW STORE LOCATION, DON'T YOU THINK?
HA-HA. DON'T GO RUSHING INTO THINGS.
THE COMPANY'S LIVENED UP RECENTLY, HUH?
I GUESS MY PEP TALK IS FINALLY SINKING IN.
NO, IT'S PROBABLY THE NEW STRATEGY.
THE NEW STRATEGY? THE ONE I PUT MISS KAZUMI IN CHARGE OF?
WHAT DO YOU MEAN? NO ONE TOLD ME ABOUT IT!
BA-NG
WHAT'S THE MEANING OF THIS?!
WHY DID YOU PROCEED WITHOUT MY APPROVAL?!
MAIN MEETING ROOM

I-I THOUGHT THE GENERAL MANAGER HAD ALREADY INFORMED YOU...

YES, I'VE ASKED HER TO PROCEED.

WHAT ?!

WE'VE DETERMINED THAT MISS KAZUMI'S STRATEGY IS EFFECTIVE.

WHA—

PLEASE REVIEW THE STRATEGY DETAILS FIRST.

I DON'T HAVE TO LOOK AT ANYTHING!

YOU THINK SO? I THINK IT'S VERY WELL-CONSTRUCTED.

DARN IT...

FLIP FLIP FLIP

WHY DID IT COME DOWN TO THIS...?

WELL, WHAT'S THIS ABOUT "NARROWING DOWN OF THE PRODUCT LINE-UP"?!

ARE YOU GOING TO WASTE ALL THE PRODUCT TYPES WE'VE DEVELOPED SO FAR?!

239

THE MORE PRODUCTS WE HAVE, THE MORE WE CAN MEET THE CUSTOMER'S NEEDS!

WE'LL NEVER INCREASE SALES IF CUSTOMERS CAN'T FIND WHAT THEY WANT TO BUY.

UM, THAT'S NOT NEC-ESSARILY THE CASE.

IF YOU WOULD LOOK AT THIS DATA OUR COMPANY HAS DOUBLE THE PRODUCTS THAN THE COMPETITORS.

BUT, WHEN YOU COMPARE THE PROFITABILITY, YOU'LL SEE IT'S NOT EFFICIENT.

SO, THE PLAN IS TO TURN THINGS AROUND BY FOCUSING ON PROFITABLE PRODUCTS.

WHAT ABOUT WITHDRAWING THE UNPROF-ITABLE STORES FROM THE DEPARTMENT STORES?!

YOU'RE GOING TO RUIN THE RELATIONSHIPS WE'VE ESTAB-LISHED!

PLEASE LOOK AT THE DATA FOR THAT, TOO.

THERE'S A DROP IN THE CUSTOMER FLOW...

CEO, THE SALES DEPARTMENT ALSO FEELS THE DEVELOPMENT OF NEW SALES CHANNELS IS A MUST.

WE MAY HAVE TO SACRIFICE SOME CURRENT POLI-CIES, BUT IT WAS INEVITABLE.

SALES MANAG-ER!

240

THE PRODUCTION TEAM SUPPORTS THE REDUCTION OF PRODUCT TYPES AS WELL.

!

THEN, WHAT ABOUT THIS?

SUI-YA

THE CEO'S QUESTIONS WENT ON FOR HOURS.

KAZUMI CONTINUED TO ANSWER WITH PASSION.

SHE KNEW SHE HAD TO CONVINCE THE CEO TO COMPLETE THE STRATEGY-BUILDING PROCESS.

AND FINALLY

...

WHAT DO YOU THINK? I BELIEVE THIS WILL BE VERY EFFECTIVE.

OKAY. YES, I AGREE.

WHY DIDN'T YOU SAY ANYTHING UNTIL NOW?

I'LL BE HONEST.

241

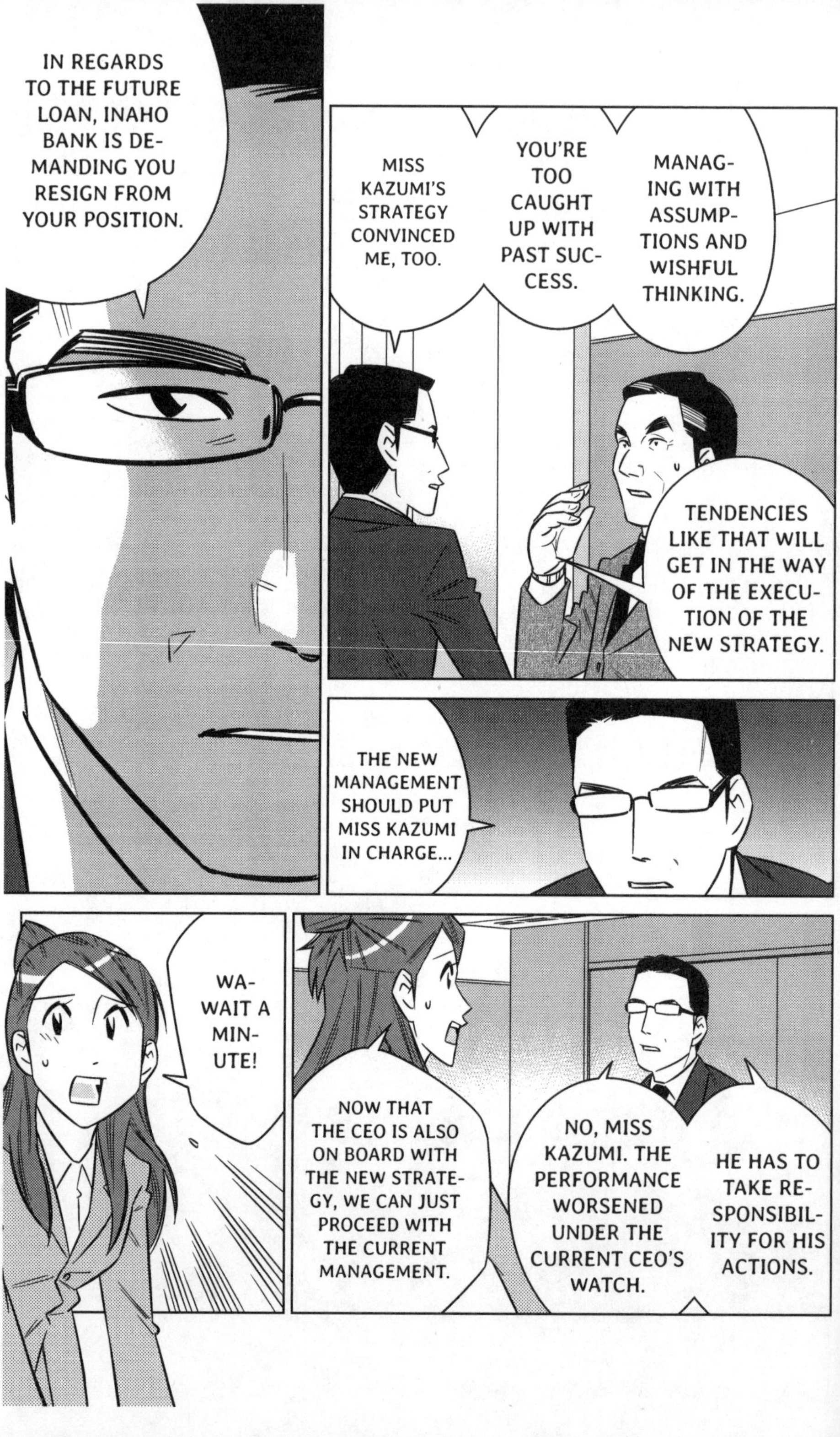
IN REGARDS TO THE FUTURE LOAN, INAHO BANK IS DEMANDING YOU RESIGN FROM YOUR POSITION.
MISS KAZUMI'S STRATEGY CONVINCED ME, TOO.
YOU'RE TOO CAUGHT UP WITH PAST SUCCESS.
MANAGING WITH ASSUMPTIONS AND WISHFUL THINKING.
TENDENCIES LIKE THAT WILL GET IN THE WAY OF THE EXECUTION OF THE NEW STRATEGY.
THE NEW MANAGEMENT SHOULD PUT MISS KAZUMI IN CHARGE...
WA-WAIT A MINUTE!
NOW THAT THE CEO IS ALSO ON BOARD WITH THE NEW STRATEGY, WE CAN JUST PROCEED WITH THE CURRENT MANAGEMENT.
NO, MISS KAZUMI. THE PERFORMANCE WORSENED UNDER THE CURRENT CEO'S WATCH.
HE HAS TO TAKE RESPONSIBILITY FOR HIS ACTIONS.

I KNOW WHAT YOU'RE SAYING, BUT...

...

THE FIRST STRATEGY I CAME UP WITH WAS UTTERLY USELESS.

BUT I GOT HELP FROM THE GROUND UP AND MANAGED TO SHAPE IT INTO WHAT IT IS NOW.

MAYBE HE LOST HIS WAY BECAUSE OF PAST SUCCESS.

BUT I WAS ALLOWED TO LEARN AND GROW FROM THE CEO.

I'LL SHARE EVERY-THING I'VE LEARNED.

WE'LL BRAIN-STORM TOGETHER ABOUT THE UNKNOWN.

ISN'T THAT WHAT THE BUSI-NESS PLAN-NING OFFICE IS FOR?!

243

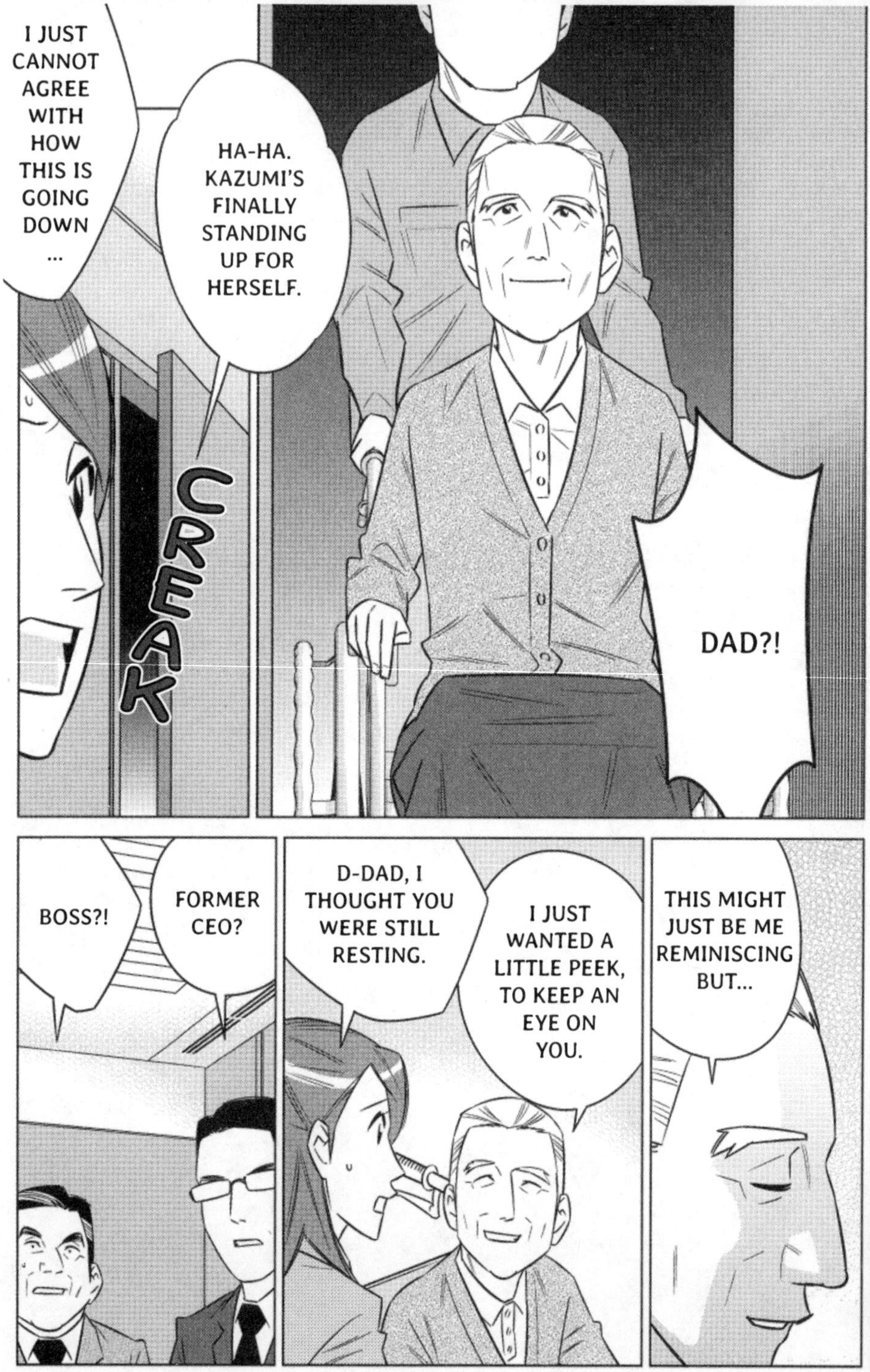
I JUST CANNOT AGREE WITH HOW THIS IS GOING DOWN ...
HA-HA. KAZUMI'S FINALLY STANDING UP FOR HERSELF.
CREAK
DAD?!
BOSS?!
FORMER CEO?
D-DAD, I THOUGHT YOU WERE STILL RESTING.
I JUST WANTED A LITTLE PEEK, TO KEEP AN EYE ON YOU.
THIS MIGHT JUST BE ME REMINISCING BUT...

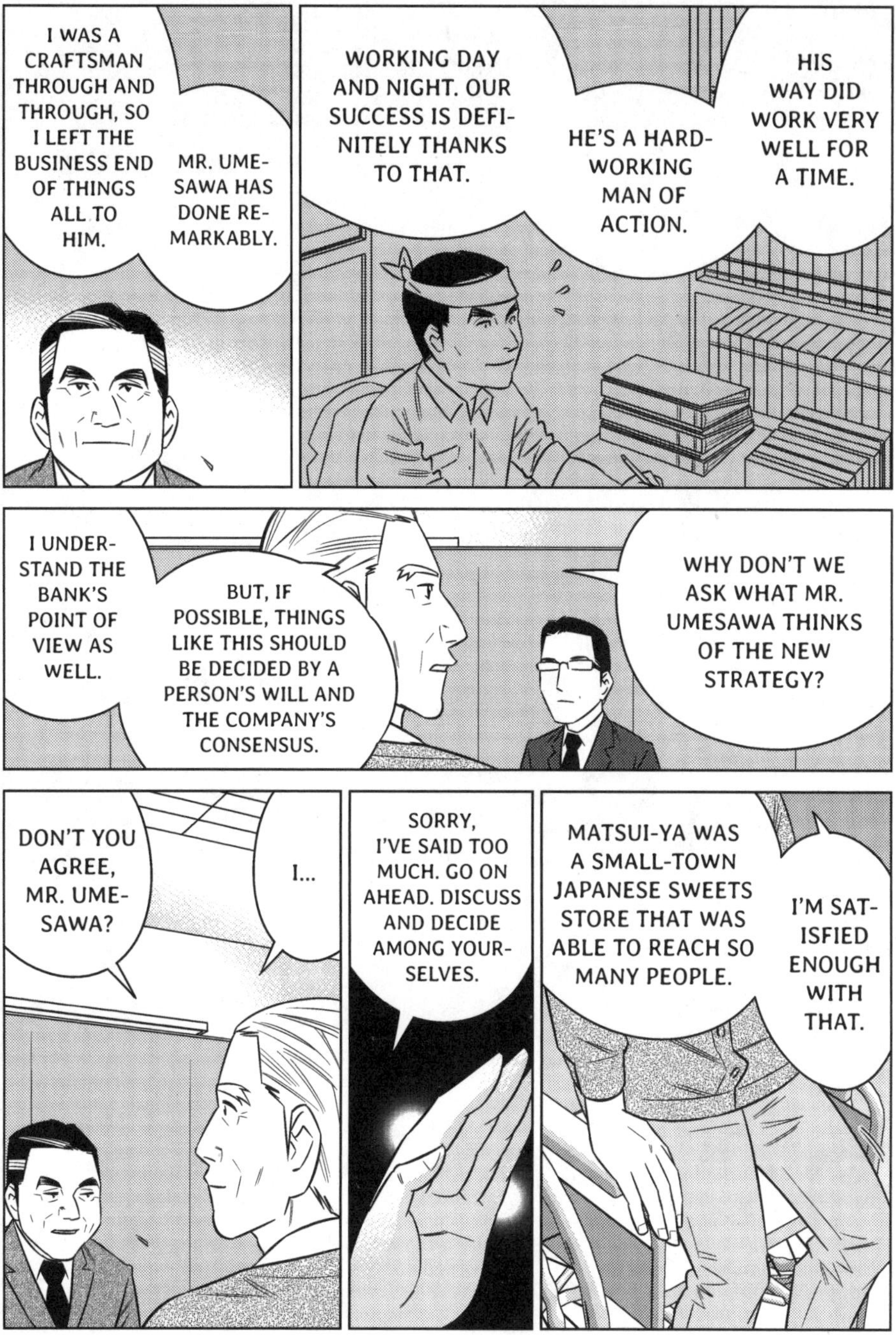
I WAS A CRAFTSMAN THROUGH AND THROUGH, SO I LEFT THE BUSINESS END OF THINGS ALL TO HIM.
MR. UMESAWA HAS DONE REMARKABLY.
WORKING DAY AND NIGHT. OUR SUCCESS IS DEFINITELY THANKS TO THAT.
HE'S A HARD-WORKING MAN OF ACTION.
HIS WAY DID WORK VERY WELL FOR A TIME.
I UNDERSTAND THE BANK'S POINT OF VIEW AS WELL.
BUT, IF POSSIBLE, THINGS LIKE THIS SHOULD BE DECIDED BY A PERSON'S WILL AND THE COMPANY'S CONSENSUS.
WHY DON'T WE ASK WHAT MR. UMESAWA THINKS OF THE NEW STRATEGY?
DON'T YOU AGREE, MR. UMESAWA?
I...
SORRY, I'VE SAID TOO MUCH. GO ON AHEAD. DISCUSS AND DECIDE AMONG YOURSELVES.
MATSUI-YA WAS A SMALL-TOWN JAPANESE SWEETS STORE THAT WAS ABLE TO REACH SO MANY PEOPLE.
I'M SATISFIED ENOUGH WITH THAT.

EVERYONE, PLEASE...

...LEND YOUR CONTINUED SUPPORT TO MATSUI-YA.

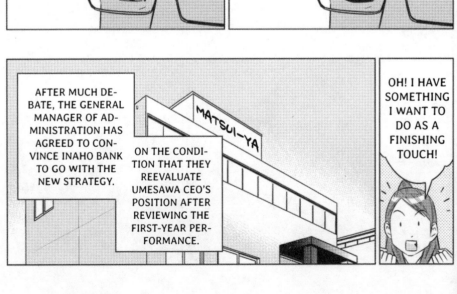

AFTER MUCH DEBATE, THE GENERAL MANAGER OF ADMINISTRATION HAS AGREED TO CONVINCE INAHO BANK TO GO WITH THE NEW STRATEGY.

ON THE CONDITION THAT THEY REEVALUATE UMESAWA CEO'S POSITION AFTER REVIEWING THE FIRST-YEAR PERFORMANCE.

MATSUI-YA

OH! I HAVE SOMETHING I WANT TO DO AS A FINISHING TOUCH!

MATSUI-YA REVITALIZATION: STRUCTURE REFORMATION MASTER PLAN

		PHASE 1 — DRASTIC RECONSTRUCTION OF THE BUSINESS FUNDAMENTALS	PHASE 2 — BUSINESS EXPANSION BY DIVERSIFYING THE BUSINESS MODELS	PHASE 3 — A LEAP FORWARD TO GROW FURTHER
FUNDAMENTAL POLICY		■ Short-term profit improvement/stop the bleeding ■ Reestablish the brand and competitive edge by utilizing the "red-bean paste" strength to the fullest ■ Reinforce the department store model	■ Shift to business expansion ■ Full-scale deployment of a multi-business model ■ Establish a reinvestment model by realizing a high-profit structure	■ Tackle the overseas markets in earnest ■ Tackle new business models
STRATEGY FRAMEWORK	BRAND REVITALIZATION	● Develop flagship products using the "red-bean paste" ● Revitalize the brand image by cultivating buzz and novelty	● Establish a "red-bean paste" means "Matsui-ya" brand image ● Expand variations of "red-bean" flavors ● Shift to new concept stores (carry out substantial storefront redesign)	● Establish brand recognition as Renewed "Matsui-ya" ● Proposing a new Japanese sweets culture

	MULTI-BUSINESS MODEL	● Reestablish the business model as a comprehensive department store Japanese sweets brand
		● Develop a personal gift business model and expand to urban commercial facilities
			● Expansion toward other sales channels
			  • Urban commercial facilities
			  • Transportation hub sales channel
			  • E-commerce and corporate sales channel
				● Accelerate the shift to a multi-business model domestically (over 30% non-department store model)
				● Stepping stone for overseas expansion
				● Evaluate new business models (cafes etc.)

	PROFIT STRUCTURE REFORM	● Implement short-term measures to stop the bleeding (eliminating unprofitable products and stores, decreasing procurement, factory reduction, etc.) ● Build a new profit-managing scheme	● Introduce a profit management structure ● Establish a new operational structure for production and sales (improve productivity) ● Turn all products profitable	● Let the profit management structure take root ● Establish a high-profit structure (operating margin ratio over 15%) ● Formulate a new investment plan
SALES GOAL		15 billion JPY (temporary reduction due to unprofitable store closures etc.)	16 billion JPY (expansion back on track)	18 billion JPY (continued expansion)
OPERATING MARGIN RATIO GOAL		5% (early stages of returning to profit)	10%	17%

WE'LL PROCEED IN PHASES ACCORDING TO THE MASTER PLAN.

WE'LL ALSO ESTABLISH PROGRESS MONITORING AND EVALUATION STRUCTURES.

247

THIS IS THE FRAMEWORK OF THE NEW STRATEGY.

DETAILED SCHEDULES WILL BE DETERMINED IN CONJUNCTION WITH EACH DEPARTMENT.

I'LL STUDY EVEN HARDER AND TAKE FULL RESPONSIBILITY.

I THOUGHT I WAS COMING UP WITH NEW MEASURES, BUT MAYBE I WAS JUST CLINGING TO PAST SUCCESS...

...I CAN SEE THAT NOW.

I'D LIKE TO GET BACK TO BASICS AND INTRODUCE THE BRAND-NEW "MATSUI-YA" TO OUR CUSTOMERS.

TO DO THAT, YOUR SUPPORT IS ESSENTIAL.

THE LEADERSHIP WILL PUT ALL OUR EFFORTS INTO ONE UNDER THIS NEW VISION.

BRINGING A MOMENT OF PEACE TO PEOPLE'S LIVES AROUND THE WORLD THROUGH JAPANESE CONFECTIONARIES

PLEASE, PLEASE LEND US YOUR SUPPORT AND UNDERSTANDING.

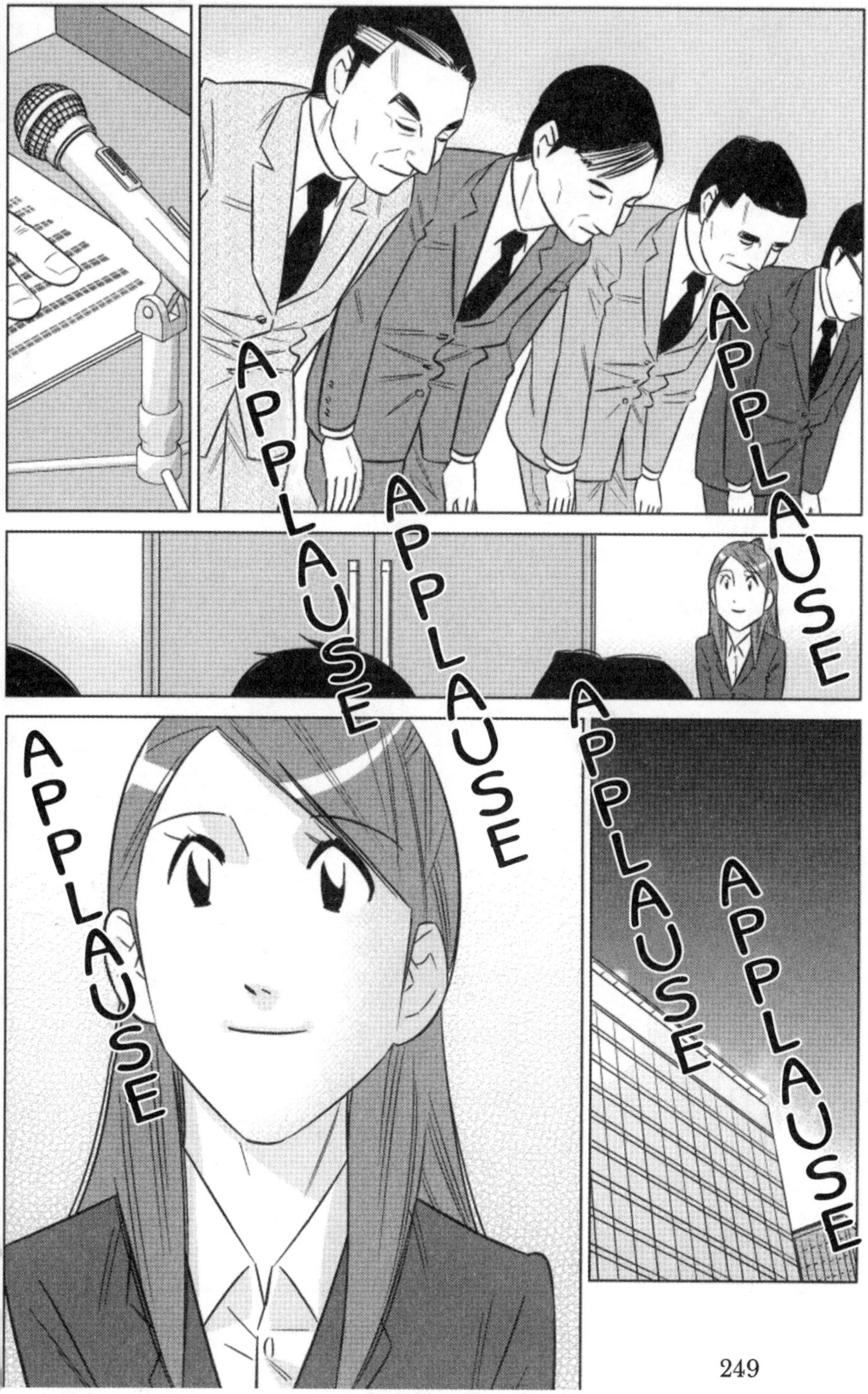
APPLAUSE
APPLAUSE
APPLAUSE
APPLAUSE
APPLAUSE
APPLAUSE

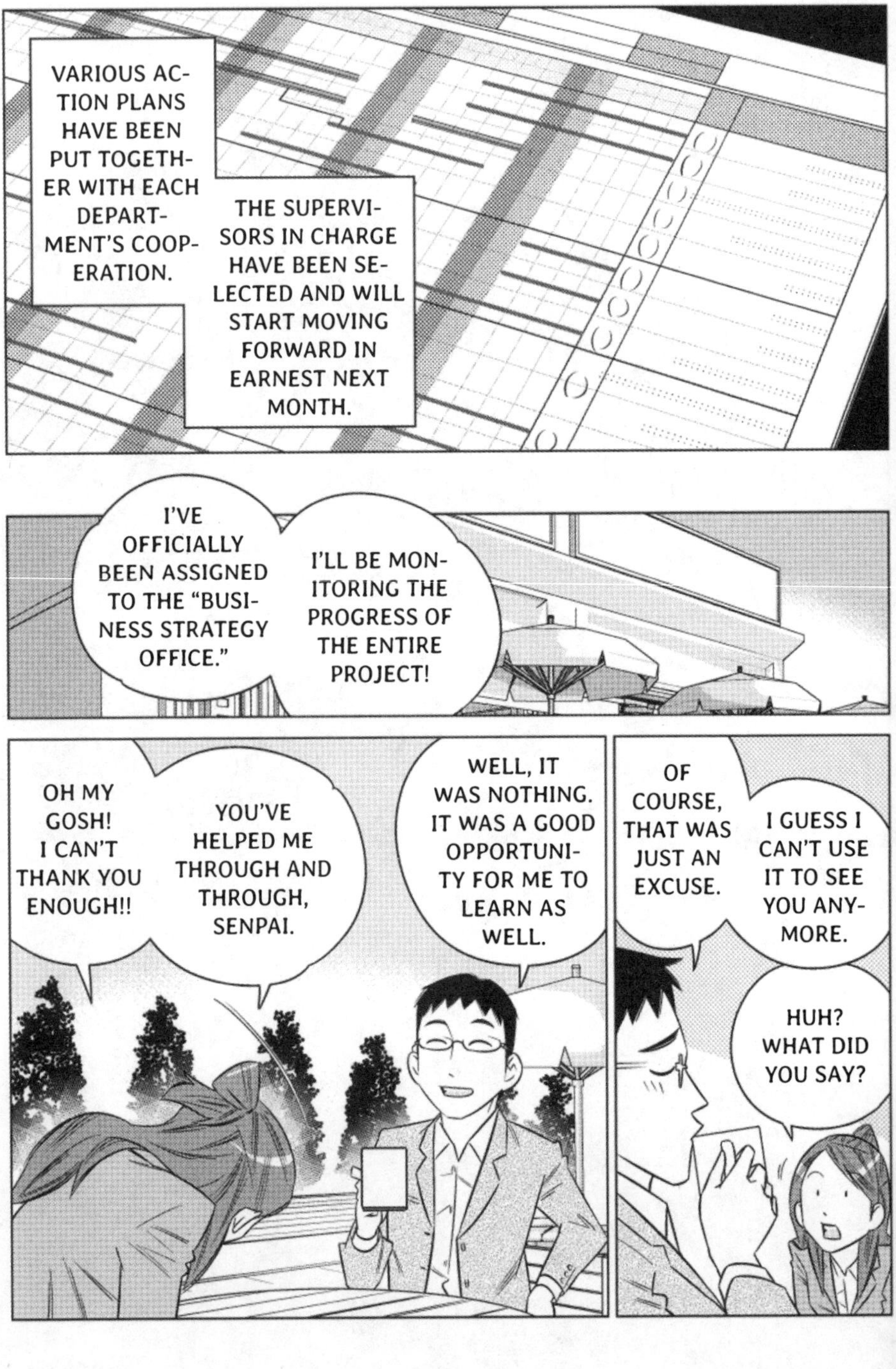
VARIOUS ACTION PLANS HAVE BEEN PUT TOGETHER WITH EACH DEPARTMENT'S COOPERATION.
THE SUPERVISORS IN CHARGE HAVE BEEN SELECTED AND WILL START MOVING FORWARD IN EARNEST NEXT MONTH.
I'VE OFFICIALLY BEEN ASSIGNED TO THE "BUSINESS STRATEGY OFFICE."
I'LL BE MONITORING THE PROGRESS OF THE ENTIRE PROJECT!
OH MY GOSH! I CAN'T THANK YOU ENOUGH!!
YOU'VE HELPED ME THROUGH AND THROUGH, SENPAI.
WELL, IT WAS NOTHING. IT WAS A GOOD OPPORTUNITY FOR ME TO LEARN AS WELL.
OF COURSE, THAT WAS JUST AN EXCUSE.
I GUESS I CAN'T USE IT TO SEE YOU ANYMORE.
HUH? WHAT DID YOU SAY?

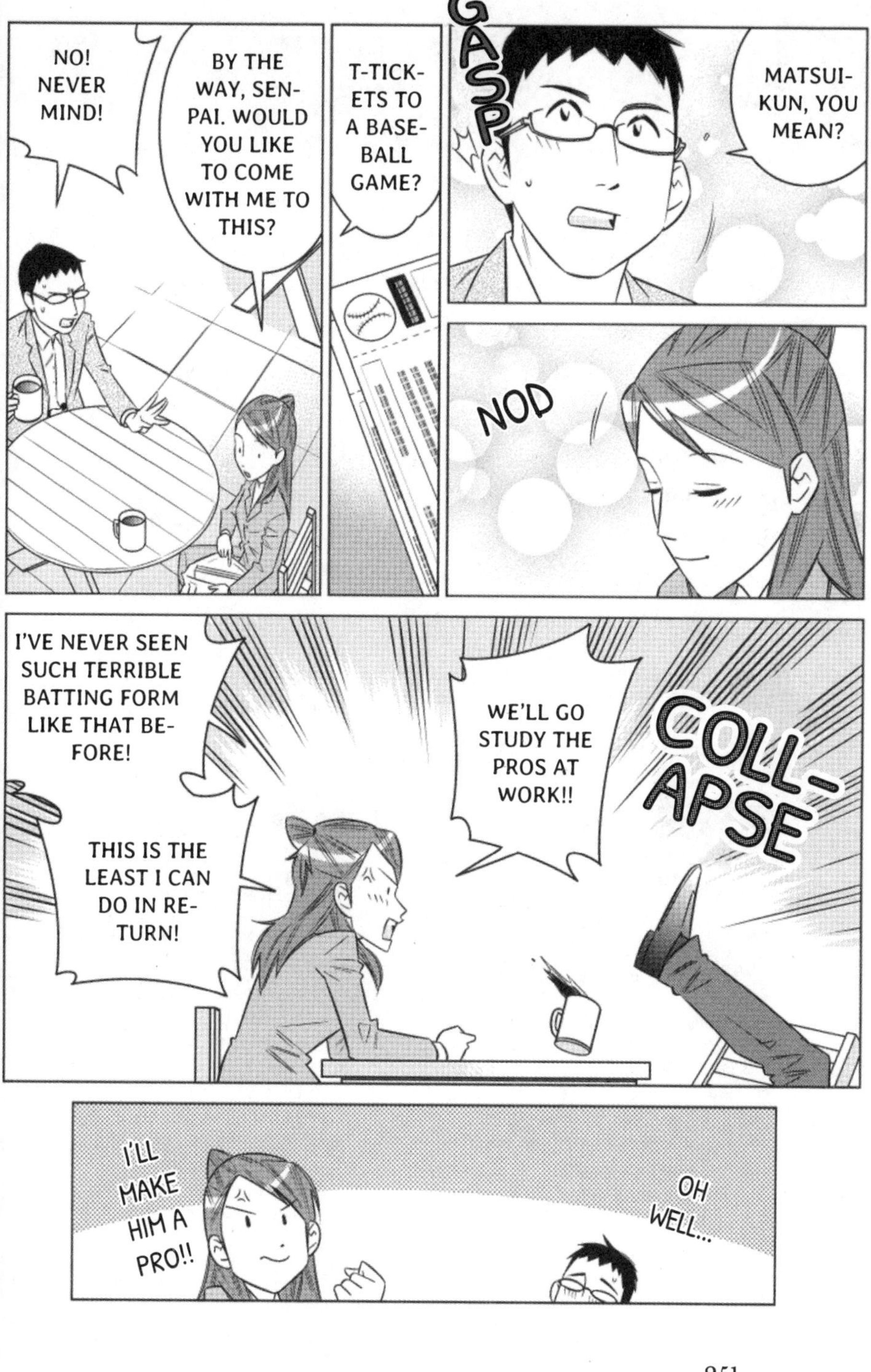
NO! NEVER MIND!
BY THE WAY, SEN-PAI. WOULD YOU LIKE TO COME WITH ME TO THIS?
T-TICK-ETS TO A BASE-BALL GAME?
GASP
MATSUI-KUN, YOU MEAN?
NOD
I'VE NEVER SEEN SUCH TERRIBLE BATTING FORM LIKE THAT BE-FORE!
THIS IS THE LEAST I CAN DO IN RE-TURN!
WE'LL GO STUDY THE PROS AT WORK!!
COLL-APSE
I'LL MAKE HIM A PRO!!
OH WELL...

1 How to Translate Strategic Options into a Plan

▶ **The Necessary Process in Executing the Strategy**

Once the strategic options are narrowed down, we'll put them into specific plans and actions. Here, executability is the key to making sure your strategy is more than just a pie in the sky.

A lot of well-thought-out strategies can end up not being executed, their progress not monitored, fizzled out, or yielding little to no result. A strategy is meaningless in such cases, no matter how brilliant it may be.

SIMPLY COMPLETING THE STRATEGY BUILDING ISN'T THE END!

To avoid this, it is crucial to put the strategy into specific actions and a detailed planning table

Diagram 5-1 Steps to Put a Plan of Action Together

Breaking down the strategy into measures (strategy structuring)	Translating measures into specific actions

● Identifying requirements to realize the strategy
● Coming up with measures to fulfill requirements sufficiently
● Set priorities to measures
  • Consider the impact on the strategy itself, or on the execution of other measures
	● Putting measures into implementable actions that can be executed on-site
	  • Come up with measures that involve on-site personnel hands-on
	● Refine the first step of the strategy execution
	  • A gimmick to create a company-wide "big wave"
	  • Early visualization of the outcome

so the progress can be monitored. Embed the monitoring system into the organizational structure and build a system to propel things forward. Only then the strategy-building process is finally complete.

So the strategy-building is not complete until you put the strategy into the action plan, implement it, and see things through by monitoring the progress. Only then you can call it complete.

To do this, the first task is to break the strategy down into specific measures. This means clarifying what measures make up the strategy and what action is needed to reach the strategic goal of gaining a competitive edge. If this strategy structuring is not done properly, you will not reach the strategic goal even if the measures are correctly executed. This is indeed the climax of realizing the strategy.

Put together a plan of action	Establish a structure to drive the strategy execution forward
● "Master plan" (core plan): Oversees the whole picture • Act as a guide in strategy execution • A plan with a bird's-eye view of the whole ● "Action plan": Broken down into executable actions • Specific tasks • Project manager • Project deadline	● Establish a system to implement the strategy • Decision-making, direction (executive level) • Progress monitoring, implementation (planning section level) • Actual execution (each department)

2 How to Apply Strategy to Execution

▶ How to Apply Strategy to Execution

To what degree should we break a strategy into each executable measure? There is no correct answer to this, but a good rule of thumb is to break it down to a measure that can be thought of as a single entity. You need to make it easy to visualize the required specific actions for it.

The type of strategy also affects the size and type of measures. If you are looking at a sales strategy, which is carried out within a limited range, you can narrow down the measures required to specific ones. On the other hand, an all-encompassing company-wide strategy could be made up of sub-strategies such as a sectional strategy, a business strategy, a larger strategic theme, and so on. An upper-level strategy like this will be made up of lower-level strategies, and in turn, those lower-level strategies will be made up of measures.

In most cases, there will be a company-wide strategy, then separate business strategies to work toward the realization of the overall strategy. Each business strategy will have different strategies required to accomplish its goal. Examples are, but not limited to, marketing strategy (targeted clientele and offered values, products to meet those needs, price, promotions, distribution channels policy and strategic branding, etc.), operational strategy (research and development,

THE SIZE OF THE MEASURES FOLLOWS THE SIZE OF THE STRATEGY!

sales, customer service, and where each function is headed), and organizational strategy (organization structure, human resources, system and policies, etc.).

Marketing, operational, and organizational strategies would be further broken down into measures needed to realize each goal (product planning, detailed pricing, ad campaigns, specialized research and development, sales efforts, etc.).

As you can see, a strategy can be broken down into different levels, and the measures required vary. It's vital to structure them to figure out what strategies will be needed at the lower level and what specific measures are needed to execute them. You must get to the bottom of what needs to be done to accomplish a strategic goal. Measures are the required steps that need to be taken and fulfilled in order to carry out the strategy. To figure out what measures are needed, identifying requirements to realize the strategic goal is necessary.

A typical way to break down a strategy into measures is to identify requirements from both marketing and operational (value chain) points of view and come up with measures needed to meet those requirements.

From the marketing standpoint, you'll have to consider what requirements need to be fulfilled, such as product and pricing, promotion, and distribution channels. Do you need more functional, more cost-effective, or more design-oriented products? Should the pricing be lower than the other companies, or go ahead with our own pricing unrelated to the competitors? You should examine each of such points.

Diagram 5-2 Relationship between Strategy and Measure

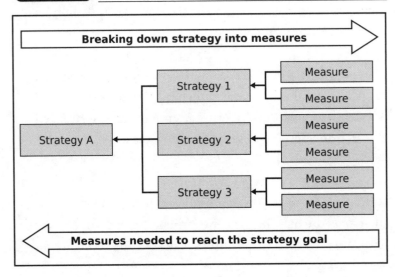

As for the operational standpoint, take a look at the requirements to realize the strategic and marketing goals and identify the business activities each operational function needs to carry out and how to structure the value chain around them.

For an average manufacturer, on top of the value chain flow such as development, procurement, production, distribution, marketing, sales, and customer service, functions such as corporate infrastructure and human resource management will also be required. Each function has requirements needed to fulfill the strategic goals, and there are measures that need to be taken to meet those needs.

The size and types of measures needed to be taken can also depend on the degree of divergence (or the degree of reform) between the current and the anticipated positions. A strategy with a larger scale of reform will have a larger degree of divergence and requirements not being met by the existing functions.

▶ Setting Priorities

Now, let's set priorities for the implementation of measures. Each measure may be important, but carrying them out all at once is not realistic. Prioritize the measures based on their importance, and carry them out in steps.

As for the priority, base it on items such as the impact on the strategy as a whole, urgency, and the impact on the execution of other measures. If the scale of the reform is larger, or the company-wide urgency is higher, then it should be of higher priority.

3 How to Carry Out Strategic Options

The next important step in building an executable strategy is to break the measures down into specific actions. The objective here is to translate the strategy into detailed, implementable actions to be executed on-site.

▶ Beyond the Possibility: Feeling and Determining

At some point, you may start to have doubts about the feasibility of the strategy, no matter how carefully you have built it to suit your need. As you try to visualize the actual execution and turn it into actions, you will start thinking, "Can this really be done?" or "How are we going to do this?" You might also find everyone agreeing to the strategy in general but disagreeing on the details of it.

But this is an unavoidable process, and only by overcoming such obstacles, you will be able to put a "soul" into the strategy in the true sense of the word. It's actually dangerous to come up with the required actions without questioning their feasibility. A true pie in the sky like this is often the case when the planning section doesn't have the frontliners' knowledge. Also, if the strategy itself is a simple extension of the current situation, the actual outcome may not be as effective.

THIS IS AN IMPORTANT STEP TO MAKE A STRATEGY THAT WORKS.

A truly effective strategy often has a large gap between what it aims for and the current situation. This means there will be obstacles when it comes to the actual implementation. In this step, it's essential to work out a way to

258

Diagram 5-3 Relationship between Measures and Actions

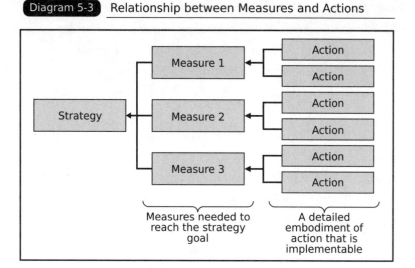

Measures needed to reach the strategy goal

A detailed embodiment of action that is implementable

actually execute the actions and how to overcome the obstacles in carrying them out.

The most important point in examining the actions is how much you can involve the on-site personnel who will actually be carrying out these actions. Consider the possible hurdles in execution thoroughly and decide on feasible actions. You'll have to discuss and work things out together with the on-site personnel. Face-to-face discussions should be quite effective here.

Overcoming these hurdles together will be the "soul" of your strategy. This will let on-site personnel have more conviction in the selected strategic actions that need to be executed.

Along with working with the on-site personnel, another key is the resolve of the leadership. As you discuss actions in more detail, there's bound to be resistance and opposition from the departments with conflicting interests. This is the typical example of everyone agreeing to the strategy in general but disagreeing on the details of it. There are times when involving the on-site personnel isn't enough to break through these boundaries. You can't execute your strategy just by listening to those who carry it out.

The leadership's resolve is needed to keep those oppositions in check, convince them, and carry things out together. The top management has to send a strong message that they are determined to carry out the strategy to the end. However, be careful not to let the strategy lose its substance when doing so.

▶ The First Step in Strategic Execution

Always keep in mind what the first step will be when selecting actions. The very first action that will launch you on the path of strategy realization is extremely important. But at the same time, getting this ball rolling is quite difficult.

The first step can't just be any step. It has to be an action that would set the course for the actions to follow. It'll also have to give an impression to everyone in the company that it will be effective. More so if the strategy leads to major changes in the company. The objective is to encourage the company as a whole to motivate everyone to work toward the goal together. For companies that had many failed strategies in the past, this first step is especially important and has to be examined carefully in order not to end up with the same result.

What action should be the first step depends on the strategy details and type, as well as the company's current situation. But the following actions are generally most suitable for the first step.

❶ Action that allows you to see the outcome
Or a quick hit, as some call it. Any action that produces a positive result, no matter how small, and a successful experience that is visible throughout the organization. This needs to be an action that is relatively easy to be carried out and yields a result fairly quickly.

In addition, the outcome should ideally be something tangible. By setting up these actions at the beginning of the strategy execution process, you will be able to make an impression of consecutive successes. Having these quick hits can be one of the keys to a steady strategy execution, especially for companies that had a past strategy falling apart or fizzling out.

❷ Action that signifies the strategic goals and aims
If you want to lay out a clear strategic course, choose a symbolic action that matches the strategic goal as the first step. Contrary to a quick hit, this action will require a more challenging execution that can transmit a message to the whole company even if it is a little more difficult.

A major organizational reform, a drastic resource distribution to the focused area, and a delegation of authority are all examples of symbolic and significant actions. Transferring key personnel is another action with a large impact on the company, and so is establishing a cross-functional project team.

❸ Action that moves the core personnel
One of the important aspects of the strategy is securing the core personnel needed to get it up and running. The vital role in this is the role of managers and leaders on-site.

Getting those key personnel involved early in the process is an important first step. Preferably this action would delegate responsibilities to those in the center of the action, motivating them to move and lead the project. Move the personnel to the core of the team and let them create a "big wave" early on to get things going.

④ Action that communicates the strategic direction to the whole company

An action that clarifies and communicates the strategy's aim and direction can also be an important first step. The previous three actions indirectly contribute to spreading the strategy company-wide as well, but combining them with carrying out an action that directly telegraphs the message to the whole company would be ideal.

On top of implementing strategy, actions can also be programs to socialize the strategy and reforms. Some good examples are company-wide surveys, workshops, Q&A sessions, dialogues with the leadership, informational booklets, and company pep rally, all aiming to send out the details of the strategy and the reform.

Matsui-ya held a pep rally where the CEO went over the framework and the details of the strategy to the whole company as a finishing touch to the strategy building.

Create a Plan of Action

Once the strategy is broken down into something feasible, we need to compile it into a plan of action in order to get it moving. A plan of action is made up of a master plan that oversees the whole project and an action plan detailing each measure meticulously.

▶ The Master Plan: The Plan of Action for Strategic Execution

A master plan is a broad plan for the strategy to be carried out. This serves as a guideline for the strategy execution from this point on. A master plan should have an ultimate goal of the plan and a road map of how the strategy should be implemented.

There needs to be an ultimate goal so everyone involved can visualize the direction and destination of the strategy. The master plan has to reiterate this goal.

The ultimate goal will show a clear vision for the company or organization and a clear direction in the decision-making. It has to be feasible, simple, and easy to understand. Set numerical goals that are challenging and stretch your limit, but at the same time, also be realistic enough to be supported by the strategy and its measures.

LET'S LEARN HOW TO BUILD A MASTER PLAN AND AN ACTION PLAN.

A "road map" is a guide map to the goal or the vision you are aiming for, identifying the

Diagram 5-4 | Master Plan vs Action Plan

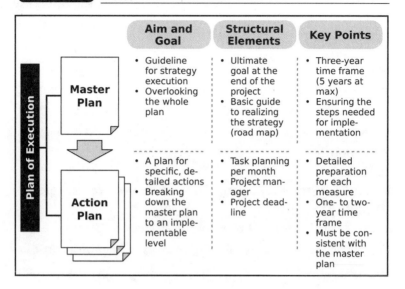

Plan of Execution		Aim and Goal	Structural Elements	Key Points
	Master Plan	• Guideline for strategy execution • Overlooking the whole plan	• Ultimate goal at the end of the project • Basic guide to realizing the strategy (road map)	• Three-year time frame (5 years at max) • Ensuring the steps needed for implementation
	Action Plan	• A plan for specific, detailed actions • Breaking down the master plan to an implementable level	• Task planning per month • Project manager • Project deadline	• Detailed preparation for each measure • One- to two-year time frame • Must be consistent with the master plan

directions and steps to take. If this road map is insufficient or wrong, you'll never make it to the goal. Many companies that failed to fulfill a strategy or a management plan often have issues with their road map.

The key to creating a road map is first and foremost clarifying the major steps needed to execute the strategy. For the master plan, what's important is a broad course of action, not a detailed plan. It is a step to decide the direction and how to get to the final goal. You need to specify what needs to be executed for each year in the period specified in the master plan.

Next, map out which measures should be carried out in what order for each step. The key here is to make sure the strategy is built with the actual execution in mind. You should have come up with detailed actions needed to carry out the strategy by this point. Examine the following points and more while you put the measures into action: Is the plan within the current means of your organizational ability and workforce? Is the order in which measures should be carried out correct? Will the strategic goal be met if we follow the designed steps?

Thirdly, set clear milestones. A milestone is a turning point within the strategy or its execution, such as a deadline that cannot be extended, or a pivotal decision-making time. Set a goal for each milestone. Define clearly what needs to be accomplished by a certain date and time. Move forward with the strategy with these milestones as goals, and monitor the process using them as standards.

Finally, incorporate the foresight into the anticipated changes in the business environment along with the road map for your company's strategy execution. Together with the milestones, this will become an important element to monitor the progress. Be prepared to make quick adjustments to the strategic course if the business environment changes faster than anticipated, or if the strategy's direction changes.

▶ Coming Up with a Realistically Applicable Plan

An action plan is the master plan broken down to an achievable level. It is a more detailed plan of action and has to be made with meticulous details for each measure. It'll have to be a plan that can be carried out by the on-site team, and an average time frame for it is one to two years. For the first-year plan, be sure to include the first step in the action plan.

Diagram 5-5 Master Plan Image

	Phase 1 (20XX/XX-XX/XX)	Phase 2 (20XX/XX-XX/XX)	Phase 3 (20XX/XX-XX/XX)	What we should aim for

The basic concept (broad design)
- Steps to realize the strategy
- Goals and aims for each step

Milestones
- Turning points where a delay is not permitted or decision-making is required

Measures implemented/strategy per department
- Actual actions/steps for each measure
- Details of implementation for each step

Changes in the targeted business environment
- "Foresight" into the business environment change
- Time frame of the environmental change that can impact strategy

Requirements that need to be met in each phase
- Requirements that need to be met in each step
- Conditions to move onto the next step

Numerical goals
- Numerical goals to gauge the progress and the outcome of the plan

What we should aim for
- Goals to aim for
- The company and/or business vision to be realized after the strategy is carried out

266

The most important element of making the action plan is its specificity. You'll have to take the measures which have been broken down into specific actions and form them into a workable plan. Actions for each measure are further broken down into tasks and scheduled at a "per month" level.

Also important is consistency with the master plan. The action plan focuses on precision and details, and is built bottom up, or by compiling required tasks. As a result, there can often be inconsistency with the master plan which represents a general direction created from the top down. Always keep both the master plan and the action plan in sync when creating them.

And finally, clearly identify the person responsible for the execution of each action. It is necessary to spell out who is responsible for what and when something has to be carried out. If you keep these points vague, you risk the chance of actions being postponed or not carried out altogether.

5 How to Execute with Certainty

We are finally at the point where the strategy is actually being executed. A strategy that is not carried out is a pie in the sky, no matter how great. This is where the true value of the strategy created is weighed.

▶ Establish a Driving Force

Key functions required for the strategy being executed are one, decision-making and taking the helm, two, implementation and progress monitoring, and three, execution.

For item number two, decision-making and taking the helm, the required elements include presenting the strategy summary, goals, and directions, as well as decision-making, course adjustments when needed, and handling issues as they arise. The actual deployment of the strategy execution team, progress monitoring of the achievable plan, and support for the execution team are needed for item number two. Concrete execution of the strategy is necessary for item number three, or the execution.

For a standard company-wide strategy, number one falls under the leadership function (management), number two is handled by the planning section, and number three is carried out by each department in charge of execution. Temporary or extra fuel may be needed if the strategy calls for a greater propellant to carry

IT'S VITAL TO KEEP THE PDCA CYCLE GOING.

out a large reform or move a new venture forward. This is the launching pad for a project.

In some cases, the whole process, from one to three, is set up separately from the normal or current streamlined organization, or a project team focused on specific measures or actions may be established.

▶ Implement a Thorough PDCA

Implementing a thorough PDCA (plan, do, check, action) cycle is crucial in realizing a strategy. Plan is the actual strategy creation step. Do is its execution. Check implies progress monitoring, and action is where you make improvements and/or adjustments based on the results from the monitoring. Some companies do the plan and do steps, but not the check and action steps, ending up with a half-baked realization of the strategy.

More often than not, things don't go as planned. In fact, you can say the plan not going as expected is a requisite. Spotting the diversion early, identifying its cause, and quickly responding to it are all as important, if not more, than carrying out the plans as designed.

Also, the business environment can often change while the strategy is being executed. In such cases, it is important to determine how and where this environmental change can impact the strategy, and adjust the course as needed. By analyzing the current situation accurately and building the strategy around it, you'll be able to figure out the range and degree of the adjustments needed. This will allow a flexible course adjustment in line with any business environment changes. The meticulousness of the strategy has a big impact on the PDCA. If you have made clear the reason and logic behind why that specific strategy was chosen, you'll be prepared to take quick action in a situation in which the whole premise of the strategy is changed due to environmental change.

Diagram 5-6 Thorough PDCA Implementation

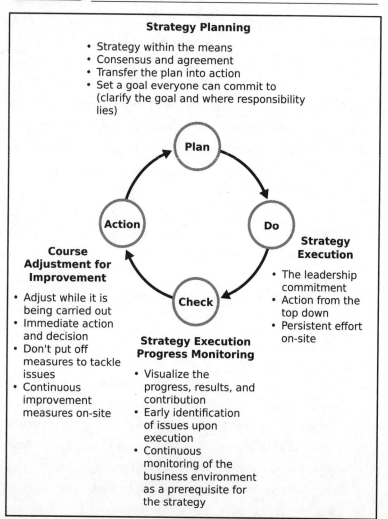

Strategy Planning

- Strategy within the means
- Consensus and agreement
- Transfer the plan into action
- Set a goal everyone can commit to (clarify the goal and where responsibility lies)

Plan

Action

Do

Course Adjustment for Improvement

- Adjust while it is being carried out
- Immediate action and decision
- Don't put off measures to tackle issues
- Continuous improvement measures on-site

Check

Strategy Execution

- The leadership commitment
- Action from the top down
- Persistent effort on-site

Strategy Execution Progress Monitoring

- Visualize the progress, results, and contribution
- Early identification of issues upon execution
- Continuous monitoring of the business environment as a prerequisite for the strategy

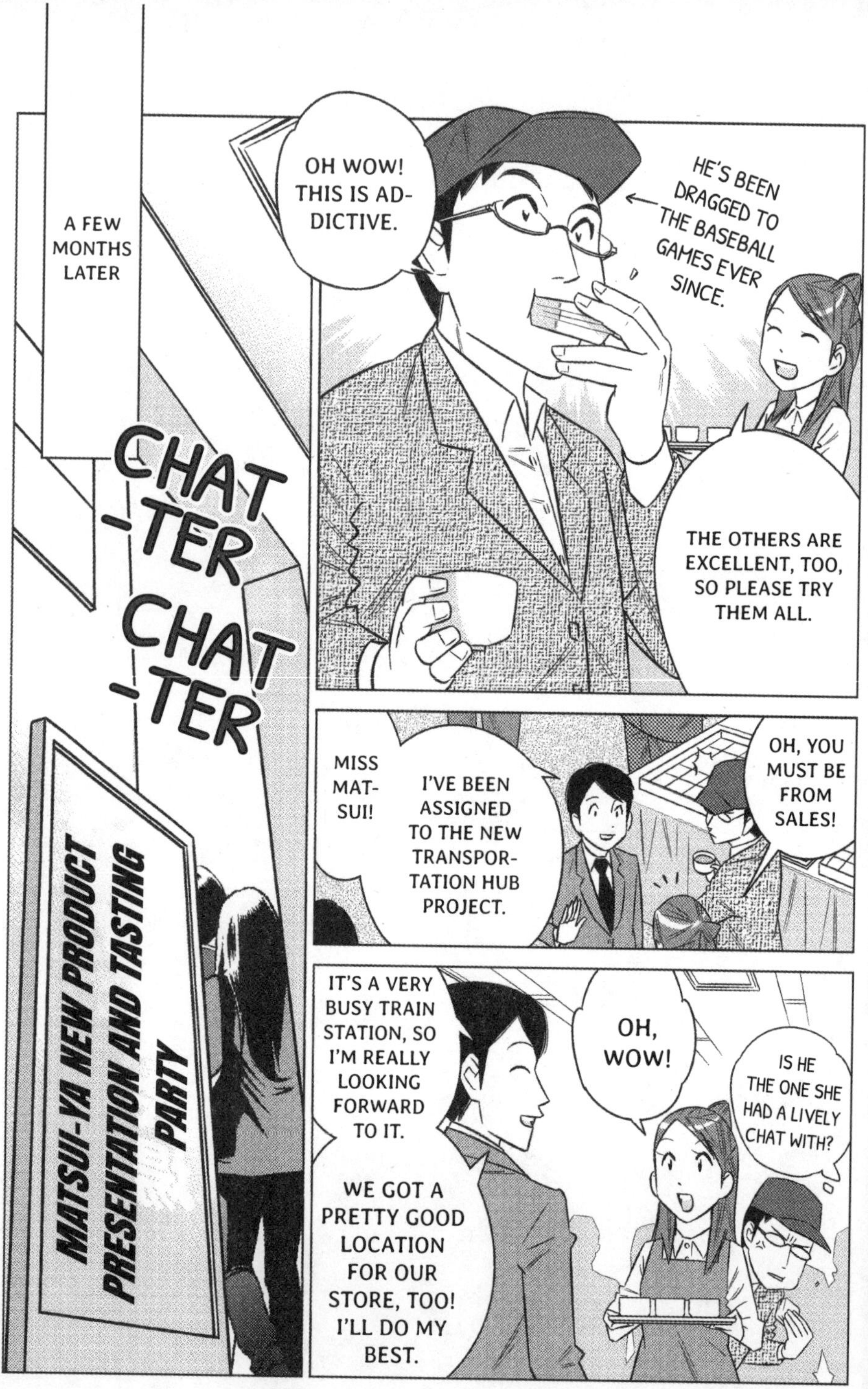

A FEW MONTHS LATER
OH WOW! THIS IS AD-DICTIVE.
HE'S BEEN DRAGGED TO THE BASEBALL GAMES EVER SINCE.
THE OTHERS ARE EXCELLENT, TOO, SO PLEASE TRY THEM ALL.
CHAT-TER CHAT-TER
MATSUI-YA NEW PRODUCT PRESENTATION AND TASTING PARTY
OH, YOU MUST BE FROM SALES!
I'VE BEEN ASSIGNED TO THE NEW TRANSPOR-TATION HUB PROJECT.
MISS MAT-SUI!
IS HE THE ONE SHE HAD A LIVELY CHAT WITH?
OH, WOW!
IT'S A VERY BUSY TRAIN STATION, SO I'M REALLY LOOKING FORWARD TO IT.
WE GOT A PRETTY GOOD LOCATION FOR OUR STORE, TOO! I'LL DO MY BEST.

MISS MATSUI!

LONG TIME NO SEE! THANK YOU FOR COMING!

TEE-HEE. I WOULDN'T MISS A CHANCE TO GET FREE JAPANESE SWEETS.

WE EVEN GOT SOME TO TAKE HOME.

YES! IT'S NOT MUCH, BUT I JUST WANTED TO THANK YOU FOR YOUR OPINIONS.

I'M ACTUAL-LY SEEING JAPANESE SWEETS IN A NEW LIGHT LATELY.

IT'S HEALTHIER THAN FOR-EIGN PAS-TRIES.

TEE-HEE. YOU CAN HAVE THEM EVEN IF YOU'RE ON A DIET.

I SEE. HEALTHIER. THAT'S AN ANGLE I HAVEN'T CONSIDERED BEFORE.

AH, YOU'RE MR. TAKE-DA.

HUH? YES, THAT'S ME.

I HEARD MISS KAZUMI GOT YOUR HELP IN BUILDING THE BUSINESS STRATEGY.

273

THANKS TO YOU, I THINK WE'RE MOVING IN A GREAT DIRECTION.

WELL, I JUST TAUGHT HER HOW TO DO IT. IT'S ALL MISS MATSUI'S DOING.

BY THE WAY, I HEARD YOU WERE WITH A FOREIGN CONSULTING FIRM BEFORE, MR. TAKEDA.

BUT YOU MOVED ON TO A DIFFERENT COMPANY IN ORDER TO REMAIN ON THE FRONT LINE.

HOW DO YOU KNOW THAT?!

OH, I HAVE MY SOURCES.

I ALSO HEARD YOU'RE STILL SINGLE.

WHY DID YOU HELP MISS KAZUMI SO MUCH?

PERHAPS YOU HAVE AN ULTERIOR MOTIVE?

YOU'RE NOT INTO HER, ARE YOU?

HOW ABOUT IT?

UMMM!

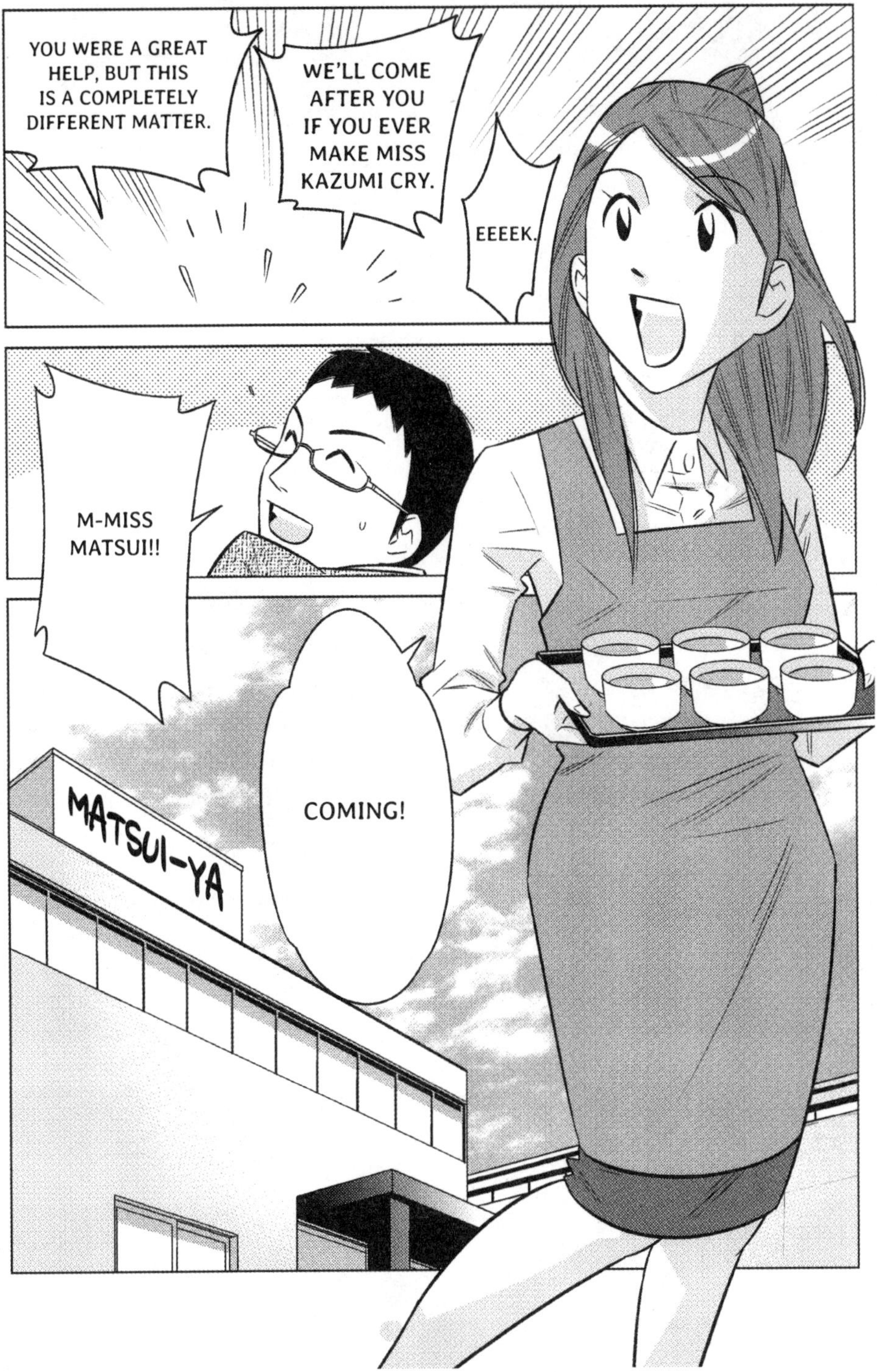
WE'LL COME AFTER YOU IF YOU EVER MAKE MISS KAZUMI CRY.
YOU WERE A GREAT HELP, BUT THIS IS A COMPLETELY DIFFERENT MATTER.
EEEEK.
M-MISS MATSUI!!
COMING!
MATSUI-YA

Postscript

This book is based on *Recipe for Business Strategy*, published by Nihon Noritsu Kyoukai Management Center. We have edited it for better understanding and added a Manga portion in hopes of offering a more detailed flow and some tricks for creating a business strategy.

It's already been six years since the publication of the original book, and we've gained experience in the consulting field during that time. We believe the things written in *Recipe for Business Strategy* are still valid to this day. However, we also felt that there are places we can improve based on the experience from these past six years.

That was when we received an offer to write this book from the publisher. We thought a manga format was a great way to present things we couldn't include in the previous book, such as the feel of real strategy-building situations and nuances. We also thought we could contribute new details and viewpoints from what we have experienced in the past six years. In a sense, this book is a sequel to the previous book, *Recipe for Business Strategy*.

This book uses the manga format to the fullest and offers the topic of strategy building, something that could be dry and hard to understand in a regular book format, as realistically as possible. This book is full of issues and common situations from our point of view as business strategy consultants assisting our clients in the strategy creation process. By reading this book, we believe you'll gain some insight into what a business strategy consultant does. The process in which Kazumi, with Takeda's help, struggles to build a business strategy for "Matsui-ya" through trial and error is just like how our clients create a business strategy with us, the business strategy consultants.

Of course, real life is far more complex, and there are things we just couldn't fit into the manga. However, we believe we've covered the most important aspects of creating a business strategy. Along with commentaries, you should be able to understand the basics of the business strategy. There were parts we had to cut due to the length constraint. This book and *Recipe for Business Strategy* together should provide a further understanding of business strategy.

There is no shortcut to building a business strategy and executing it. There is no one right answer, either. You need to have an in-depth understanding of the situation, look ahead into the future, let your imagination run wild, and get everyone involved to carry it out. This is the only surest way to yield desired outcomes. For this purpose, we've included the "Secret Recipes for Success" in this book. We hope to provide our readers with the true essence of the business strategy.

On behalf of the writing team, Takayuki Kito

Author and Editor

TAKAYUKI KITO

A graduate of Tokyo University Law School and a former Roland Berger employee with ample experience mainly in the consumer goods and distribution industries, cosmetics, apparel, food and drinks, retailers, expansion to the overseas market and emerging countries, brand management, marketing strategy, and business strategy planning and execution assistance. Kito has published and lectured on brand and global strategies. The author of *Recipe for Business Strategy* (co-writer), *Brand Recipe* (Nihon Noritsu Kyoukai Management Center), and *Brand as a Strategy* (Toyo Keizai Inc.).

Author

KEISUKE YAMABE

A graduate of Hitotsubashi University Business School and a former Roland Berger employee with extensive experience in planning and execution of company-wide strategies including sales and marketing, brand, emerging countries, and business reform strategies, in industries such as restaurant and service, automobile, aviation, consumer goods, and construction. The author of *Recipe for Business Strategy* (co-writer).

About Roland Berger

Roland Berger Strategy Consultants is a leading European business consulting firm headquartered in Munich. Since its founding in 1967, Roland Berger Strategy Consultants has built an impressive track record and has been praised for offering drastic solutions for issues the top management of the industry's leading global companies have been facing for over 40 years. With over 2,700 employees and 52 offices in 36 countries, they offer consulting services from a borderless, global viewpoint. Currently, approximately 100 consultants work out of the Tokyo office, which was established in 1991. They offer consulting services on corporate strategy, marketing, brand management, operational, and organizational issues. Their broad range of clients includes businesses from the automobile industry, consumer goods and distribution, machines and electronics, pharmaceutical and health care, financial, IT and communication, transportation, real estate, energy, and public sectors. In recent years, they have been dispatching Japanese consultants to locations in Europe and Asia as Japan Desk to support Japanese companies' global expansion. With their motto, "Consulting that yields actual results," their grounded consulting style has been commended by many corporate clients.

Roland Berger LLC
Ark Mori Building 23F,
Minato-Ku, Akasaka 1-12-32
Tokyo-To, Japan
107-6023
Phone: 03-3587-6660
Fax: 03-3587-6670
Email: Office_Tokyo@rolandberger.com
Website: http://www.rolandberger.co.jp/

BOOKS IN THE  SERIES

TAKASHI YASUDA

MANGA FOR SUCCESS

MARKETING

THE FUN WAY TO LEARN THE BASICS OF MARKETING

ALL THE IMPORTANT CONCEPTS YOU NEED TO KNOW, INCLUDING:

» THE 4 "P'S" OF MARKETING
» THE CUSTOMER JOURNEY
» ANALYZING YOUR COMPETITOR'S STRENGTHS & WEAKNESSES

AND MORE

KOJI KUZE

MANGA FOR SUCCESS

RESILIENCE, CONFIDENCE, & POSITIVE THINKING

CREATE A STRESS-RESISTANT, STRONG MIND & HEART

MANAGE NEGATIVE EMOTIONS AND DISAPPOINTMENTS

GET THE SOCIAL SUPPORT YOU NEED

RESTORE YOUR SELF-CONFIDENCE AND USE YOUR STRENGTH!

TOSHINORI IWAI

MANGA FOR SUCCESS

THE PSYCHOLOGY OF PERSONAL GROWTH & BETTER RELATIONSHIPS

» CHANGE YOUR PERSPECTIVE, AND YOUR LIFE WILL BE EASIER!
» FIND THE COURAGE TO HAVE DIFFICULT, BUT IMPORTANT, CONVERSATIONS
» GET THE SUPPORT YOU NEED FROM OTHERS

BASED ON THE GLOBALLY INFLUENTIAL WORK OF PSYCHOLOGIST ALFRED ADLER

KAZUHIKO NAKAMURA

MANGA FOR SUCCESS

MANAGING the CHANGE

LEARN POWERFUL TECHNIQUES FOR OVERCOMING OLD MINDSETS AND RESISTANCE TO CHANGE

THE SCIENCE OF ORGANIZATION DEVELOPMENT CAN MAKE IT EASIER

BECOME A CHANGE AGENT, AND CREATE A CORE TEAM FOR CHANGE!

TAKAYUKI KITO
KEISUKE YAMABE

MANGA FOR SUCCESS

BUSINESS PROBLEM-SOLVING & STRATEGY

USE "SWOT ANALYSIS, "5 FORCES" AND OTHER TOOLS TO UNDERSTAND YOUR MAJOR CHALLENGES

DEVELOP A STRATEGY FOR ANY BUSINESS SITUATION

MAKE AN ACTION PLAN AND EXECUTE SUCCESSFULLY!

MASUMI TANI

MANGA FOR SUCCESS

LEADING MEETINGS & TEAMS

LEARN BASIC FACILITATION SKILLS TO IMPROVE GROUP PERFORMANCE

GET FULL PARTICIPATION, HIGHER ENERGY, AND STRONGER BUY-IN FROM ALL TEAM MEMBERS

ASK GREAT QUESTIONS THAT WILL DRAW OUT EVERYONE'S OPINION

AVAILABLE WHEREVER BOOKS ARE SOLD

WILEY